The Un-Natural State

The Un-Natural State

Arkansas and the Queer South

BROCK THOMPSON

The University of Arkansas Press
Fayetteville
2010

ISBN-10: 1-55728-943-3
ISBN-13: 978-1-55728-943-8

14   13   12   11   10   5   4   3   2   1

Designed by Liz Lester

⊛ The paper used in this publication meets the minimum requirements of the American National Standard for Permanence of Paper
for Printed Library Materials Z39.48-1984.

LIBRARY OF CONGRESS
CATALOGING-IN-PUBLICATION DATA

Thompson, Brock, 1977–
     The un-natural state : Arkansas and the queer South /
Brock Thompson.
          p.   cm.
     Includes bibliographical references and index.
     ISBN 978-1-55728-943-8 (cloth : alk. paper)
     1. Gays—Arkansas—History. 2. Gays—Identity. 3. Gay
community—Arkansas—History. 4. Gay culture—Arkansas—
History. 5. Arkansas—Social life and customs. I. Title.
     HQ76.3.U52A885   2010
     306.76'609767—dc22
                                        2010022422

A version of chapter 10 appeared previously in a collection of essays
on southern masculinity. Reprinted by permission of Louisiana State
University Press from *White Masculinity in the Recent South* by Trent
Watts. Copyright © 2008 by Louisiana State University Press.

For my mother and father.

. . . and for Opal.

I should like to flee
like a wounded hart
into Arkansas.

—OSCAR WILDE

CONTENTS

Acknowledgments ix

Introduction ■ Outing Opal, Outing Arkansas 3

PART ONE   **The Diamond State**

1 ■ Powder-Puff 17

2 ■ Drag and the Politics of Performance 19

3 ■ Drag in the Daylight 43

4 ■ Rags to Drag Riches 51

5 ■ The Current Reigning Symbol of Excellence 63

PART TWO   **The Natural State**

6 ■ A Crime Unfit to Be Named 75

7 ■ The Ingredients of Offense 83

8 ■ Race, Sex, and Queer Renegotiated 89

9 ■ Redefinition 95

10 ■ Public and Private Prejudice 109

11 ■ Constructing a Gay Life 121

PART THREE   **The Land of Opportunity**

12 ■ Creating Space, Separating the Self 131

13 ■ Losing Space, Separating Identities 137

14 ■ Mansion on the Hill 157

15 ■ Economic Opportunity and the
Queer Community 167

16 ■ And Then *She* Came 177

Epilogue ■ Queer Comes Home 183

Notes 191

Selected Bibliography 225

Index 239

ACKNOWLEDGMENTS

There are so many people that deserve my gratitude that the task of thanking them all is near impossible. My roommate at the time this project was wrapping up joked that a more accurate title for the work should have been *The Un-Natural State and Acknowledgments*. All kidding aside, what follows are my attempts to include all who shared in this work's completion.

At Hendrix College I am deeply indebted to Jay Barth who provided not only countless leads and encouragement but also gave me the title for this project. In the History Department Deborah Skok provided me with the venue for sharing my findings and thoughts with faculty and students. Also, Garrett McAinsh was a great teacher of history and deserves mention here simply for that. He also was a very receptive audience to my early research in gay and lesbian history. For that I am also thankful. Eric Binnie in the Theatre Arts Department was also extraordinarily helpful in this project's early days. In the English Department Alex Vernon was a thoughtful critic. At Bailey Library at Hendrix I also wish to thank Britt Ann Murphy, Peggy Morrison, Sheila Peters, Amanda Moore, and Dianne Edwards for putting up with me through this entire project and dealing with what seemed to be innumerable interlibrary loan requests.

At the University of Arkansas I wish to thank Lynda Coon, Patrick Williams, and Jeannie Wayne. Also in the History Department, Trish Starks and Michael Pierce, Charles Robinson, and Richard Sonn deserve my gratitude. In the Political Science Department the dynamic husband-and-wife team of Janine Parry and Bill Schreckhise proved to be great friends and colleagues. Also, I wish to thank the staff of Special Collections at the University of Arkansas Library for both their patience and assistance in compiling the research for this project, specifically, Tom W. Dillard, Andrea Cantrell, Anne Prichard, Ethel C. Simpson, Cassandra McCraw, Geoffrey Stark, and, at the reference desk, Debra Lee Miller. Also lending their talents and remarkable collections were the staffs and directors at the archives at the University of Arkansas at Little Rock. There I am particularly indebted to Linda Pine, Jennifer McCarthy, Kaye Lundgren, and Jillian

Barnett. The Arkansas History Commission and the Butler Center for Arkansas Studies have my gratitude as well. At the University of Arkansas Press I wish to thank the ever-patient Julie Watkins and Katy Henriksen for their efforts in getting these pages in shape.

At King's College, University of London, I am, of course, indebted to my advisor John Howard and his colleague Kimberly Springer in the Department of American Studies. In the Department of English I wish to thank Mark Turner for his assistance in interpreting theory as well as providing the surface off which I bounced countless ideas dealing with this project and postgraduate life in general. Socially, there was Paul Fairley. Thanks, Paul.

There were also colleagues from across the academic world who gave me advice and encouragement that proved essential to this project's completion. At the University of California at Berkeley, Whitney Bauman gave a thorough reading of an early draft. Jon Bell at the University of Reading gave me the opportunity to present early research findings at departmental seminars. Also, I would also like to thank Pippa Holloway at Middle Tennessee State University for including me and my fledgling research on a panel at the American Studies Association's annual meeting. I would also like to mention John Kirk at Royal Holloway, University of London, for serving on my thesis committee. His thoughtful suggestions have been incorporated throughout this manuscript. At the University of Central Arkansas I am grateful to Ken Barnes for my first teaching job out of graduate school. Also, Sondra Gordy, herself a leading figure in Arkansas history, gave a thoughtful and encouraging reading to an early draft of this project. At the University of Arkansas at Little Rock, Julie Steel, a lifelong friend to be sure, was supportive throughout. At Oklahoma State University, Lindsey Smith gave feedback and valuable suggestions. Back in my hometown of Conway, Arkansas, Jim Owen began as a history teacher, now a friend; he deserves mention here.

I brought this work to a close working at the Library of Congress in Washington DC. There I benefited from a wonderful and supportive environment that scholars often dream about. At the library I wish to thank Robert Newlen, Monica Lira, and Dorothy Almanza.

Certainly, there are many cherished friends and cohorts who were there for me from the beginning, of whom many deserve inclusion here.

In Fayetteville, Arkansas, Sarah Brooke Malloy. In Little Rock, Tucker Steinmetz, who gave invaluable editorial advice on several drafts and opened to me an extraordinary friendship and his almost encyclopedic knowledge of Arkansas history. In many ways this work owes its completion to him, and I am deeply in his debt. In Washington DC, my home for the final year of this project, a big heartfelt thanks goes out to Brian Greer. Also in Washington, Jason Abel, a talented musician and keen editor, gave me a push at a critical juncture to complete this work. He also gave a very insightful reading of a final draft. Also lending their time and talents to the entire manuscript were Matt King and Paul Scott Thacker.

This work remains so many different endeavors at once. First and foremost as a genealogical experiment, this work begins and ends with new revelations about my family as I attempted to resurrect a personal queer past. The herald of these revelations was my father. His endless capacity to love never ceases to amaze me. He listened throughout this project and peppered me with questions, and we both took away so much from each other during this time. I honor him here. My mother makes me extremely proud, and I hope I am able to return that favor. My brothers, Mike and Jay, shaped my life and who I am more so than anyone else. For that, I am in their debt. Two particularly cool cousins, Brenda Mize and Robin Fuhrman, should be recognized.

And there are, of course, the scores of gay and lesbian Arkansans whose work this is. There are too many to thank in these pages—too many I cannot thank because I never managed to get their names—though these pages belong to each and every one of them.

The Un-Natural State

"New Girl/Old Girl Wedding" at Arkansas State Teachers College, now the University of Central Arkansas, circa 1930. *Files of Author.*

Outing Opal, Outing Arkansas

To repent is to own oneself entirely.

—SOREN KIERKEGAARD

L et me start with telling you this. She was actually my great-aunt, my grandmother's half sister, but everyone, including me, referred to her as simply "Aunt Opal." I have few memories of her that are entirely my own. The vague recollections I do have of her are of a kind woman who was fanatical about college football, especially her beloved Arkansas Razorbacks, and who always gave me circus peanuts the few times my grandmother took me to see her. Beyond this I remember nothing. I have no memories of Jerry, the woman with whom she lived for most of her adult life.

Suddenly in my late twenties, some time after Opal and Jerry had died, I was desperate for more memories. Coming out as a young gay man, first to myself and then to my family, involved a coming out as a family. A few years after I had come out to my parents, they began to reveal details about our extended family altogether new to me. My father, stoic but still deeply emotional in his own way, told me that Aunt Opal was most likely a lesbian. Subsequent talks with aunts and uncles only confirmed his suspicions.

I was enthralled. I peppered cousins, aunts, and uncles with questions seeking any details, any personal memories they could share about Opal and Jerry. No one really had any. Opal and Jerry, my father later explained to me, were always kept at a distance from the family, not primarily due to a suspicion of a taboo same-sex attraction but more so because my grandmother's side of the family always annoyed my grandfather. He saw them as poor and unsophisticated and did not want any of them around. Now, more than twenty years after her death in 1986, no one can really recall precisely where she is buried or whether Jerry, who died a short time afterward, is beside her.

I wish I knew more, but I don't. My drive and determination to learn more about my family's queer lineage inadvertently began to unearth episodes of Arkansas's queer past. This project began in graduate school and coincided directly with my own coming out to my family. As I struggled with my personal identity, my own private history, I discovered that Arkansas had its own queer leanings. Poked at and made fun of by the rest, Arkansas as a state has always struggled with how to define and defend itself against the rest of the nation. Arkansas, along with the South in general, has long been considered a redheaded stepchild of the union, a poorer cousin of sorts. Its long-standing state motto, "The Land of Opportunity," was commonly a source of ridicule within and outside the state, mainly because Arkansas afforded little economic opportunity to citizens compared to more prosperous neighbors. After years of both informal and official debate, the motto was dumped for one that could ideally tout the state's positive aspects and lure the highly prized tourist dollar.

Branding the state proved to be serious business. The Arkansas legislature debated the topic in the late 1980s. The state's leading newspaper, the *Arkansas Gazette,* opened a "nickname the state" contest. More than a thousand entries were submitted from citizens across Arkansas. Possible slogans ranged from the comical "Arkansas: Not as Bad as You Might Think" and "Arkansas: Now Tick-Free" to more serious and catchier slogans that, it was hoped, would attract visitors and their wallets. Some suggested "The Diamond State" as a nickname, as Arkansas, with its diamond mine open to the public, was the only state where one might find a diamond in the rough. The question of how the state would redefine itself was the order of the day.[1] Among myriad entries, state officials narrowed the contest down to three possible slogans. I have adopted these slogans and use them as three part titles for three distinct queer Arkansas histories: The Diamond State, The Natural State, and The Land of Opportunity.

The Diamond State

That Sunday morning in the summer of 1956 was hotter than usual, even for Arkansas. While most Arkansans sat fanning themselves in church, ten-year-old Robert Howard sat on the side of the road.[2] It was an act he had played out before, but something was different about this day's running away from home. He had adopted not only a new look but also a new identity to accompany it. Young Robert became a little blonde girl. He often modeled his sister's dresses. He enjoyed taking strolls around his hometown of Marvell, Arkansas, in those same dresses and donning the small, blonde wig he had ordered at the downtown five-and-dime. No one paid it any mind. No one gave the boy any trouble. Nevertheless, Howard wanted nothing more than to leave his home in the Arkansas Delta.

Throwing a few of his favorite dresses into a suitcase, he sat on the side of the road, thumb out, intent on hitchhiking to anywhere with anyone willing to give a little blonde girl a ride out of town. On Sunday morning cars were scarce. Finally, after some time, a black family traveling south to New Orleans to identify the body of a slain relative stopped to pick up the young hitchhiker. The family had driven the distance from Chicago to southeast Arkansas without incident or any real notice by anyone on their journey southward. Determined to keep it that way, they hid their white companion in the back of the car, placing Howard under blankets and quilts as they drove through the small towns and swamps of Arkansas and Louisiana.

Having dealt with their grisly family business in New Orleans, the group headed back north to Illinois and home. Approaching the town of Marvell, they tried desperately to convince their little blonde companion to come home with them to Chicago and live as a member of their family. She declined and was dropped off outside the town limits not far from where she started a few weeks earlier. Taking off her wig but leaving on the dress, Robert Howard made the walk home along those old familiar town roads where he in a dress had become a familiar sight. He was not entirely sure if he was able to fully pass as a little girl, never determining whether the black family had known or simply did not care whether he was a boy or a girl. He passed for the time he was with them, and he was tempted by their offer to let him live with them as their child in the big city. However, during their journey on the back highways along the Mississippi, he grew homesick for Marvell, Arkansas. It was his home, and though he had run away, all he wanted to do was run back.

Robert Howard's story is our first foray into Arkansas's queer past. Small-town drag shows were a tremendously popular means of rural entertainment and community fundraising, and little Robert most certainly would have been exposed to them at an early age. By the time Howard was an adult, drag in Arkansas, with glitzy showcases of queer talent in queer venues, would have changed from a means of rural entertainment to the principal means of gay community expression. Part one of this book will illustrate, through an analysis of the politics behind the performance of drag, how Arkansans used gender-bending numbers not only as an outlet for both subtle and explicit queer expression but also to showcase for those in attendance a number of social messages that ranged from racial subjugation to identity pride.

The Natural State

The fact that he was from Chicago made him a bit of an outsider already, but if his northern breeding were not suspect enough, the fact that unmarried Wellington Stephenson traveled with a black servant made him even more so. Stephenson arrived in Harrison, Arkansas, in the Ozark Mountains, on the morning of January 3, 1926, in his new position as the president of the North Arkansas Railroad. He troubled locals with his "city-type" mannerisms but probably much more with the company he kept.[3] Jesse, a black man Stephenson referred to as his "servant," lived right in the house with Stephenson and cooked all his meals. From the beginning, the townsfolk were suspicious of the relationship between the two men. Whatever it might have been, it surely was unacceptable. Though the two would live together in Harrison for another eight years, Stephenson never gained the respect and, indeed, acceptance of the local rank and file in that north Arkansas railroad town. Finally, his superiors cited poor job performance and dismissed Stephenson from his position during the depths of the Great Depression when the railroad industry began to bottom out. The railroad had brought Stephenson, his big-city mannerisms, and his black male lover to Arkansas, and those in Harrison never treated Stephenson as anything but an outsider. Perhaps he could have passed living with another male, a white male. Many southern men managed to live together discreetly as confirmed bachelors, just as women lived quietly together as spinsters or old maids. But Stephenson's queer combination of being from the dreaded north and having not just a male companion but a black male companion could not be ignored by the people of Harrison. Ultimately they could neither accept nor overlook these transgressions.

After the Second World War and as mobility increased, Arkansans found pride in the natural beauty found in the rolling hills of hardwoods and pines around small towns like Harrison and hoped to trade on it with the growing number of tourists moving across the country. But with the defining of the natural of course comes the defining of the unnatural. "The Natural State," the slogan that Arkansas would eventually settle on, illustrates the state's almost constant preoccupation with the natural and the unnatural. What is unnatural in the Natural State was continuously undergoing renegotiation and redefinition. Indeed, *unnatural* came to be used synonymously with queer desire, but this was not always the case. The unnatural and the abnormal, part two will demonstrate, changed along with societal discourse and cultural paranoia in an ongoing production of human difference by a larger heteronormative society. This part will focus on the Arkansas sodomy statute, exploring issues of power, resistance, and increasing gay and lesbian visibility in the state. Arkansas lawmakers distinguished themselves as the first in the nation to throw out their sodomy law in deeming it outdated and unnecessary. Then in a stunning reversal a year later, the sodomy law was rewritten to specifically address homosexuality, reflecting a trend of nascent queer visibility during the turbulent decade of the 1970s. The law was a peculiar means of discourse in society. Shown in this section, the sodomy law, with its in-flux definitions and applications, stood as a barometer of what society saw as abnormal and unnatural.

The Land of Opportunity

During the 1683 French expedition from Canada south along the Mississippi River, the explorer René Robert Cavelier, Sieur de La Salle, himself said to be intimately fond of his young and handsome valets, encountered tribes of Caddo Indians in what was then the Louisiana Territory. La Salle's aide, Henri Joutel, made a curious entry into the official log: he wrote of what he called the "hermaphrodites," male Indians who expressed and acted upon same-sex desires.[4] This is the only reference found in Joutel's journal to the homosexual identities of Indians who "passed among" the tribes in the Arkansas Territory. One thing is certain: the larger tribes in Arkansas had no real qualms with what we could consider gay Indians. The specific "hermaphrodite" encountered by Joutel later became the personal guide to La Salle's expedition.[5]

One of the few references I could find to same-sex desire in pre-Arkansas, that part of the Louisiana Territory that later became Arkansas, indicates that queer Indians were treated at worst with a passing disregard and perhaps as full and valued members of their tribes. This suggests to me that in the land that would become Arkansas, there was opportunity for the expression and larger acceptance of queer desire and sensibility long before Europeans would leave their mark on the land. As part three will illustrate, queers from both within and outside the state's boundaries eventually would construct, defend, and maintain personal spaces closely linked to their identities, whether they were simply a discreet queer bar in the basement of a hotel or, in one instance, the entire city limits of a tourist town in rural Carroll County. In any case Arkansas would be a "Land of Opportunity" for many gay people. By chronicling the establishment of rural communes, gay and lesbian tourism, and queer capitalism, this final section will focus on issues of creation and maintenance of gay and lesbian space, community, and queer expression and visibility in the age of queer capitalism.

But why a "queer" Arkansas? Many times throughout this work, I employ the word *queer* when speaking of both same-sex desire and identity in Arkansas. Throughout the text I use terms such as *gay* and *homosexual* interchangeably to describe an identity, using *homosex* to reference an act. When the term *queer* is employed, it is meant as far more than simply shorthand for gay and lesbian Arkansans. Used here, *queer* is meant as a descriptor, encompassing those who would claim to be gay or lesbian as well as those who engage in homosexual sex but would not or could not necessarily label themselves as such. I see *queer* acting as an umbrella used to summarize these various complicated identities as they are revealed in this work. Also, as seen in the events that unfold in subsequent chapters, *queer* can be seen to signify acts—not just identities—in certain cultures that contradict societal norms, whether by means of sexual, gender, or racial transgression.[6] It is not my intention to comb through Arkansas history, waving some sort of post-Stonewall magic wand, christening this person gay or that person lesbian. The identities and acts I have encountered here are far too complex at times to be labeled as simply *gay* or *lesbian*. There, *queer* can come in handy.

Each part provides an analysis of queer episodes of Arkansas history. Each will also detail a period of transformation, a queer segue from one period to the next within these sections. Also, within these pages, the queer histories are presented chronologically. Generally, histories are far more accessible this way. But I intend to steer clear of offering any timeline of a shared queer past. Any such timeline gives a false impression that history moves in a linear, progressive fashion so that we may look back and subtly scoff at the way things used to be. Arkansas was never behind; Arkansas never played catch-up to modern alternatives found elsewhere in the nation. Rather, Arkansas offered and operated under specific social and cultural conditions that shaped it as an alternative modernity.[7] To have a dialogue with these modernities, new parameters of discussing sexuality and desire become necessary, parameters that allow us and our historical gaze to look beyond rigid boundaries of homosexuality as the only frame-work in which to view our past. The alternative queer modernity I offer here will question and adjust the use of sexual topography to include alter-native queer lives that operate outside the dominant mode of addressing queer histories within the large "privileged metropolis."[8] This approach, by using a spatially defined rural environment, Arkansas, will illustrate that while urban queer lives were enjoying a new modernity after the Second World War, this modernity was never fixed or confined within the urban framework. Arkansas, this work will prove, operated within its own framework of modernity, buttressed by and defined within specific cul-tural circumstances found in the rural South.[9] Being there, Arkansans were able to construct enabling spaces in which to negotiate sexuality and desire. Once a friend asked why gay southerners do not simply pack up and leave for the city. Many do. I did. Many can't. Moving takes money. More impor-tantly to note is that many don't want to move. There are certain things about southern culture—the closeness to the land, church on Sunday—that so many do not want to give up to be another face in the city. It is their version of modernity that they cling to. No other will do.

Within the borders of twentieth-century Arkansas, queer Arkansans were regularly able to create and cordon off physical spaces which were their own, spaces ranging from backwoods drag clubs to lesbian communes tucked away in the Ozark Mountains. These venues were often protected from the intrusion of straight Arkansans and their social norms. Beyond these enclaves, expressions of queer life often were seen within larger straight communities where they were given casual and often unspoken approval of some deviation from accepted sexual norms. Encroachment of queer individuals and spaces in Arkansas came about when the larger heteronormative society within the state, in a postwar adjustment of social attitudes and perceptions, restructured what exactly Arkansans should see as deviant and threatening. Also, as the Second World War ushered in the civil rights movement, only then was queer really politicized. Only then, in the postwar reconstructing of America's families, their homes, their jobs, and the roads that connected them, would queer become a deeper transgression in Arkansas. It is at this time that the state began a rearticulation and transference of fear that had less to do with racial transgressions and more to do with sexual ones. It is here, as we will see in the The Diamond State, where rural drag shows performed in churches and schools lost their popularity, only for drag to reemerge decades later in gay bars across the state as not only a lucrative business practice but also as a larger means of community expression and articulation. It is at this point that, as will be seen in The Natural State, the sodomy law is rewritten, with the same language once used to condemn interracial sex now used to denounce sexual acts between those of the same sex. During this time, illustrated in The Land of Opportunity, lesbians from across the country, seeking peace from the growing animosity toward queer sexuality, retreated into the Arkansas hills to construct communities on their own land and on their own terms. These disparate sections come together to form a large narrative on southern history and will illustrate the complex contradictions that are characteristic of gay life in a southern context.

This work will focus on ideas of community and community building. I will illustrate the relationship between identity formation, community articulation, political mobilization, and cultural visibility within a proper contextual background and historical episodes such as the Second World War, the civil rights movement, post-Stonewall visibility, and the AIDS epidemic.[10] How these episodes work to redefine and renegotiate cultural understandings will also be addressed. For example I will examine how queer Arkansans, within specific cultural conditions, build sustainable queer communities within seemingly hostile southern environments.

In examining these cultural and social circumstances that shape daily queer lives in the South, this work builds upon John D'Emilio, George Chauncey, Estelle Freedman, Esther Newton, Lisa Duggan, and, more specifically, John Howard. In his collection *Carryn' On in the Lesbian and Gay South* Howard offers up the "three Rs," three useful analytical rubrics of race, religion, and the rural that cannot be avoided when speaking of southern life.[11] Race and religion shape the daily lives of queer Americans, but more so and in different fashions in the South. The rural landscape, the fabled and feared backwoods of America, is more complicated as it shapes both race and religion. In Arkansas, a state where so much of daily life deals with land and land extraction, the varied topographical regions found in the state produce varied populaces. Arkansans shape the natural landscape, and the natural landscape is constantly writing itself on the landscape of the body, from the callused hands of the Ozark plowman to the dirty, sweaty faces and sun-baked necks of the Delta cotton pickers. All Arkansans, all queer Arkansans, sit within the same larger state boundary, under the same political system, but the lay of the land produces a law of the land that shapes rural lives perhaps more than any other factor. No one map of Arkansas will suffice. Clearly, no one map of gay Arkansas will do either, as there is a need for multiple queer mappings across multiple and varied landscapes. Indeed, the varied landscapes across the South produce different queer results, and this work builds upon many who have detailed queer lives in the rural. John Howard is chief among them.

The rural lives and landscapes presented here depart from rural histories like those found in John Howard's hugely important *Men Like That: A Southern Queer History.* The most important of these departures stems from Howard's assertion that the majority of queer lives in Mississippi operated under a norm of "quiet complacency" offered by the larger heterosexual/white society. Though this may well have been true for queer Mississippians, it seems that queer Arkansans demanded something different than what Howard deems a "culture of quiet accommodation."[12] Simply judging from the photographs explored later in drag productions as early as the 1930s, the word *quiet* would hardly work to accompany *queer.* But at other times queer life was extremely quiet. Queer Arkansans lived and negotiated around these contradictions every day. Beyond this, these pages will work to construct a more complete history of the queer South beyond the entirely male (and largely white) study that Howard has given us in that it seeks to include the queer rural woman.

In finding queer on the landscape, let us turn to the land itself. Arkansas, as the nation's twenty-fifth state, has always been concerned with its land in some capacity, seen in both the old and new state mottos touting the land in either the opportunity it affords or the natural beauty it offers. This diverse land is seen in five distinct geographical areas.[13] Little Rock, the capital, sits almost dead center in the state. It is a city where the streets in one fashionable, upper-middle-class neighborhood are named for presidents but manage to skip Lincoln and pick up again at Grant. To the north toward Oklahoma and Missouri lie the Ozark Mountains covering most of the northwest quadrant of the state. To the south of the Ozarks sit the Ouachita Mountains. Dividing the entire state is the Arkansas River, carving out the Arkansas River valley as it flows between the mountain ranges from the Oklahoma border and then turns more to the south at Little Rock to flow across the flat Delta region toward the Mississippi River. The fertile Delta is a vast wedge of land running the length of the state's eastern border on the Mississippi River inward to a point east of Little Rock. Below the river and Little Rock, the Gulf Coastal Plain is wedged between the Delta and the Ouachita Mountains and runs to the southern border of Arkansas. All of these regions shape Arkansas culture and politics.

The diverse regions and landscapes found in Arkansas produce diverse and, at times, divided communities. The stark economic and social variances within Arkansas produce tensions between the agricultural southeast and the industrial northwest over interests still very much tied to the land. Focusing on smaller communities within the larger boundaries of the state is absolutely necessary not only to bridge these gaps between regions but also to examine common and contrasting aspects of race and class found within smaller communities across the state. With this in mind, this work is creating a community history. I do not intend to simply offer more historical threads in the overall tapestry of Arkansas history. Instead, I have created a specific past that seems to have been lost in a fit of queer aphasia. To achieve this, I have depended heavily on oral history. Just as so much of southern culture is passed down orally, so too does this work rely primarily on the spoken rather than the written word. Difficulties in researching a project of this nature were abundant. Oral histories not only helped to solve many of these problems but also played an essential role in building the textual framework for the arguments found here.[14] This work uses oral histories to record personal experiences and larger community histories that would otherwise be lost. The South as a region seems to constantly replay history so that the past never really passes in the South. Battles over the use of the Confederate flag, civil rights issues, controversial laws against teaching evolution in the classroom, as well as issues of sex and sexuality are all written across the South's tortured brow and are constantly revisited by both layperson and legislator alike. As I articulate these histories here, people will have their own memories of them. We differ in that I intend to collect them, bring them into a proper context, and share them with my fellow queer Arkansans in an effort to work against any aphasia, to write these histories again across the landscape of the South but this time in a queer voice and from a deeply personal perspective.

Even while constructing this history, my intentions remain quite selfish. In digging up what I could about my queer lineage, in an effort to own myself entirely, I discovered a queer past that moved beyond my family. Nevertheless, this work remains a highly personal journey. All good history is in some way personal, and how it is important to the historian, I believe, must be articulated. In keeping with that, I will remind the reader throughout this work of its personal meaning to me, my personal take on things, as well as my own queer history as it relates to this work. I came to realize that a better understanding of myself over time provides not only a better understanding of those who came before but also a possible connection to people and places now gone.

What legal scholar Casey Charles calls "autohistory," this relaying of the personal, shifts historical perspective to invite the audience into a constant conversation with countless others within and outside the text.[15] It is a journey that began with the outing of a relative I hardly remembered and became a personal memory of a private and now public queer Arkansas.

Most importantly, throughout this work, I was always reminded of Opal and never deviated from her legacy as my interest grew into a larger focus. And for that, I am grateful to her.

PART ONE

The Diamond State

ONE

Powder-Puff

Aged thirteen, eighth grade, junior high, I was a female cheerleader. Not a male cheerleader but a female one. I safely wore my miniskirt and danced with pompoms in front of my fellow students and proud parents in what was the most anticipated football match of the year, or at least it was to me. It was, as they called it, a Powder-Puff football game. As a charitable event whose beneficiary I now forget, popular female students donned football pads, jerseys, and helmets in a game that matched the eighth-grade girls against their freshman counterparts.

The boys were not left out. Our task was to cheer them on from the sidelines sporting cheerleading skirts while brandishing the discarded pompoms. Ideally, the boys who would be cheering would be of the popular set, those normally on the field not on the sidelines. Acting silly and playing for laughs, these boys would be part of a gender inversion show of their own. This was not me. Lanky, awkward, and a bit feminine, I was neither popular nor did I ever pretend to play football. I simply wanted to wear a dress in what was the only possible moment in an otherwise stifling junior high setting when one could get away with it. Such an opportunity could not be passed over.

Some of the girls, I remember, were just as eager to seize this opportunity for school-sanctioned inversion. For a few this was their only opportunity to play football in front of bleachers of roaring fans, without raising suspicious eyebrows or, God forbid, fears of a true female invasion of the sacred precincts of male football. The role of quarterback for the eighth-grade girls went to the daughter of the school's groundskeeper. The toughest, most stubborn girl in junior high, everyone agreed with no debate that she would be the logical choice. She did not require the after-school tutoring on play calling and pass throwing, punting and tackling, that other girls needed. She already knew the ins and outs of the sport. The night of the game, leading her team onto the field, she proudly wore the school's jersey and carried the game ball, perhaps as she had done a hundred times before in the safe arena of her own backyard. She must have wanted to play so badly. In retrospect I think she must have been looking forward to that cool night in October for months. I know I had.

What I was participating in—what we all were participating in, though I could not articulate it until now—was a merging of traditional southern drag with new queer sensibilities, personal sensibilities that our school practically encouraged, if only for that night. Early drag performances in Arkansas were charitable undertakings that counted on locally respected and recognizable figures to display gender roles and humiliate themselves by playing on opposites, a trend seen later in hypermasculine junior high football players posing as cheerleaders in a Powder-Puff football match. Drag in Arkansas would become, certainly by the time I was in junior high, the most popular and profitable means of gay community expression, though I would not be exposed to that aspect of drag culture for another decade or so. But, as I remember, I intended to use the Powder-Puff opportunity to safely satisfy a maturing queer curiosity and to perform in a dress in front of crowded stands of eager fans, my own little drag show of one, shining like a new diamond in a state of queer euphoria. Even my parents came.

TWO

Drag and the
Politics of Performance

Internees had their weekly dances and other social events, but causes for any real celebration and merriment must have been few and far between. However, on August 19, 1944, the *Rohwer Outpost,* the newspaper for the Japanese American interment camp just south of Pine Bluff, Arkansas, announced that the camp would host a most peculiar wedding ceremony and the first of its kind at Rohwer.[1] The groom for the occasion was A. G. Thompson, superintendent of the Rohwer schools. The identity of the bride remained a "closely veiled secret" until the day of the ceremony. The newspaper revealed only one clue about the bride: she was to be performed by a *he.* What was to be performed at the camp for the entertainment of those held there was a "womanless wedding" production. Presented by the Camp Rohwer Recreation Association and sponsored by the camp canteen, the womanless wedding was a popular folk production and a farcical parody of a Protestant wedding ceremony. These productions were staged by white men, usually prominent town figures, who played both the male and female roles and obviously required a great deal of cross-dressing for those involved.[2]

For the audience the cross-dressing represented only a portion of the real entertainment performed that evening. For this particular performance the production notes clearly call for "leading men" to take on the roles that require cross-dressing.[3] Specifically, in portraying the institution of marriage as more of a pragmatic and practical undertaking rather than any sort of sentimental union, the script calls for the bride to weigh at least two-hundred pounds and recommends that she appear to be pregnant, wearing a hastily assembled gown with two or three window curtains sewn end to end for her train and holding a bouquet of seasonal vegetables rather than flowers, all done in an attempt to make the obese and obnoxious bride the focal point of the comedic production.[4]

The script also called for the "smaller the better" groom, forced to marry a woman he does not love, to appear in a tight-fitting suit that would "augment his smallness."[5] In employing comedic gender inversion in folk drama, the man chosen to play the groom for the production would be a smaller, indeed almost feminine, man, while the man chosen to play the bride, burly and unshaven, was to be overly and overtly masculine. Because the script called for prominent town figures to play not only the bride but also other female roles, the audience would surely delight in witnessing the ludicrous inversion in which the town's more authoritative figures—the local banker, the mayor, the sheriff—appear ridiculous. The play brought these highly masculine figures down to a more manageable level where, if only for a brief while, those over whom they exercised their authority could comfortably reply with ridicule.[6] This was rural folk drag at its best. The play takes an everyday and entirely recognizable occurrence, a wedding, and mixes with it both the bizarre and the absurd and, along with the cast, produces a distorted mirror into which the audience can gaze.[7]

Shortly before 8:00 p.m. on Wednesday, August 23, the night of the performance, hundreds of Japanese Americans, paying a dime for adults and a nickel for the kids, filed into the camp's recreation center to witness the ceremony. That morning, the camp newspaper revealed the identity of the bride. This particular role was to be played by C. B. McGowan, a low-level administrator and aide to the camp kitchen.[8] Besides McGowan, the paper announced that many low-level and "masculine members" of the camp personnel would be "shedding their daytime Simon Legree personality" to join the wedding festivities.[9]

Given the attention to casting and the willingness of a truly captive audience to view, the production was a complete success. Besides the superintendent of schools' marrying a member of the kitchen staff (surely to the delight of the school children in the audience), the two men were joined by forty members of the grounds crew and motor pool who were all "fittingly dressed for the roles."[10] According to the *Rohwer Outpost,* this combination left those in attendance "rolling in the aisles."[11]

When taking into account the actual script of "A Womanless Wedding," it is clear that the comedic value is built upon the visible and

The cast of the womanless wedding assembled on stage. *Courtesy Arkansas History Commission.*

performed difference of gender and class. Though the most obvious difference is that of gender and the creation of a staged gender confusion, the script also paints the characters as members of another class, with general mockery of the uneducated, the hillbilly mountain folk who by all accounts know no better than to involve themselves in such foolhardy endeavors.

The play opens with the arrival of the aunt and uncle of the bride, entering the church through an archway again decorated with garden vegetables rather than flowers; beyond that, the script dictates that the wedding decor be meager, as if to suggest lack of funds to purchase such

The minister conducts the ceremony while the father of the bride watches nervously. Notice the minister reads from *Esquire* magazine. *Courtesy Arkansas History Commission.*

materials. From the opening dialogue the audience knows immediately of the poor family roots and the unfeminine gluttony of the female guests.

> FIRST USHER. Allow me to present the uncle and aunt of the bride. (*Confidentially.*) I don't think they're bragging folks. He can't help it.
>
> UNCLE. Is this where th' war . . . I mean th' wedding t' be at?
>
> AUNT. Shore it is. (*Surveying room.*) Ever'thing's purteyed up right elegant too.
>
> UNCLE. Huh! They better save their money t' buy victuals with. (*Strolls backstage, steals large cookie from tray.*) Say, whur is ever'body?
>
> AUNT, *snatching cookie.* Gimmie that teacake! Hain't ye got no fetchin'-up a-tall? (*Eats cookie greedily, talks with mouthful.*) Umm-ma mum-m mum mum?

The mother of the bride. Notice the baby at her feet. *Courtesy Arkansas History Commission.*

UNCLE. Huh?

AUNT. Um ma mum ma ma!

UNCLE, *disgustedly.* Try United States, Maw, we might git along better. (*Aunt swallows cookie painfully. Uncle watches her.*) You know, a pig wouldn't git killed if he didn't make a hog out uv hisself.[12]

Besides their general entertainment value in observing the ludicrous behavior of country yokels in confused states of gender, womanless weddings (and their sister production, the womanless beauty pageant) often doubled as fundraisers for local organizations and were fast to spring up and be performed by those who wished to assist wartime causes. Arkansas chapters of the American Red Cross were all too eager to use the popularity of womanless weddings as a fundraiser during the

The bride being escorted by the groom after the ceremony. *Courtesy Arkansas History Commission.*

First World War. Holding their ceremony in the local Methodist church and encouraging townspeople to remember the Red Cross and "buy liberally of the tickets," the local chapter of Marked Tree, Arkansas, advertised that their production would include a local judge, a college professor, and other well known men playing "leading ladies in short socks and short skirts."[13] Though it might seem bizarre for a Methodist church to host such a drag production, it also makes the most sense. In a small rural town such as Marked Tree, the church would provide both the largest venue in town, often serving as the community center for secular matters as well as the natural backdrop for a mock wedding ceremony. In that era a rural Protestant church was primarily used as a religious venue (and certainly a masculine one, as southern denominations at this point are dominated by men in both lay and spiritual roles) on Sunday mornings and Wednesday nights as well as other select times during the liturgical calendar. With the production of a womanless wedding it becomes, if only for a few hours on a Saturday night, a queer space that allowed for church-sanctioned institutions such as marriage to be mocked by the members of the community.[14] Indeed, in this part of the rural South what is queer one minute is not the next; the desire to display or perform queerness fluctuates between available spaces in Arkansas. Though productions such as those mentioned here can be seen as queer in their bending and blending of both race and gender, there is an important distinction to make. Whereas queer behavior is primarily seen as a reaction or contrast to accepted social norms, in these cases the performances operate well within and are even sanctioned by those norms and their enforcers.

Churches were not the only spaces used to host such productions, as they were also not the only institution that remained polarized by class and gender or segregated by race and sexes in Arkansas; public schools were also quick to host drag productions to raise funds for drastically underfunded coffers.[15] With boys and young men encouraged to display their masculinity in school-sanctioned sporting events and girls encouraged to cheer them on, the southern school offered an environment of extreme and polarized genders with little to no space in between wherein one might operate with confidence or dignity.[16] It is this environment that also seemed to foster drag productions, providing an extreme take on the purposes and services normally provided in southern public schools and small Protestant churches. Not even twenty miles from Marked Tree sits the odd little town of Wilson, just a few miles west from the Mississippi River in the heart of Arkansas cotton country. Members of the Wilson family, for which the town is named, owned nearly everything from the drugstore to the beauty parlor. They were large-scale landowners operating under a new plantation system, the pinnacle of southern aristocracy. Under the new system sharecroppers who worked Wilson land were paid in a created currency known as "doodlum script," thereby forcing them to spend their earnings in Wilson businesses.[17] Charging themselves with the welfare of the townspeople, members of the Wilson family were fond of womanless productions and their ability to raise funds for local causes, especially those championed by the white schools. Productions were mostly performed in the white high school's auditorium, and proceeds almost always benefited the white-only schools.

Photographs taken in Wilson during the 1930s show white men in a seasonal beauty pageant sharing the stage with other white men in blackface. In the thick of the American South this suggestive mingling of "black" men and white "women" went to the core of both racial transgression and sexual disobedience.[18] For the people of Wilson the production was undoubtedly humorous and festive, although in actuality any real mingling of black men and white women would certainly have incited swift retribution by white men. In the segregated South a white man in an authoritative position not only delighted in flirting with the permeable boundaries of gender and sexuality but also openly mocked the social construct of race through the coupling of rural drag and blackface minstrelsy. Also, judging from the images produced here, it is essential to call upon arguments made concerning sex and racial violence. In her essay "'The Mind That Burns in Each Body': Women, Rape, and Racial Violence" Jacquelyn Dowd Hall writes that the South "maintained order through a system of deference and customary authority in which all whites had informal police power over all blacks."[19] Furthermore, in a system based on an informality that bred such injustice, southern whites heavily manipulated rape fears both to provoke and excuse violence against African Americans. Showing men in comical blackface onstage with women clad only in black lace conveniently plays on popular themes of race and sexual violence, perpetuating images of a buffoonish, perhaps animal-like, negro capable of morphing at any moment into the "black beast rapist" common in American popular culture of the period.

Womanless weddings and blackface minstrelsy were popular across Arkansas, as Arkansas used both secular and religious backdrops to see just how far those onstage would probe and reinforce the limits of acceptable behavior. That is not to say, however, that they were performed in every small town and hamlet in the state. Productions of these styles had a stronger appeal and indeed a more essential function where there was a stark divide between race and class as seen in the sharp juxtaposition of race in a Mississippi River sharecropping town or the obvious divide between white guards and imprisoned Japanese Americans. The stark racial difference between black and white in northeast Wilson, Arkansas, is clear. One must also realize just how dramatically the racial composition was altered in southeast Arkansas with the sudden arrival of over eight thousand Japanese and persons of Japanese decent. Both drag and black-

Miss December. *Courtesy of the Special Collections, University of Arkansas Libraries, Fayetteville.*

face were more established in environments where those in power, who were often the performers, saw the didactic nature of illustrating class and race control through low-brow entertainment as entirely necessary.

Beyond any entertainment value, scholars commonly treat black-face minstrelsy as a social exercise that illustrates white superiority over blacks but mixes with it a voyeuristic ethnic and racial envy.[20] Through productions of blackface minstrelsy, southern white males borrowed from cultural peripheries to produce perverted interpretations that would be on display in towns like Wilson. This interpretation was born

Beauty pageant contestants assembled on stage at Wilson. *Courtesy of the Special Collections, University of Arkansas Libraries, Fayetteville.*

out of the intrusive gaze of fascination into a subculture that was forbidden and largely inaccessible to whites.

Could the same be said for onstage gender bending? The southern culture apparent here prized the whiteness of the southern male as well as his masculinity. As Pete Daniel points out in his treatment of such transgressive showmanship in the American South, white males controlled household economics, local and state politics, the larger economy, and race etiquette and could both violate and enforce all barriers with impunity.[21] Minstrelsy and drag were all the more thrilling because they flirted with boundaries of sexuality and mocked the southern patri-

Miss February. *Courtesy of the Special Collections, University of Arkansas Libraries, Fayetteville.*

archal and supremacist order. Beyond witnessing these shows, as with most folk dramas and similar productions, the audience was supposed to walk away having taken in a vital social lesson in southern living. To borrow from gender theorist Simone de Beauvoir, one is not so much born a white American, or more importantly a white southerner, but rather one becomes one through the lessons of a didactical onstage farce.[22] This message can be seen in the "A Womanless Wedding" script when the bride's uncle instructs his wife to try speaking "United States" so that they "might git along better." A message perhaps not altogether lost on the Japanese Americans in the audience.

Miss August. *Courtesy of the Special Collections, University of Arkansas Libraries, Fayetteville.*

It is clear that while productions of womanless weddings allowed for a certain degree of self-humiliation, some used the show as an opportunity to display their manliness and masculinity center stage in an effort to illustrate southern masculinity and whiteness. In the Hayes script for "A Womanless Wedding," if the audience had any doubt as to the actual gender or sex of the characters, all was to be revealed by the final curtain but only after the portrayal of marriage as a less-than-maudlin institution undertaken hurriedly by the uneducated underclasses. The final exchange takes place just as the enormous bride, Tiny Oats (a characternym suggesting small testicles), and the elderly groom, J. Flivverton Barley (a characternym suggesting an old and out-dated man), are exchanging vows.[23]

DRAG AND THE POLITICS OF PERFORMANCE

MINISTER, *to Bride.* Young woman, do you really want this sorry wad?

BRIDE, *giggles.* You'll never know how bad.

MINISTER. Very well, but remember, you brought it on yourselves. (*Arranges book.*) Join lunch-grabbers, please? (*Bride and Groom join hands.*) My friends, this couple has sworn before unreliable witnesses that they feloniously desire to sail the malicious ship to Get-the-Money. Therefore, I know nothing else to do but proceed. (*Pause.*) J. Flivverton Barley, do you take this relic . . . I mean, this woman for better or for worse?

GROOM, *looks at Bride, pause.* I'll take her for better. If she gits any worse, I'll kill her.

MINISTER. Wisely spoken, indeed! And now, Tiny Oats, do you take this souse . . . I mean, this spouse for worse or better?

BRIDE, *pause.* I'll take him for worse, till I can find better.

MINSTER. Very good! Now, you both agree . . . as just punishment for this unthinking act . . . I repeat, do you both agree to never flirt over ten times on week days and fifteen times on Sunday? Answer, please.

BOTH. We do.[24]

After the final exchange the paternal grandfather rushes the stage in a fit of sexual craving for the bride.

GRANDPA, *coming forward.* Granny's bin gladeyin' the parson, an' I'm a donkey mule if I don't kiss the bride! (*He rushes Bride.*)

(*She fights him away, trying to run. In the tussle, the Bride's skirt drops off, exposing gaudy BVDs and garters. Bride rushes out r., flinging her bridal bouquet into audience as she leaves. Curtain falls.*)[25]

Just as the curtain falls, the bride's skirt is removed to display oversized and ostentatious men's underwear held in place by women's garters. In this display of the actor's masculinity and ability to humiliate himself, the masculine is altogether unhinged, downplayed, and, in some ways, reinforced. Also, by performing the normative, or in the case of womanless weddings the non-normative attributes of masculinity, masculinity and its chief characteristics can be seen as contingent on certain social circumstances rather than entirely inherent in or independent from them.[26] Beyond this, it is important to note that the actor who portrayed the underwear-exposing bride, in this instance the camp cook, had the power to self-humiliate whereas the Japanese Americans for whom he cooked had no such opportunity.

Other productions of womanless weddings, not using the popular Hayes script, were also quick to invert and display overt masculinity. At Hendrix College in Conway, Arkansas, students who wished to join the "H" Club, an organization for athletes who had lettered in a particular college sport, had to endure three days of intense pledging.[27] At a school that provided no Greek social system of fraternities and sororities for its students, student organizations such as the "H" Club provided students with the social interactions and events that a Greek system normally would have offered. Robert Meriwether, himself a future Hendrix College history professor, lettered in basketball as a freshman in the spring of 1946. Since he was the tallest of the initiates that year, he was chosen as the bride for the womanless wedding that took place in the center of campus. Meriwether looked forward to it, seeing the production as an opportunity to meet girls through self-humiliation and campus-wide notoriety.[28] With the war in Europe over for a little more than a year and in the Pacific for just eight months, returning servicemen were just beginning to trickle home, making available men on college campuses in short supply. Meriwether and his fellow male classmates seized every opportunity to benefit from this advantage.

Though, as Meriwether noted, the Second World War plucked many of Arkansas's men and boys out of their typical existence, it did nothing to hinder any tradition of cross-dressing and female impersonation. Indeed, in the almost entirely same-sex environment established by the U.S. Army, cross-dressing was encouraged by the armed forces. GI drag was a popular form of entertainment for servicemen who often found themselves in strict same-sex environments for long periods of time, and as historian Alan Berube contends, it offered a haven for gay soldiers looking for an outlet for an otherwise-taboo behavior in an often hostile military atmosphere.[29]

At Arkansas military bases Camp Robinson, Camp Pike, and Fort Chaffee, drag seemed to flourish as a form of entertainment for enlisted men, bringing urban and rural drag traditions and performances to a

Robert Meriwether in his womanless wedding. Hendrix College, 1946. *Courtesy Hendrix College Archives.*

common location. Men often performed original scripts with titles such as "Queens of the Companies" and "The It Girls."[30] Though at times resembling their rural counterparts of cross-dressing entertainment, GI drag shows differed in that they often sought to impersonate pin-up models and Hollywood starlets (such as the popular Carmen Miranda), figures and personalities recognizable to almost anyone. Here we see the first departure from the rural tradition. Servicemen took these shows with them "on the road," as they were transferred to various locations during the war. Given their nature, rural womanless wedding productions could not travel easily simply for the reason that a local audience would not see the humor in another town's mayor dressing in women's

Hazing ritual, Hendrix College. *Courtesy Hendrix College Archives.*

clothing; it was important for ridiculed characters to be recognizable. However, scripts often did travel from community to community, as church congregations and social organizations sought to capitalize on fundraising techniques that proved successful elsewhere.

Again, as with the productions of womanless weddings and beauty pageants, the chief roles often went to authority figures, though like at Camp Rohwer, they were often performed by low-level officers and enlisted men. More often than not they were corporals and sergeants who allowed themselves, and their masculinity, to be openly mocked by the troops they commanded everyday. In an article on the "Circus Daze" production, the *Camp Robinson News* also reported that Corporal Conrad, who played Lola the Lady Lion Tamer, wore the most "resplendent costume."[31] Her "symphony of color" ensemble was "tipped by a glamorous red pompadour, trimmed in kelly-green ostrich plumes with white garnish print trimmed in yards of black mosquito netting, ruffles, and large gold sequins."[32] More extravagant costumes, though at times still absurdly displayed, lent an air of professionalism quite different from the rural productions that encouraged the use of such things as seasonal vegetables and window curtains. The trend of splendid and often excessive costuming seen in the urban drag scene won out over the rural trend of using the cheap and common.

Though largely confined to the camp, some GI drag shows did eventually make their way into local towns, either intentionally fulfilling a duty of entertainment to the civilian population or for other reasons. One company, staging its production of "This Is the 66th" to boost local civilian morale, performed a three-night run at Little Rock's Robinson Center. The production ended with a "girlee" line weaving in and out of the audience. A newspaper article mentioned that "girls" drew a number of "howls from the crowd" from men and women. Drag was becoming larger than the simple one-night, one-show performance that many Arkansans were used to; drag was slowly becoming a profession.

GI drag made its way from rural locals into mainstream culture in other less conventional ways as well. In one instance, when soldiers were preparing for a drag production of "The It Girls," they were allowed to travel across the Arkansas River from Camp Robinson to Little Rock to shop for costumes at the Ladies Ready-to-Wear department store. Sgt. Harry Houston of Camp Robinson Headquarters Company played the role of "Peaches," a "silky siren with a petty larceny disposition."[33] When Sergeangt Houston found himself the instigator of a "near riot of laughter" from the female patrons, he offered his services to the department store as a model of women's fashion.[34] Although his offer was turned down by store managers, this nonetheless demonstrates that GI drag was moving off the base and into town, and both performers and locals not directly affiliated with the military desired more.

Though the majority of drag shows performed in Arkansas military encampments lacked any real professionalism, this is not to say that servicemen and civilians were not treated to the occasional star production. One man, Harvey Goodwin, performed one "gratis" show as his female persona "Harvey Lee" Goodwin. One of the nation's more famous female impersonators and a native of Little Rock, Goodwin performed in venues all over the nation, such as San Francisco's famous cabaret club Finocchio's, and toured through many cities with the "Jewel Box Review."[35] He was a favorite of servicemen and local civilians, and even of Pres. Franklin Roosevelt, who often commanded birthday performances. As far as the professional drag circuit, comprising shows hosted mainly in cabaret-style venues in large urban centers, Harvey Goodwin was indeed world famous.[36] And now he was in Arkansas. Before Goodwin, before the war, Arkansas drag operated within a specific cultural context defined by both rural and southern social parameters that often included charity. More peripatetic and visible, drag was now being allowed to flourish beyond these boundaries as a purely entertainment-minded, profit-making venture seen mainly in large urban centers such as San Francisco, Paris, and Berlin. Such undertakings also allowed for a certain amount of professionalism, as stars tried to distinguish their acts and personas from competitors, with door cover charges and drink prices helping to pay for the expensive gowns and props for acts and routines that the performers would become known for.

From an early age Goodwin suffered from tuberculosis. He was born in Little Rock in 1912, and when he graduated from Little Rock High School in 1930, in a move of early queer diaspora, he left. Goodwin sought to start his career in entertainment in Washington DC, where he quickly found daytime work as a low-level government secretary and saved his earnings to pay for weekend dance lessons and a wardrobe of upmarket female attire. He returned to Little Rock only briefly, between 1941 and 1943, for treatment at local sanitariums but did not sit idle. Locals were well aware of what talent was now at their doorsteps and quickly coaxed him to perform his shows at the victory balls held at the Little Rock ordnance plant, a munitions factory employing hundreds of Arkansans on both day and night shifts. Harvey Goodwin was delighted to bring his talents back home to contribute to the war effort in his unique way. Billed as a once-in-a-lifetime experience, tickets quickly sold out for the event. On September 25, 1942, his drag persona, Harvey Lee, made her first appearance at the factory's auditorium. He walked onto the stage that night accompanied by two full orchestras. The auditorium, "the biggest barn I could appear in," was filled to capacity with

Harvey Lee performs at the Arkansas Ordnance Plant, 1942. *Courtesy University of Arkansas at Little Rock Archives.*

five thousand factory workers, their families, and various other Little Rockers delighted to have such talent in the city.[37]

Lee stayed in Arkansas until the spring of 1943 headlining at three victory balls. When his condition became manageable, he left to resume his drag career, and after the end of the war he took his act to cabaret venues in postwar France and Germany. Retiring in 1967, he would not return to Arkansas until 1989. Despite his poor health, the war made Goodwin. Though he certainly would have remained popular without the help of the war, the worldwide engagement made Harvey Lee a drag persona recognized by soldiers and civilians alike well beyond the confines of urban popularity.

The war had a peculiar effect on drag, as seen in the shows and productions in Arkansas. It is important to note that not all of those who participated were closeted gays simply looking for an outlet for taboo behavior. But did some of those who participated find it curiously liberating? Were some men more eager than others to try on their wives' stockings and hats, or their mother's or sister's? Were some more conscious of matching handbags to shoes? The popularity of drag originated with prominent locals in outlandish costumes, uttering corny dialogue and wobbling across stages in heels two sizes too small. Behind it all was a subtle political message. These patriarchal figures were willing to be openly mocked by their fellow townspeople to illustrate the ridicule certain to follow anyone else's deviation from established codes for gender and sexual behavior. In the process of self-ridicule, these southern white males again asserted their authority over blacks and women by flaunting their exclusive ability to cross lines of gender and race with impunity. They drew the lines and made the rules; they alone could violate those boundaries.[38] However, the practice and production did not carry the same meaning for all involved, or indeed all who observed then and now.

This is especially evident with the first production noted here. With hundreds of Japanese Americans, mainly from Los Angeles and Orange counties, now finding themselves in the thick of the segregated South, those responsible for their internment deemed necessary certain lessons and displays of American whiteness. Beyond the production of "A Womanless Wedding," Japanese Americans at Rohwer and Jerome were regularly treated to films such as *Little Black Sambo* to illustrate that "others" are indeed a source of comedy and should be openly mocked. Clearly, camp officials were showing Asian Americans that to be a successful American, one must be white and masculine. This lesson was important given the fact that when the detainees had leave to visit local towns, they were often confused as to which public facilities to use: white or colored. Asian Americans were told by camp officials that, when in doubt, use white restrooms.[39] After all, they were training detainees to become more white than Asian, and what location to better illustrate the differences between white and the lesser, the other, the *queer,* than the American South? And the point was illustrated in a spatially defined area: Arkansas, where the differences are everyday, far more pronounced, state sanctioned, and strictly enforced. Here, drag productions helped to accomplish all of this. Indeed, it took these locations of pronounced divisions for rural drag to flourish. The sharp divides of class and race evident in the Japanese internment camp are distinctly similar to those found in the churches and schools of Delta sharecropping towns, stark divisions of race enforced with often tangible barriers.[40]

The Second World War had turned society, along with its sexual and racial norms, upside down as the wartime atmosphere uprooted and mobilized millions, and drag was brought along too. Rural drag shows, which normally were only performed locally so that the audience would recognize and appreciate the performance of those in them, were now at the forefront of society and quickly moved around, mobilizing as swiftly as the army personnel that performed them. If during the rural production of drag shows, schools and churches provided the most extreme cases of segregation and male-dominated institutions, the army did so on a far more impressive scale. In the enormous same-sex environment that it created, the armed forces provided yet another extraordinary situation in which drag could flourish.

The war gave voice to those who wished to question established institutions that had provided a delicate equilibrium of race and sexuality for Arkansans. As southern blacks returned from the war, having witnessed and enjoyed greater access to rights and opportunities, many began to demand an increase in civil rights on the home front. This rejection of the status quo by southern blacks eventually led to the civil rights movement, and one of its first and most tangible victories in the dismantling of the extreme institution of segregation unfolded in Arkansas.

For the first time a southern governor, Arkansas's Orval Faubus, defied the law when it came to civil rights. He refused to adhere to a federal court order attempting to enforce the U.S. Supreme Court's 1954 decision in *Brown v. Board of Education of Topeka, Kansas,* which called for the desegregation of public schools. In 1957 Faubus mobilized the Arkansas National Guard to prevent nine black students from entering Little Rock

Central High School. He eventually withdrew these men, leaving local law enforcement in charge of crowd control. Pres. Eisenhower, witnessing the escalating scene as it played out on national television, dispatched federal paratroopers to escort the students while on campus. The spotlight fell on Arkansas as the nation waited to see what might come of segregation and other racist institutions of the American South. In 1958 Faubus closed all four of Little Rock's high schools, locking out close to four thousand students and locking in dozens of teachers and administrative personnel forced to honor contracts. Although many court battles lay ahead, this was the beginning of the end of segregation in Arkansas schools.

The yearlong school closing gave Arkansans a brief period to adjust to the idea of desegregation.[41] This period of adjustment for race relations in Arkansas could also be seen as a transition period for Arkansas at large. The now nationally notorious Faubus, born and raised in the Ozark Mountains, had briefly attended Arkansas's Commonwealth College, an institution founded in Mena, Arkansas, by socialist organizers founded on the principles of southern progressivism and the development of coal mining and farming unions.[42] He spent the majority of his early political career devoted to the plight of rural working families and efforts to industrialize the state. Later, as he and other southern political figures abandoned progressive politics for race-baiting and incendiary politics, Arkansas's more progressive past, the past that allowed for a greater degree of nonconformity and queer theatrics on the rural level, began to disappear. Arkansas entered a new modernity at the beckoning of the Second World War and would see a great politicization of sex and sexuality.

Just as the postwar years brought increasing policing of race, so too did the policing of sex and sexuality shift in this period. Gay and lesbian servicemen and women returned home from the war to find an increased climate of paranoia and hostility. Paradoxically, the American military, which generally saw homosexuals as a threat to national security and to the strength and morale of the armed forces, had provided ample venues for those same young men questioning their sexuality to find others within the system, or perhaps within the numerous cities where they found themselves stationed. Servicemen might discover a queer bar or catch a Harvey Goodwin performance in San Francisco as they awaited further deployment. A young man unsure of his sexuality, or at least the possibility of a concrete identity based on his sexuality, could now locate a vast network of others like them in the large, same-sex environments established by the military.[43] For many, GI drag shows offered not only a safe haven but also a form of condoned self-expression in the overly masculine military system. For gay men in military drag shows, this odd feeling of acceptance and the facilitation of queer space and venue proved to be only temporary. Indeed, their return to the home front found an America weary of the fast-paced uncertainty and extraordinary circumstances of the war years and longing to return to a "normal life" that no longer included the vibrant sexual expression of rural and GI drag productions. Such activity was rapidly being deemed dangerous and a threat to postwar America, and those who performed them were quickly portrayed as nonconformists.

In the cold war climate of the 1950s and 60s, sexual deviation was now a trait assigned to the "outside agitator," and homosexuality was looked upon as something to fear. The homosexual was painted as a perverse and dishonest individual, a threat to the nuclear family that Americans sought so hard to reconstruct, or perhaps altogether invent after the turbulent war years.[44] Though all these threats and attributes were assigned in order to isolate homosexuals from a southern white norm, a strange case appeared on the front page of the *Arkansas Gazette* in 1961 just before Christmas, one that only seemed to confirm Arkansas's concerns that they indeed had something to fear from homosexuals.

THREE

Drag in the Daylight

I f the war enjoyed an interesting union with drag, the war's end
made drag a most peculiar widow. The atmosphere following the
war dictated a return to a normalcy that truly never was. The new
look-a-like American suburb was evidence of an increasingly homoge-
nized national culture. New television icons such as Donna Reed, donning her string of pearls and kitchen apron, showed American audiences
the value of an orthodox American family. Helped along by such things
as growing public fascination with the emerging field of sexology, drag
was seen less as a valuable, if not lucrative, form of rural entertainment
and fundraising and more as a subversive potential challenge to the new
model of the American family. With this, the popularity of productions
such as womanless weddings began to subside. Even the administration
at tiny Hendrix College openly discouraged freshman males from participating in them.[1] This trend was helped along by a most unusual and
high-profile case involving the state's notorious penal system.

Although many considered Arkansas's penal system the most corrupt and inhumane in the nation, most Arkansans turned a deaf ear to
the tales of sadism and brutality that filtered out of the prison farms.
After all, the prison system caused few public problems and at times even
turned a profit for the state. Arkansas prisons achieved this through their
largely self-sufficient system, producing useful materials such as cotton
and lumber at cut-rate cost for all-too-eager state buyers. The two principal institutions were Cummins Prison Farm, built on land acquired by
the state in 1902, and Tucker Prison Farm, constructed in 1916. After
the end of the Second World War, the institutions sprawled over a combined 21,000 acres of southeast Arkansas farmland, not too far from the
Japanese American internment camps at Rohwer and Jerome. Both
prison camps were facilities built with self-sufficiency and profit in mind.

Both locations had road gangs, chicken farms, and forestry camps, not to mention thousands of acres of cultivated crops tended by prison hoe gangs.[2]

Like stories of abuse and brutality that seemed to filter out to the Arkansas populace, so did stories of sex and gender "confusion." Homosexuality, or perhaps more so the act of homosex, has been closely associated with prison life for some time.[3] It was common at both Tucker and Cummins for older and often physically larger, male prisoners to adopt a "punk," or younger male sexual partner, usually in an arrangement tantamount to brutal and systematic same-sex rape inside a power system already based on exploitation and abuse. It was estimated by some Arkansas prison officials that perhaps 80 percent of prisoners had raped, been raped, or had same-sex sexual experiences with other inmates.[4] And since virtually all prison guards were themselves prisoners, called trusties, pay-offs, bribes, and demands for sexual favors from other inmates were high. Homosexuality and homosex were a viable issue at both prisons, at times considerably slowing down production. To combat this, prison officials routinely made "known-homosexuals" trusties, giving them guns and making them tower guards, positions that insured that they would be alone all day. Still, brutal and sadistic homosex persisted. But not all sex was nonconsensual, as men in a prison, much like its army counterpart, found comfort in the arms of others. Also, beyond these occurrences, tales of male prisoners in drag, often taking on female names and personas, made their way to the free-world parlors of Arkansas.

One such inmate, Hazel, had achieved notoriety at Tucker and throughout the entire penal system. Hazel, whose actual name is unknown, wore a red wig and bib overalls and stood over six feet tall. Prison officials remember Hazel as a good worker and a valuable asset to the farm teams, though the only real problem they had with him was that Hazel had to be constantly moved from prison job to prison job due to her "seductive nature." Jimmy Carlin, a trusty long-line rider in charge of the tractor squad at Tucker, complained to his supervisors that "he . . . she, whatever it is, is always out in the ditch laying one of my tractor boys. Every time I see a tractor with nobody on it I find Hazel down in the ditch blowing someone. Hazel is getting all the action, and I'm not getting any plowing done."[5] Administrators were truly torn. Hazel was providing a service of sorts by offering a sexual outlet to men in a strict same-sex setting while satisfying her own need for homosex and those of fellow inmates as well. Prison officials were willing to recognize if not accept this. However, the prison was a working, for-profit institution. Plowing had to be done. Hazel was moved from the tractor squad to the carpenter team, then on to the vegetable shack. All the foremen complained of the same problem: Hazel was severely slowing down production. Finally, Hazel was transferred to the chicken house, a prison job that required no more than one person at a given time. Once in charge of the chicken house, prison officials noticed that Hazel grew increasingly lonely, and they grew sympathetic. They tolerated her bribing other inmates to keep her company by letting them pinch valuable chicken eggs for their own use or to sell to other inmates, a lucrative trade to say the least. Guards turned a blind eye to it as they were well aware of the need that Hazel met and the pleasure she gave and received.

Stories such as this were commonplace in the Arkansas penal system. Indeed, when examining Hazel's experience within Tucker Prison, it seems that she was more than simply tolerated by other inmates and officials within the prison, a space seen as entirely male but hardly entirely masculine. Hazel, after all, did provide a service beyond that of working the chicken coops and plowing dusty fields. Strict same-sex environments such as the Arkansas penal system often fostered the sexual situations that prison officials later regarded as problematic. Problematic to some, not so much to others, institutions such as churches, schools, and military establishments, and certainly prisons, were not merely fostering queer behavior by providing the appropriate environment for it but were openly encouraging it by providing space and opportunity.

Hazel was not the only transsexual to inhabit the Arkansas penal system and certainly was not the most legendary. Arkansans who heard of her would have certainly recalled the strange case of David Van Rippey. Just two weeks before Christmas 1961, an article appeared on the front page of the *Arkansas Gazette,* the state's leading newspaper and the oldest continuously operating newspaper west of the Mississippi River. It sat on the page top center, right above an article on the Soviet Union's nuclear capability entitled "Reds Threaten to Test Again," showing both the anxiety of the atomic age and the routinely articulated fear of the communist so closely linked with homosexuality during the McCarthy years.[6] David Reginald Van Rippey had been in the Monroe County jail for four months when he was transferred to Cummins just south of Pine Bluff in southeast Arkansas. He was arrested for bigamy after his second wife, Glenda Smallwood Van Rippey, filed a complaint with the Monroe County sheriff's office.[7] On December 13 Van Rippey was escorted to the infirmary for his routine prison physical. Prison physician A. H. Hollins was surprised when Van Rippey refused to remove his clothes for his physical, a procedure for all newly arrived inmates. He finally called in guards who were able to wrestle the prison uniform off of Van Rippey. What they found would become the stuff of Arkansas legend. The prison superintendent, Lee Henslee, was immediately called to the Hollins's office. Henslee told a *Gazette* reporter that "we have had a lot of feminine looking men come here but this one didn't seem quite right," and that he was suspicious of Van Rippey from the start.[8] He had no idea that *he* was actually a *she*.

More baffling details began to unfold. Not only had Van Rippey fooled everyone into thinking that she was a he, but she had also pleaded guilty and received a one-year prison sentence for bigamy, a crime of a sexual nature considered immoral and entirely undesirable by southern norms. On top of this, she also was the father of two boys, ages seven and eight. She later admitted to prison officials that, as the father in her first marriage, she had adopted them.

As for vocations prior to arrest, authorities were dumbfounded when Van Rippey listed that among other things she had owned a service station and women's shoe store and had been an ordained Church of Christ minister since 1953, the year of her first marriage. Besides this information, Van Rippey was not telling much, and she refused to reveal her true identity. Prison officials had no idea what to do with her. Superintendent Henslee immediately moved Van Rippey to a prison cot outside his office and transferred her from the brutal farm detail to more appropriate "woman's work."[9] Van Rippey would spend the rest of her prison sentence working in the prison laundry and the kitchen.

All questions were answered when a high school acquaintance who spotted her prison photograph and the accompanying story in a Tennessee newspaper wrote to Henslee and explained that he remembered Van Rippey from public school in Wayne County, Tennessee. As the story spread across the front pages of the South, Henslee called Van Rippey into his office. In a voice that Henslee described as "fine-pitched masculine," she admitted it was all true.[10] Her real name was Dorothy

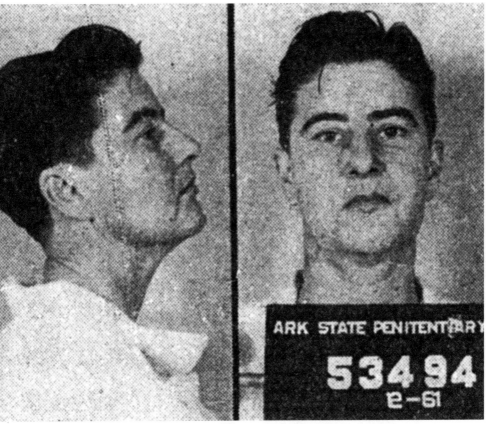

Dorothy Van Rippey's 1961 prison mug shot. *Courtesy Arkansas Department of Corrections.*

Van Rippey, and she was born in Waynesboro, Tennessee. Van Rippey also lied about her age; she was thirty-eight years old, not twenty-nine. She had decided about twelve years ago "to be a man" and had done so until the prison doctor discovered her act of passing.[11] Henslee updated the prison records accordingly.

Since the marriages she had entered into were considered void transactions by Arkansas law because they were based on misinformation, the Arkansas parole board granted Van Rippey parole from Cummins Prison. She was released to the custody of her relatives. She quietly left the state with her relatives and moved back home to Collinwood, Tennessee. After all was said and done, Henslee was sad to see her go. Van Rippey had been a model prisoner, and, as Henslee remembered, quite the entertaining piano player.[12]

The Van Rippey case commanded headlines across Arkansas and was picked up by newspapers across the South, adding to the growing discourse in the region that queers are of a subversive set. Arkansans were baffled that Van Rippey had not only masqueraded as a man but had also convinced two women to enter the holy bonds of matrimony. Though the institution was the focus of jabs and jokes in womanless wedding productions, many Arkansans were now quick to defend it as not only sacred but crucial to the American family. Van Rippey had also fooled members of the Church of Christ, a staunchly conservative Protestant denomination, that she was the right man for the job of minister, further mocking religious institutions beyond the level allowed in the occasional sardonic womanless wedding. In one charge of bigamy, Van Rippey had insulted two sacred institutions, marriage and the church, and had made a mockery of the family. Bigamy appeared in the Arkansas criminal code under the heading of "Crimes Against the Family" and was listed among such offenses as sodomy and incest.[13] Indeed, if anything, those following the Van Rippey story in the *Gazette* could not have imagined a better pairing of words to describe the bizarre case. Posing as a father, a husband, and a minister was seen as a slap in the face to white southern values and institutions not open for scrutiny.

All this was unforgivable. Though Superintendent Henslee might have seen Van Rippey as a likable and entertaining inmate, for many Arkansans she personified the fear that there were those in the state, outsiders perhaps (even though she was just from across the river in Tennessee), whose deviant sexual behavior threatened the idea of the family so highly cherished in American society.[14]

One can only speculate as to Van Rippey's motives for passing. Unlike her male counterparts who crossed the gender line for a night or two to entertain their fellow townsfolk, or Hazel who sought to fulfill certain sexual and emotional desires that an all-male environment seemed to foster and protect, Van Rippey crossed the line daily for almost twelve years. For her, passing as a man could mean much more and might yield more than just the one-night-only drag production Van Rippey saw during childhood. Van Rippey held jobs almost entirely reserved for men while posing as one. She saw the possibility of fulfilling

not only sexual desires but economic needs as well. Thus, she helped secure possible long-term economic security for herself independent from men and the traditional domestic obligations so adamantly placed on women.[15] Van Rippey bypassed this, and with the income earned he secured his own home and sought after female company in a move to perhaps fulfill ultimate ends to his desires and wants and, by doing so, achieved his own model family in spite of forbidding social norms and all on his own terms.

It is unclear, however, if Van Rippey was a lesbian, by modern terms, who was simply doing what she had to do to get by or if she actually considered herself a man. In a larger sense she did perform the everyday tasks associated with masculinity.[16] Doing it so well, in fact, she fooled many. However, many still claim to have never been fooled. Townspeople in Clarendon, Arkansas, the location of her second marriage, still insist that they knew all along, simply going along with the charade to avoid a most egregious intrusion into a private family matter. Beyond that, many just did not care. Van Rippey all but vanished from Arkansas after being released from prison in 1962. All attempts at finding any trace of her proved unsuccessful.

The Van Rippey case, and others like it, seemed to play directly into the hands of the amateur sexologists of the day trying so desperately to unlock the dark sexual secrets of ordinary Americans.[17] In the growing field of sexology, in many ways a response to Alfred Kinsey's *Sexuality and the Human Male*, so-called scientific writings sought to illustrate what sort of perversions stem from same-sex desire. For many Arkansans laughing and joking about the story as it unfolded in front of them in the daily newspapers, Van Rippey did just that. Sexology played a strange role in the lives of Americans. Hearing of the new "sexualities," many could not get enough of it, and the science was as popular (and perhaps as factual) as science fiction. To counter the increasingly popular *Leave It to Beaver* postwar model of American existence, many became increasingly fascinated with the other side of the cultural spectrum, and sexologists were all too willing to feed their desires.[18] To those who had heard of this growing field of study, and even to those who had typical sexual curiosities, Van Rippey's sexual transgressions only lent credence to the now-ubiquitous warnings swarming around so-called and oft-described deviant behavior. Drag was no longer something delivered on stage for

entertainment and subtle didactic purposes. Somehow, when Arkansans were not looking, or at least pretending not to, deviancy had seeped into their daily lives, and drag as Arkansas had known it fell out of favor. With the end of the Second World War and driven by episodes such as the one described above, drag was cast into the underground. After the war, drag would become a principal means of clandestine entertainment and the queer community's greatest and most recognized, and indeed the most profitable, means of self-expression.

Rags to Drag Riches

In less than ten years Norman Jones would go from a dental assistant on an aircraft carrier to the belle of the southern drag-queen circuit.[1] Soon after, Jones would amass a small fortune owning and operating the Discovery Nightclub, one of the South's largest drag venues. In Arkansas drag was moving from rural entertainment to the principal means of gay community expression and the most visible means of queer capitalism, and Norman Jones would be along for the ride. The story of his adult life does more than simply chart the progression of drag in Arkansas; it is both exceptional and representative of rural queer lives in the second half of the twentieth-century Arkansas.

Long before his drag-queen career began, Norman Jones was a sailor. A native of Hot Springs, Arkansas, he volunteered for the navy in 1967 at the height of the Vietnam conflict to avoid the draft and get his choice of service. Before enlistment he had lasted only a year at Ouachita Baptist College in Arkadelphia, Arkansas, leaving in 1966 with a 1.8 grade-point average. He was twenty-one years old when he left Hot Springs for the naval hospital in Bethesda, Maryland, to receive his training as a dental technician—a field, according to Jones, "most of the gays in service would flock to."[2] For Jones it was certainly better than the highly demanding and gritty, greasy food service, which he had heard was absolutely the worst service a seaman could find himself in.

Jones said in the navy he "screwed everybody."[3] His first real love affair, one that would continue until he was discharged, was with a young supply officer. The affair would "come in handy from time to time." The greatest advantage was that every time Jones was granted weekend leave, he was also given a U.S. Navy automobile in which to cruise Bethesda and neighboring Washington DC. When he drove down Connecticut Avenue and took the curves at Dupont Circle in his borrowed car, he used electrical tape and a piece of cardboard to conceal the navy emblem on the car door.[4] Using a concealed though nonetheless government issued automobile, he cruised around late-night DC looking for queer networks and undergrounds.

After becoming a dental assistant, Jones was assigned to the USS *Forrestal* out of Virginia Beach, the first of the navy's supercarriers and a monument to the military's cold-war spending policies.[5] On board, he became known affectionately as the "Tooth Fairy."[6] To supplement his navy income of fifty-two dollars a week, he and his cohorts from dentistry stole powdered orange drink from the ship's sick bay and vodka from the fficers club and mixed crude screwdrivers for the ship's crew in a makeshift floating night club of their own. They also would show a "fuck flick," though Jones laments it was always a straight one. It was two dollars to get into the room and a dollar a drink. Jones and his friends made a small fortune, and the only reason they were caught was that the line to get in stretched outside the room and far down the corridor. The club was broken up, but Jones was not reprimanded for either stolen alcohol or the make-shift porno theater.

Having an affair with an on-ship navy supply officer was not the only beneficial relationship one could have in the U.S. Navy. Having an ongoing sexual relationship with an admiral's son would certainly be a close second. While playing the organ in the ship's chapel, Jones was approached by the son of a navy admiral. Though the relationship granted Jones a great deal of leeway in his duties and certainly spared him any punishment for the pornography club or the stolen liquor, he considered the admiral's son to be "one of the worst fucks I had ever had." However, he would not dare end the relationship for fear of reprisal.[7] With the relationship, Jones had a sort of crude insurance policy for in-service queer undertakings.

Reprisal did come, but not in the way Jones might have thought. One afternoon he was summoned to the admiral's quarters aboard the *Forrestal*. The admiral sat behind his large oak desk and behind him stood the military police. In their file on Jones were dozens of pieces of personal correspondence he had written to Anthony Perinelo, a civilian love interest. The letters were turned over to naval authorities by a jealous girlfriend of Perinelo's. Nervously thumbing through the love letters, the admiral asked the police to leave the room. He then told Jones that he knew about his homosexuality and his involvement with his son, who he hoped would one day reach the rank of admiral just as he had. He told Jones that he could leave the navy immediately with full benefits and nothing in his record regarding the queer events. Jones, in a burst of confidence that startled even him, demanded proof. In front of him the admiral scribbled on his record that he had been granted an honorable discharge with full benefits from the U.S. Navy. He left the *Forrestal* by helicopter just an hour later. He waited only a week in Bethesda for his discharge to go through. When it did, he packed his GI bags and headed south toward Arkansas.

In the navy Jones had found an outlet for his homosexuality, whether it was cruising the suburbs of DC in his navy-supplied car or getting his kicks while onboard his assigned ship. He went home to Hot Springs, a town famous for its healing waters and infamous for treating servicemen for venereal disease during the Second World War.[8] Now home, Jones sought to locate a similar world. Nothing was immediately visible, though he knew it had to be there. He took to the streets in his white convertible Chrysler Valiant and continually cruised Hot Springs's Central Avenue. It did not take long to catch on to the tricks of cruising. Cruising for sex in one's automobile had long been a pastime in the American South, practically dating back to the introduction of the automobile itself. Those who owned cars quickly realized their potential. The availability of the automobile, and perhaps to a greater extent the *used* automobile, allowed for those once entirely confined to rural areas to retreat to the big city, if only for an afternoon or evening, and offered a new sense of freedom for those who could afford them. Truly, the automobile afforded gays and lesbians with a new means to assemble, and this fact had a greater significance for Jones and his rural companions.[9] With this increased freedom, gay men were no longer compelled to stay where they were not wanted, and now many, like Jones, sought private company elsewhere.[10]

Men cruising for sex devised a language of sexual signaling using the automobile. Applying the brake lights meant having at least some interest in the person in the car behind you. Flashing your high-beam lights could signal a desire for the person to follow you to another location, perhaps deep into the woody Hot Springs National Park for anonymous sex, or back to one's home, or to a cafe for a cup of coffee. These signals were not always related to cruising for sex, though, and it took Norman Jones three months of this automotive back and forth before he finally worked up the nerve to stop. After all, these were not the streets of Washington DC; this was his hometown of Hot Springs, Arkansas. Though many used the automobile as a sexual space, as the back seat became a sort of mobile space that facilitated quick and secret sexual encounters in backcountry roads, it also was used simply as a means of introduction, as Jones and rural Arkansans used their automobiles to find gay communities within their society. When Jones finally did stop, it was for a car of three gay men roughly his age who were simply looking, as Jones had been doing, for others like them.

Although a popular tourist destination since the turn of the century attracting those from across the nation to its healing mineral bathhouses and horsetrack betting, Hot Springs had no real gay community, at least not one that could compare in size and visibility with the likes of Washington DC. Jones, cruising about town in his white convertible Valiant with a leaky top, stumbled onto a close-knit gay community of house gatherings and Sunday-night dinner parties.[11] Exclusively gay and very white, the gay dinner and house-party circuit that Jones discovered was entirely middle class. They were older, often well-to-do gay professional men who were largely unwilling to participate in queer bar culture for fear of losing social status and employment. Instead, they sought to form a secure network with other gay men safely within the most private of queer spaces: the home. Within the walls that protected private property, queer hosts and guests found themselves the protectors and facilitators of their social identity and queer networks. Working-class gays and lesbians were altogether removed from such settings as lack of wealth and social status excluded them from these home-based queer communities. Thus, working-class gay men sought other settings. However, unlike their less privileged counterparts, upper- and middle-class queers could move freely between the bar and home scene. With this too were professional gay men often removed from the bar scene, as a potential raid or even a mere scuffle in the parking lot—anything that might attract the flashing blue lights of a police car—could threaten their employment and social status. For this reason many were often wary of venturing out to such establishments. Working-class gays and lesbians could visit back road bars and clubs, many not fearing loss of job or social status.

There was one bar, more of a speakeasy really, to which Jones and others could venture. Jones, at twenty a good-looking professional with his own automobile, enjoyed the luxury of being able to move fluidly between middle -and upper-class social settings and those popular among the working class, though he would always prefer the latter. Together with his newfound friends, Jones set out for The Royal Lion's Club. To discourage the uninvited and possible disruption that might attract authorities, the bar had no clear markings or advertising outside the building. One simply approached a locked door and rang a buzzer. Behind it, a doorman had to recognize at least someone in the party if they were to be allowed in. It was a popular place, and people came from as far away as Little Rock to the north and Texarkana to the south to socialize with their fellow subversives and enjoy the privilege of dancing together. After all, it was forbidden by town ordinances for same-sex couples to dance together in clubs and bars in many urban areas such as Little Rock. Hot Springs had no such law, illustrating that a large urban center is hardly a prerequisite for gay and lesbian communities to flourish. Indeed, as seen with Jones and his cohorts, such communities thrived in rural spaces and perhaps afforded a greater sense of privacy as gay men traveled from nearby cities and towns to the backwoods and back roads of Hot Springs to meet and dance with friends and partners miles away from intrusive urban eyes. Gay men from Little Rock used the power of the automobile to flee the city and antihomosexual ordinances to the more social and less rigid rural gay space.[12]

Little Rock, only forty-five minutes or so north by automobile, had a bustling underground gay scene from the beginnings of Arkansas's mobilization for the Second World War, with some gay bars opening close to or in the actual basements of Little Rock hotels to attract the gay men from out of the city. The first of Little Rock's gay bars to identify itself as such was The Brass Rail, located downtown in the basement of the Grady Manning Hotel, itself only a few blocks from the city's train station. The Brass Rail quickly grew in popularity with the local soldier populations from nearby army bases. Little Rock was by no means a bustling metropolis, but for troops that came from extremely rural areas it must have appeared as such, dangerous but perhaps altogether liberating. The thrilling actions now associated with putting a name to an identity, a face to deviance, the army mixed together the rural and urban man. The army bases in Arkansas brought the urban queers from cities such as New Orleans, Atlanta, Chicago, and as far away as San Francisco and mixed with them the country boys. These men brought with them their rural and urban queer desires when seeking out new experiences in and around the back alleys and basements of Little Rock.

The Brass Rail had been open for nearly twenty years when the Manning Hotel was demolished. Other bars quickly took its place. Crowds simply shifted from The Rail to private bars such as The Continental and The Pit.[13] Even more popular was The Gar Hole. Complete with a large fish tank containing an enormous alligator gar, The Gar Hole was located in the basement of the regal downtown Marion Hotel. The Gar Hole was well known throughout the region as a gathering place for gay men, and the fact that it was located in the cellar of a hotel made it all the more appealing for passing sexual encounters.[14] Men from as far away as Alabama, knowing of the hotel's reputation, drove to Little Rock to meet men in the basement Gar Hole then move upstairs to a convenient room. Thus, they could stay privately within the same building and never venture outside, lessening the chance of being recognized.

The Gar Hole closed in April 1970 and was replaced by The Drummer's Club across from the Manning Hotel in the heart of downtown close to the Arkansas River. Though bars existed within the city, restraint within them was extremely harsh. In The Drummer's Club, which by 1971 was Little Rock's only gay bar, displaying same-sex affection was completely verboten. In fact, it seems that The Drummer's Club was far stricter than earlier spaces, as Little Rock bars began to resemble other southern urban social venues that also restricted physical affection among their clientele. The Drummer's staff was quick to point out to patrons that the place would certainly not identify as a gay bar but that queer dollars would always be welcome. Queer men were so desperate for a space, as well as desperate for the fragile community that the bar helped sustain, that they grudgingly agreed to the austere rules barring same-sex displays of affection. Like most bars, The Drummer's was popular on Saturday nights as gay men came to enjoy dinner first and then to listen to the jukebox and converse with friends (staying in their seats, as moving about was frowned upon by management). After a certain point in the evening, a sign was posted on the door stating that there was a "private party" inside in an effort to discourage unknowing would-be patrons from wandering in from the street. Throughout the evening, The Drummer's employees constantly monitored patrons' tables for displays of affection. Even holding hands under the table was enough to have a man barred from the establishment, and dancing, of course, was very much out of the question.

Facing such a hostile environment, many men from Little Rock's stifling gay scene and from the surrounding areas were now willing to drive the back roads and country highways and soon joined Jones and his friends at The Royal Lion's Club, using their freedom provided by the automobile to find new places and others like them as word spread of a more hospitable queer venue.[15] People excitedly told others that The Royal Lion's Club in Hot Springs allowed men to dance together. Here, men fled the city for the less restrictive rural venue where a sparse country landscape could afford a transient man a certain degree of anonymity (shedding their daytime persona and putting on their queer one) as well as greater freedom to express his sexual desire and identity. The rural gay bar discovered by Jones and friends was constructed as a far more fashionable, tolerant space than its urban contemporaries. The bar was also far more democratic regarding race and sex than most southern institutions were at the time. All were welcome, though, of course, all did not always get along. At most, the welcoming atmosphere stopped at mere tolerance for African American clientele. Jones remembers:

> The [white] gay kids fought a lot over their boyfriends. And the lesbians liked to fight no matter what. Then the black queens would come in, and they thought they were better than everyone else. I don't know what their deal was. They would start a lot of arguments. Twenty of them at a time would crowd into the bathroom and wouldn't let anyone else in. It was kind of sad.[16]

It seems that in The Royal Lion's Club all were welcome. However, one would know exactly which area of the bar was reserved for members of his or her social status as the bar and its patrons relied on self-segregation once in the door. In a space used by a marginalized group, there were some within the group who saw themselves further marginalized. According to Jones, black gay men congregated near, or even in, the bathrooms. Though this was possibly the worst space in the establishment, it was a defined area within a larger one that they could cordon off as their own.[17] White and heterosexual bars, roadhouses, and honkytonks could remain white and certainly heterosexual by using devices ranging from required membership to outright intimidation toward would-be black patrons. However, with only one gay bar for miles around, many queer Arkansans could not afford to be so selective when it came to race and social space, nor did they necessarily wish to be. At first glance, a newcomer might applaud the queer setting as varied in its makeup. However, once inside, they would find the interior space of the bar even more segregated than most public spaces in the American South. According to Jones, blacks knew their corner, and whites knew theirs. Rarely did they mingle, and rarely would they dance together. Even more rarely still would they leave the bar with one another. Needless to say, beyond the racial division, the space was almost entirely male.

Jones and his friends, after becoming somewhat regulars at The Lion's Club, asked the owners if they might perform the occasional drag number. Although he had been dressing up in drag since the age of fourteen, Jones gave his first public performance as Miss Norma Lou at The Royal Lion's Club in the spring of 1973. For the stage the pool table was moved to the center of the room, and a large piece of plywood was placed atop. His hastily assembled costume was an empire-waist evening gown of white chiffon and a black train. It cost him fourteen dollars at a local secondhand store. For breasts, Jones used Kleenex.

The night of Norma Lou's debut, the bar was packed wall to wall with patrons eager to see the night's entertainment and the variations on the drag that they were raised on. For his first number Jones chose a religious tune, singing "Put Your Hand in the Hand of the Man from Galilee," borrowing both from his training as choir director at a local Baptist church and the religious roots of rural drag. After a brief intermission he returned to his makeshift stage and wooed the crowd with Barbra Streisand's "Secondhand Rose." He closed with Dionne Warwick's "What the World Needs Now." The crowd adored him, and the owners, ecstatic and seeing the possibilities, demanded more. From that night on, Jones performed once a month at The Royal Lion's Club to packed audiences.

It was appropriate for Jones to choose for his first drag number an old-time gospel favorite. By wooing his new found audience with "Put Your Hand in the Hand of the Man from Galilee," Jones was borrowing from earlier traditions of southern drag that often incorporated or was incorporated into larger religious spaces and functions. By singing lyrics that encouraged those who heard it to "take a look at yourself, and you can look at others differently," Norman Jones stood on rural drag traditions for his first auspicious public performance. For the followup numbers, he chose distinctly secular but still distinctly sentimental songs by popular gay icons Barbra Streisand and Dionne Warwick, signaling that drag was on the move away from such traditions to the glitz and glamour of Hollywood starlet impersonation. Recognizing both, the audience must have been pleased with the entire set.

Jones had performed regularly at The Royal Lion's Club for three months when a flyer arrived from a gay bar in Nashville announcing the first ever Miss Gay America Pageant. Jones did not hesitate to enter. The pageant was organized and promoted by Jerry Peek, owner of a Nashville club he named The Glass Menagerie as a not so subtle tribute to the southern queer playwright Tennessee Williams. The pageant was held on June 25, 1973, at Nashville's largest gay-friendly venue, the Watch Your Coat and Hat Saloon.

After arriving, all Jones wanted to do was leave. Seeing his competition, contestants who had been performing on the professional drag queen circuit for some time, Jones was sure he had no real chance of winning. Seeking to enhance his appeal, Jones quickly changed his drag name from Norma Lou to Norma Kristie, the surname of that month's Playboy centerfold, in an effort to overcome his folksy, down-home roots and adopt a more sophisticated and professional drag persona.

After paying the hefty entrance fee and the travel expenses for himself and his entourage from Hot Springs to Nashville, Jones could not afford the pricey gowns and Max Factor makeup that the other contestants sported. At that point in his career most of his drag accessories either were borrowed from friends or purchased at local thrift shops. Staying in a Nashville motel, he and his friends, having spent most of their funds on gasoline, stole ketchup bottles from the motel kitchen and mixed the contents with hot water from the bathroom sink. This crude soup would carry them through two days of rehearsal.

The show would start at seven o'clock on June 25. Act one was evening gown and talent, and Jones delighted the packed house with his usual gown and his rendition of Shirley Bassey's "Diamonds Are Forever." Act two was the interview. The judges asked Jones what he would do if he were president of the United States for a day. Jones replied simply that he would not want the job, adding that the current president, Richard Nixon, was doing a fine job. Act three was sportswear, and Jones wore a black-and-white-checked tennis outfit.

In order to sell more alcohol and to pay the winner the promised $2,200 prize, Peek repeatedly announced a judges' tie in selecting the winner, making Jones and all other contestants perform their talent number five additional times. By two o'clock that morning, the judges had finally narrowed it down to five contestants. Jones was one of them. When he was called onto the stage as the winner of the first annual Miss Gay America Pageant, Jones, who had been doing drag shows for only a few months, was in complete shock. He could not understand, thinking his act and drag stage persona was strictly amateur compared to the competition.[18] Later, he cornered a judge, who told Jones that he "looked like a real woman, the southern girl next door, and that is the kind of person we wanted to select" as Miss Gay America.[19]

Jones made his triumphal return to the Royal Lion's Club the following week. For this welcome-home performance, a curtain now surrounded his pool-table stage and three nail kegs were placed on top so that he could now stand a bit taller than usual in front of his faithful fans and well-wishers. Attendance swelled. Jones had become a local celebrity.

In 1975 Jones bought the rights to the Miss Gay America Pageant from Jerry Peek and toured the country with the pageant. He attracted contestants from every state and made a great deal of money franchising preliminary pageants in drag venues across the nation. Being the coordinator of the pageant carried its share of troubles. In October 1982 the night Jennifer Fox of Detroit, Michigan, was to be crowned the tenth Miss Gay America, dozens of Ku Klux Klan members, who had unsuccessfully lobbied the Dallas City Council and its mayor to shut down the pageant, harassed contestants and patrons alike as they entered the Dallas Convention Center, holding signs reading, "Homosexuality is a curable disease, one bullet to the head will do it."[20] The following year, when Franchesca Wakeland was crowned Miss Gay America 1983 in Charlotte, North Carolina, local Baptist ministers greeted the patrons by taking photographs, hoping to capture prominent citizens and those who held public office so that they could be blackmailed into denouncing any future pageants and homosexuality in general. Despite their efforts, 2,500 people paid fifteen dollars a

Norman Jones at the first Miss Gay America Pageant. *Courtesy of Norman Jones.*

ticket to enter Ovens Auditorium in Charlotte.[21] It was hugely popular and hugely profitable as drag and the increasingly nascent gay communities became increasingly inseparable.

Touring the Miss Gay America Pageant proved to be a huge success financially for Jones, and for him that was always the bottom line. The Miss Gay Arkansas Pageant, still held in Little Rock annually, packs the forty-thousand-square-foot Discovery Nightclub, which Jones purchased in 1985, making it one of the south's largest gay club and drag venues. The Miss Gay America Pageant continues to be one of the most anticipated social events of the year in the gay community in the South.

Long after performing in Second World War variety shows as his drag persona Harvey Lee, Harvey Goodwin retired back to his home state after the San Francisco earthquake of 1989. Goodwin would often serve as a judge of the Arkansas pageants. Having such a background in early

Norman Jones receiving the crown. *Courtesy of Norman Jones.*

cabaret, he was more than willing and much sought after to evaluate the new crop of contestants.[22] When not performing this service, he often would sit quietly at the bar with his scrapbooks open, hoping to catch the curious eyes of passersby. He died in 1993 at the age of eighty-one.

Drag meant different things to different people, different performers, and different audiences. Arkansas drag, beginning in the 1980s, clearly became more of a professional undertaking, but this is not to say that Arkansas drag simply caught up with larger national urban trends of drag entertainment seen in such characters as Harvey Lee Goodwin. Though the intentions behind the performances may have changed, drag remains surrounded in politics, with the political context changing to reflect social trends. Womanless weddings and womanless beauty pageants pointedly illustrated the social ridicule awaiting those who deviated from the rigid social norms of the American south. Borrowing on this rich history, GI drag brought gender bending to the forefront only to have society declare it deviant as the end of the war ushered in the conservative 1950s.[23] With this, drag quickly came to embody for many a form of political self-expression stemming from the need for increased visibility for the transgendered and the gay community as they created and shared space.

FIVE

The Current Reigning
Symbol of Excellence

She says you could wear the whole damn
> *black sky and all its spangles. It's the only night*
we have to stand on. Put it on,
> *it's the only thing we have to wear.*

—MARK DOTY, "ESTA NOCHE,"
FROM *MY ALEXANDRIA*[1]

Alone in his house, he put on his mother's dresses and applied her makeup for his own personal amusement, a personal experience and a private pleasure. Drag was just a hobby really, something David Lee enjoyed doing but nothing he ever would consider as a career. After all, the future Miss Gay Arkansas 2001 already had a full-time job. He worked as a computer programmer and earned a good living at it. Lee enjoyed numbers, math, and all things technical. He graduated from Hendrix College with a degree in mathematics in 1998. He went to Hendrix after graduating from his local high school in Bee Branch, Arkansas, a town boasting a population of only sixty-three. Besides math, Lee also enjoyed dressing up in women's clothing, a pastime he favored far more than the rigorous logic of mathematics and something he had been doing since childhood. As a child he emulated those he saw on television, namely popular entertainment figures of the time, his favorites including Daisy Duke from the *Dukes of Hazzard* and Lynda Carter's Wonder Woman.

He chose Hendrix because the school enjoyed a statewide reputation as a gay-friendly space where one could discover or cultivate a gay identity in the safe confines of higher education. He also became intrigued, even before his arrival, at an annual event held at the college every spring, the Miss Hendrix Pageant, created in 1983 in the thick of the Reagan years as a fundraising event for Hendrix's spring charity week. Students at Hendrix, riding the wave of progressive second-wave feminism, borrowed from earlier rural drag to provide a recognizable event, the beauty pageant to mock not only the idea of the pageant but societal norms concerning gender and sexuality.

By the time Lee was a freshman the pageant was the highlight of the Hendrix social calendar. He never "came out of the closet" until his senior year, his last chance essentially, when he finally worked up the nerve to sign up for the pageant as Fonda Cox.[2] Competition was not as hard as he had expected. Most acts, he recalls, were quite vulgar, performed by men who made a point of looking as masculine as possible, similar to earlier, rural drag productions. In keeping with that tradition, few took their acts seriously. For many contestants it was a complete joke, something done for a laugh or to gain campus notoriety. Lee remembers one act where a drag queen hit golf balls into the crowd off the butts of volunteers. Lee saw the opportunity to perform as something much more, a glitzy coming-out performance and a stepping stone to what could be a real career.

His main competition came from a drag queen named Reagan Bush, an underclassman sponsored by the College Republicans organization. Being a senior, Lee was better known to the audience and soon was their favorite. He dazzled them with his talent, showing off what he had learned in the ballroom dance class that he taken for credit in place of physical education. After he tangoed tastefully with a popular campus jock, Fonda Cox won and was crowned Miss Hendrix 1998.

The pageant was strictly an amateur occasion, although the student body provided more than adequate funds so that the performance and performers had everything required from proper lighting and sound to wigs and makeup. Lee used this amateur pageant to make a foray (though it would hardly be a brief one) into a larger professional scene. He enjoyed the performance, and the popularity it afforded the once quiet and reserved Lee was too good to resist. He was amazed at how good he looked and at how much he enjoyed doing it. He described at as "being set free."[3] He turned his attention to the amateur night at Norman Jones's Discovery. He remembers being incredibly intimidated by the professional numbers put on by others, and though he did not win, he soon was taken into the tutelage of other more established drag queens who were determined to make Lee a contender.[4] In the often cramped and chaotic backstage areas of drag venues, Lee quickly discovered a close-knit community of professional drag queens, as well as their friends and partners, who operated in a queer entrepreneurial spirit. Some, such as Jones, often owned performance spaces. For Lee, gaining the favor of these seasoned performers was essential to a budding career. Lee peppered them with questions ranging from makeup tips, how to hide an Adam's apple if one wanted to, or how to deal with an unruly customer or a prickly club owner. The drag queens from whom he sought performance advice recognized him immediately as real drag talent. Many of them were matronly toward him, taking him under their wings and teaching him the tricks of what was becoming an increasingly lucrative and popular trade. With their help, Lee's confidence grew, and he was able to please crowds, though not necessarily judges, at this point. However, an ever-growing fan base and familiarity with crowds and venues would soon change that.

From there, he looked to Hot Springs, Jones's hometown, and host city of the Miss Gay Hot Springs Pageant, a preliminary to the statewide pageant. He won that competition in the fall of 1999, and though he did not win the Miss Gay Arkansas crown that year, he did claim runner-up, a position that guaranteed his place in the pageant the next season. He took the year to develop his drag skills, touring the state's drag venues and changing his name from Fonda Cox to Fonda Le Femme, a drag name that Lee thought would make him appear classier and afford him more respect as a serious artist with the judges. The name change also illustrates the further move of drag from the rural, slapstick comedy routines to the sleeker, more metro performances typical of today's drag. He re-entered the pageant the following year and won.

Fonda Le Femme performed regularly at The Factory, a popular downtown Little Rock gay bar in the heart of what is considered by day a financial district just down from the venerable, and now empty, old *Arkansas Gazette* building. Even Norman Jones's Discovery is located in a series of warehouses near the Arkansas River, a place abandoned as night falls. Under Little Rock's mini-skyline, gay men flock there and to the downtown stretch of deserted avenues, with ample parking spaces

David Lee as Fonda Le Femme as Lynda Carter's Wonder Woman. *Files of author.*

after five o'clock, to a section of the city that is otherwise a ghost town during off hours. Fixed spaces do not have fixed identities. Night and day, they are maneuvered and adjusted by those who use them for entirely different purposes. Just off nightly deserted streets, boys found comfort in a negotiated space of their own.

For the Arkansas gay scene, drag at times seems to be the only thing to wear. Almost all of Arkansas's gay bars, now and in the past—Our Place in Hot Springs, Ron's Place in Fayetteville—offer a drag show at least one night a week, and it constantly proves to be the most popular night for the bar, usually bringing in the most money in drink sales and from cover charges ranging from five to seven dollars. Like many others The Factory operates as a gay bar, a drag club at times, and as a community center for gay men in the area as owners recognize the importance of bars to queer culture. In the spring it offers pride events and pride-themed pageants. On Saturday mornings clubbers from the night before are treated to a free breakfast, HIV/AIDS information, and, if need be, free and confidential testing in the same space that only the night before offered the best in club music and mixed-drink specials for loyal patrons.[5]

Offering a social scene as well as actual services to the Arkansas gay community solidifies the gay bar as a choice space to form an identity as a gay and lesbian Arkansan, a social comfort zone where one can operate with greater dignity.[6] And, as the Internet either takes the place of or provides an alternative to the road system in bringing these men closer, almost all men in the Arkansas gay chat rooms have at least heard of The Factory and Discovery. Many living miles away have driven to Little Rock with friends to hit the bars then pitch in for a cheap motel room together. Cruising Internet rooms from a rural locale, gay men can now look for those willing to travel to either the clubs or their homes. Though The Factory and Discovery are both located in Little Rock, it would be unfair, as Donna Jo Smith writes, to cast "the closet into the rural areas, small towns, and small cities," as the Royal Lion's Club and other venues like it thrived in rural places.[7] Examining the narratives provided here, one could easily discredit such assumptions. Smith explains that these commentaries constantly raise questions as to what "kind of community we are expecting to find and to whom they should be visible" as historians offer alternative queer histories outside the urban.[8] Gay men knew of the bars, or the bar, another town had to offer, even if it sat hours away by car. They would look upon it as a queer get-away of sorts, opening onto endless possibilities in fulfilling queer desires. Sharing expenses, a car full of gay men would drive off to a bar that they had only heard about or that one of them had visited in the past, all to see what another queer venue had to offer. What were they doing differently? What was going on in their lives? They would have had to have known more than the just the address. One might have to phone ahead or ask around. What night is it busy? Is Friday better than Saturday? Are patrons more likely to spend time and money at a different bar and then at a certain time move on to another, leaving one bar empty while the other gets crowded? Space is tricky that way. In a particular drag show a patron might know the performer or the routine or might recognize a face in the group of men at another table. Perhaps they met at another bar or on the grounds of an interstate rest area just west of North Little Rock that for a time flourished as a gay venue. Even if the visitors did not recognize a face in the crowd, they would at least feel comfortable in their sense of identification that a gay bar offered: they knew that they had at least one thing in common with everyone in the room.[9] Communities are built on such commonalities.

When David Lee was crowned Miss Gay Arkansas, I was in the crowd to watch. Sitting with friends in the smoke-filled Discovery Nightclub, I sipped my beer and quietly listened to master of ceremonies Norman Jones in his deep, roughly textured voice, offer up camp slogans of drag and refer to onstage talents as the "current reigning symbol of excellence." I cheered on David Lee as a fellow Miss Hendrix, having won the crown myself the year after Lee in 1999 with my glitzy Audrey Hepburn *Breakfast at Tiffany's* style costume and my Mama Cass Elliot talent number. After graduating I went on to graduate school in Fayetteville, Arkansas, where a popular gay club and drag venue on Sunday nights, Club Xanadu, had found space in a downtown building that was home to an evangelical Christian church on Sunday mornings.

After his graduation Lee worked as a computer programmer for little more than a year, long enough to win the company Halloween costume contest as Wonder Woman. When he quit, drag became his career, and a campy one to him, as a growing queer audience sought familiarity in the places they chose to spend their money and the acts and stage personas they chose to entertain them. As sexuality met the age of profit, it was all camp to Lee, and camp was play, and for him play was work.[10] He could not have been happier.

After winning the Miss Gay Arkansas Pageant, Fonda Le Femme became a household name among those who enjoyed Arkansas drag culture. He did well, earning the regular performance fees at clubs and two to three hundred dollars in tips from eager audiences across the state each time he performed.[11] Every bar, no matter where across the state, was like a homecoming for him. As gay bars increasingly represented community, and community increasingly equaled solidarity, gay bars in Arkansas became *the* premier space for forging and performing an identity, and Lee made a living of it.[12]

It even paid for the plastic surgery on his nose, which Lee thought would make him appear more feminine. He had to stop there, for the Miss Gay Arkansas rules made any cosmetic surgery below the neck and hormone therapy strictly forbidden. For Jones, having drag queens in his pageants with actual breasts (silicon or otherwise) would diminish the theatrics, the fantasy, the production. They were *female impersonators,* men in dresses, and anything more would somehow defeat the purpose and remove the mystique that made the entire performance so popular to begin with. Men with wigs; that's all it was. For some, like Jones and Lee, and many others, that's all it should be. For many in the drag queen circuit the entire performance is based on the maleness and masculinity of the performer. Altering the body by adding breast implants or even the taking of hormonal therapies is not only strictly forbidden by Jones and his pageants, but it is tremendously shunned by Lee and his fellow performers. If a drag queen were to "go woman" as Lee described it, it would be understood by them that they would then leave the performance and pageantry circuits.[13] Jones, by putting strict limitations on what his drag queens could undertake as far as plastic surgery, was also putting his own limits on gender and gender formation. The narrowing of the nose, a little work on the chin, anything above the neck was okay. But a surgical procedure below the neck—a boob job, penis removal—was completely off-limits. To have any alterations done that could confuse in any way for the audience as to what they were watching, men in dresses, would tamper with the illusion and diminish the entertainment value of it all.

As for the popularity of the pageants, whether it was the Miss Hendrix or Miss Gay Arkansas, Lee reckons it was the blending of the familiar with the taboo. Like the womanless weddings, these drag pageants mix the popular southern institution of the beauty pageant and the absurd and extraordinary art of drag, making a combination entirely irresistible for an audience. And though the goal remained the same, to entertain, the political and social messages were dramatically different. Though Lee's drag performances were more in tune with those that had been going on for a long time in large urban centers with highly visible gay communities such as New Orleans or San Francisco by earlier professional performers such as Harvey Lee, this is not to say that Arkansas drag evolved, or caught up, to meet those trends. For Arkansans drag was used by those performing it to communicate different social messages, whether it be less-than-subtle suggestions of social dominance expressed through queer comedy or that of community expression. One thing is certain, as seen in the images here: drag was never solely a gay phenomenon, but it was and remains queer.[14] Seeing the images of womanless weddings and womanless beauty pageants, one could easily argue that they were homosocial, bringing together an all-male cast of the same race and similar class for the purpose of performing the abnormal for community entertainment. Looking backward, one could also argue that these events were queer in their representations and motives. Given the arguments here, it is easy to see just how sexual political discourse can be at times. With these queer images, sexual and political discourse can often provide a unique blend of ideas concerning sex, gender, and racial transgression that can either uphold or contradict popular southern norms, depending on the dominant social discourse of the day.

Drag is not a gay phenomenon nor is pageantry solely a southern institution. It seems, however, that both drag and pageantry are more popular in the South than other parts of the United States. In an article in *Southern Exposure,* essayist Jere Real writes:

> Indeed today "drag," or female impersonation, is far more popular and more prevalent in the South than in San Francisco, New York, or Boston. Drag shows, once mostly limited to convention cities like New Orleans or San Francisco, are now a regular staple in places like Longview, Little Rock, Shreveport, Baton Rouge, Lafayette, Jackson, Biloxi, Mobile, Montgomery, Birmingham,

Memphis, Knoxville, Nashville, Chattanooga, and Johnson City. It is big in Oklahoma, widespread in the Carolinas, and down home in Georgia.[15]

When Fonda Le Femme sat down with *Girl Talk* magazine, a publication dedicated to "enjoying the fun of the transgender lifestyle," the article noted that she was a "five-alarm fire with an engaging charm that the South seems to have patented."[16] When asked about the popularity of pageantry and drag in the South, Fonda Le Femme noted that "female impersonators are well loved in the South because we really cherish pageantry, grace, grandeur, and all things elegant."[17]

Fonda Le Femme, in describing both her talent and her popularity, often uses words such as "professional" and "artistry." Clearly, Arkansas drag has come a long way from its humble beginnings in isolated farming towns. Drag has become different and was used differently. Drag also was Fonda Le Femme's livelihood. Lee dressed up in the clothes and accoutrements of the opposite sex and made a living at it much like Van Rippey had done some forty years before. In that regard Lee was a lot like Van Rippey in that both sought to create a reality, a modernity, different from the one that was most readily available or even acceptable. David Lee took his one step further. Fonda Le Femme last appeared on stage in 2006 not long after The Factory closed down. Lee retired the character after that and transitioned completely into a female in 2008 in a sex change procedure that was chronicled on *The Tyra Banks Show*. She currently lives in Little Rock.

PART TWO

The Natural State

SIX

A Crime Unfit to Be Named

Many Arkansans saw it as inconceivable. Many more thought it was about time. Arkansans sat over their breakfasts the morning of July 1, 1986, peering at the *Arkansas Democrat* headline that read "High Court Upholds Georgia Sodomy Law."[1] It had been nearly four years since an Atlanta policeman arrested Michael Hardwick in his home after he failed to show up for a court appearance related to a charge of public drunkenness. After entering the home the policeman observed Hardwick and another man engaged in oral sex. The officer arrested Hardwick for violating the state's 1816 statute that made oral and anal sex, on the part of either homosexuals or heterosexuals, punishable by a prison term of one to twenty years.[1] An arrest in a private home for consensual fellatio among adults was an extraordinary event, and the challenge to Hardwick's case would find its way all the way to the U.S. Supreme Court.

Gay advocacy and legal groups looking to challenge the constitutionality of sodomy laws could hardly imagine a better test case. There were no other issues—no participation of minors, prostitution, or public indecency—that could obscure the fact that the state of Georgia presumed to regulate sexual behavior in the home and the bedroom. Georgia attorney general Michael Bowers argued before the Supreme Court that "the most profound legislative finding that can be made is that homosexual sodomy is anathema to the basic units of our society: marriage and the family."[2] Bowers concluded that the possible decrimalization of sodomy would demote "those sacred institutions to merely alternative lifestyles."[3]

The *Democrat* reported that the ruling dealt only with homosexual sodomy, noting that by a five-to-four decision the court upheld the principle that "consenting adults have no constitutional rights to private homosexual conduct."[4] Justice Byron R. White, writing for the majority, argued that the "issue presented is whether the federal Constitution confers the fundamental right upon homosexuals to engage in sodomy and hence invalidates the laws of the many states that still make such conduct illegal and have done so for a very long time."[5] After asserting that the *Hardwick* case was asking the Supreme Court to establish "a fundamental right to engage in homosexual sodomy," White declared, "This we are quite unwilling to do."[6]

Although White's position promoted the state's role as guardian of traditional morality, his argument dealt mainly with the question of privacy and the individual and was written in coldly objective prose. It was Chief Justice Warren Burger, writing a separate concurring opinion, who went further in condemning the crime of sodomy, and indeed homosexuality, on the grounds of religious ideology. Burger called sodomy the "infamous crime against nature," an offense of "deeper malignity than rape," and a heinous act "the very mention of which is a disgrace to human nature."[7] For Burger, sodomy was truly a "crime not fit to be named." Invalidating the Georgia statute would "cast aside millennia of moral teaching."[8]

Commentary soon followed the front-page article in the *Democrat*. The newspaper published an essay by the syndicated columnist William Raspberry who argued that "you don't have to be gay or kinky to believe that the state has no business sticking its nose into private bedrooms."[9] The *Democrat* itself, however, was not as quick to disagree with the court. Eighteen days after the Supreme Court handed down the *Bowers v. Hardwick* decision and after several editorials, the newspaper offered a final opinion on the case. The editorial stated that "the court has made good public policy by flinching away from any declaration that a sick, socially valueless, widely outlawed minority practice merits constitutional protection as a social good."[10] The *Democrat* went on to say that Arkansas should look to the Supreme Court's decision as a forerunner to overturning *Roe v. Wade,* the 1973 Supreme Court decision that invalidated state laws prohibiting abortions.

Despite the great concern and debate surrounding the Supreme Court's decision, not a single state created or reinstated a sodomy law as a result of it. Besides the editorials and the front-page articles detailing the Court's decision, the *Arkansas Gazette* also noted that the state of

Georgia's sodomy law was stricter than that of Arkansas. Truly, anyone convicted under the sodomy statute in Georgia could face a penalty of imprisonment of up to twenty years. In Arkansas the sodomy statute was a mere misdemeanor charge, with a maximum penalty of a thousand dollar fine and a one-year prison term if convicted. Written in 1976, the Arkansas's sodomy statute read:

A: A person commits sodomy if such a person performs any act of sexual gratification involving:

1: The penetration, however slight, of the anus or mouth of an animal or a person by the penis of a person of the same sex or an animal; or

2: The penetration, however slight, of the vagina or anus of an animal or a person by any body member of a person of the same sex or animal.

B: Sodomy is a Class "A" misdemeanor.[11]

Gay and lesbian Arkansans, according to the *Gazette,* could perhaps take some consolation that the Arkansas sodomy statute was less stringent than the Georgia law and that prosecutions and convictions were few and far between. Even in Georgia, Michael Hardwick had to sue the state to force his trial so that the nearly two-hundred-year-old law could be reviewed by the U.S. Supreme Court.

At the core of the *Hardwick* case was its power of language. The Georgia sodomy statute did not criminalize homosexuality per se, but the Court's majority opinion written by Justice White made it clear that the Court considered the act of homosexual sex itself criminal. Focusing on and constantly using and interchanging the words *homosexuality* and *sodomy* to describe Hardwick's intimate relationship and sexuality not only devalued instantly both the sex act and the relationship but also upheld Georgia's right to outlaw such conduct and a nascent identity. In none of the states in which sodomy laws exist is the word *homosexual* used within their text. Under statutes that deal with sex crimes, homosexual offenses are often identified as unnatural or as crimes against nature. Some of the statutes use such terms as *sex perversion, buggery,* and *lewd and lascivious acts.* Arrests and prosecutions for homosexual behavior have been made under statutes concerning obscenity, public indecency, lewdness, vagrancy, or indecent exposure.[12] Depending on the state and the offense committed, homosexuals can be prosecuted under a variety of penal statutes, many of which have been criticized by legal scholars and gay-rights activists as being catchall in character. However, under the Georgia sodomy statute and similar laws in other states, it was the sex and the sexual being that became outlawed through the interpretation of the courts. The sodomy law includes both anal and oral sexual conduct. When a state legal body outlaws a means toward homosexual sex, it thus makes the practicing homosexual a criminal.

Though the *Hardwick* case brought state sodomy statutes to the national spotlight by arguing the constitutionality of the law, there are two distinct differences between it and the Arkansas statute that must be addressed. First, to provide a sexual balance to the challenging argument, the defendants in the *Hardwick* case were both a single homosexual male and a heterosexual couple. This is important in that the Georgia sodomy statute penalized *all* anal or oral sex regardless of the gender or marital status of the participants. The Arkansas statute outlawed only sexual behavior (or penetration of the anus or mouth) of same-sex couples. Secondly, Hardwick brought suit against the state of Georgia for being arrested under a law that, at the time, had been on the books for 167 years. Clearly, the statute had been in Georgia since the state's conception, a relic of imported English common law. At the time of the *Hardwick* decision in July 1986, the Arkansas sodomy statute had been on the state books for only nine years. However, given the prevailing social discourse of the day, both laws were products of their time.

If laws are set forth to establish normativity in a given society, as is the case with sodomy laws in the South, then these laws not only put limits on sexual behavior but also define what behavior the society is willing accept as normal. Also, in this case the law attempted to prevent an abnormality by clearly specifying the sexual behavior of sodomy.[13] When one examines the Arkansas statute, a law forbidding only same-sex behavior, we see a creation of what is abnormal versus what society has deemed as normal and thus acceptable. The abnormal in the *Hardwick* case is the sexual contact either by penetration of the mouth or anus by a person of the same sex. Though the state does not go on to define what would be normal, one could automatically assume that it is the exact opposite, that is, sexual contact of the mouth or anus by a person of the opposite sex. The laws and their constantly in-flux definitions of the normal and the abnormal are a more subtle use of power that works on the transgressor from the inside and consolidates what is normal or what is implied as normal against everything that is recorded now as the abnormal opposite. In this sense the law works paradoxically by creating and defining the abnormality it wishes to control.[14] In this use of legal discourse, lawmakers only add to the contradiction by further lending identity and collective agency to those who might fall under such categories of abnormality. In this cyclical fashion the power of the law, once enacted to be read as such, only provides the situation necessary for those to now resist it, as the law works to solidify the abnormality it wishes to control. With the exercise of power there is always resistance.

Though the sodomy statutes outlaw sexual contact between same-sex participants, the laws have the potential to be far more comprehensive in effect. Sodomy laws, as so many homosexual civil rights advocates claim, are the bedrock for discrimination against a queer minority. Some may argue that if the sodomy laws go largely unenforced, the *Hardwick* case being the most extraordinary exception, their presence on the books is simply innocuous. But for gays and lesbians living under such laws, the threat of criminal prosecution looms over them as long as they engage in acts of homosex or as long as their identity is closely linked with their sexuality. Beyond prosecution from the state, the danger of an arrest and the public ordeal surrounding it reaches far beyond that of an actual arrest. For many Arkansans arrest and prosecution under the law were tantamount to loss of employment, family, and social standing. Legal scholar Walter Barnett explains that being prosecuted under a law that stands on moral grounds could have profound social repercussions. To their peers and the larger society, the prosecuted would be labeled not only criminal but abnormal and sexually deviant by the larger society.[15]

According to Barnett, a further repercussion of laws like these is explicit creation of legal disabilities for gays and lesbians. Sodomy laws stigmatized gays and lesbians in many ways beyond the initial branding as criminal. The simple presence of sodomy statutes in state legal codes has been used to deny employment to gay job applicants, to deny child custody and visitation rights, and to bolster a rationale against enacting civil rights laws that would bar discrimination based on sexual orientation.[16] Even in colleges and universities in Arkansas, gay student groups have been denied proper funding based on the Arkansas sodomy statute with school administrations refusing to subsidize "criminal" behavior.[17]

Barnett adds that, as a third consequence, these laws foment discrimination and intolerance within a society. Having been defined as unnatural and criminal by law, and thus by society, homosexuals are under threat of being treated as such by members of that society.[18] Still, the most ominous threat from sodomy statutes, beyond the real threat of criminal prosecution, is that they can and do spawn legally sanctioned discrimination and prosecution often outside the protections of privacy.[19]

In the *Hardwick* case, not only had a police officer entered the queerest and most private of spaces, the home of a gay male, and arrested him under a law that many saw as archaic, but the Supreme Court had also upheld the state of Georgia's right to do so. For the most part, disregarding the Hardwick arrest, sodomy laws went largely unenforced. However, often their mere presence on the books provides the state with a margin of power to hinder the lives of a minority group that is encouraged, if not entirely forced, to define itself based on an officially outlawed sexual practice. Also, given the discourse of the day, sodomy laws are molded and used at most peculiar times depending on what social group is being defined by the larger society as dangerously abnormal.

Like many of its southern counterparts, Arkansas adopted a sodomy law when it achieved statehood in 1836. However, given the common law language of the statute, it neither defined what actually constituted sodomy nor specified the proper punishment that should be given to anyone found in violation of the law. Concordantly, it is important to note that this particular sodomy law made illegal sexual contact by the mouth or anus by members of the opposite sex as well as members of the same sex. The first two sodomy cases to appear in Arkansas, *Smith v. State*, involving a married couple, and *Strum v. State*, with an adult male and two male youths as defendants, allowed the Arkansas courts to define exactly what sodomy was, although these cases would have distinctly different outcomes. Indeed, homosex was hardly a preoccupation of the legislature. It seems, judging from remaining documents, that given Arkansas's rural makeup, bestiality was seen as more queer than any sort of same-sex act of desire. Also, it seems that Arkansas considered interracial sex to be the queerest of all acts, and the Arkansas legislature scrambled to define it as such.

As early as the 1950s, it was clear to many that state legal codes were in complete disarray. The Arkansas criminal code particularly was in dire need of revision. In Arkansas some laws either completely contradicted one another or were found to be totally redundant. In 1976 the Arkansas Criminal Code Revision Commission drafted the a criminal code for consideration by the legislature. It was approved. However, the following year saw some legislators baffled that the new code contained no sodomy statute, as the older code had been removed with little debate during the revision process. With orange juice spokeswoman and gospel singer Anita Bryant at their side, the Arkansas legislature drafted an entirely new sodomy law. Not wishing to make criminals out of husbands and wives, the new legislation targeted only same-sex sodomy.

The third section will deal with the most recent and successful challenge to the Arkansas sodomy statute. It was clear to many who wished to topple the law that, given the *Bowers v. Hardwick* decision, any challenge to the state sodomy statute in front of the U.S. Supreme Court directly after the 1986 decision could prove futile. With this in mind, many gay and lesbian advocacy groups sought to dismantle sodomy statutes from within the particular state in which they were based. A challenge to the Arkansas sodomy law based on the state constitution would be, according to plaintiffs, a more direct and advantageous route toward the eventual removal of the law. On January 28, 1998, seven gay and lesbian Arkansans filed a suit to declare the Arkansas sodomy law unconstitutional. The Arkansas plaintiffs were represented by two local attorneys in cooperation with the Lambda Legal Defense and Education Fund, a national New York–based organization specializing in homosexuality and the law.

Also, in the third section, the issue and idea of space as an analytical rubric will be brought into question. From the perspectives of all involved, those passing such laws, those responsible for their enforcement, and especially those wishing to engage in such acts, the question of where the act was to take place was always a primary concern. Beginning even before the modification of the sodomy law in 1976 to target only acts of homosex, the state now expanded spheres of influence in both public *and* privates spaces. Finding illegal homosex was an increasing concern of Arkansas public officials. Though this was a chief concern of Arkansas legal and law enforcement bodies, the state sought jurisdiction well beyond the controlling and regulating of a certain act of homosex. The eventual destruction of created and maintained queer spaces would also be a priority.

It is clear that the sodomy statute of the state of Arkansas, though considered to be archaic by many, was, when employed, a tool of legality and power meant to hinder the lives of individuals that a heteronormative and often racist society had deemed as abnormal. The Arkansas sodomy statutes, though conforming to the descriptions and definitions set forth above, are also unique compared to other southern states. Arkansas was the only state to rewrite its sodomy law one year after lawmakers removed it. In examining the cases that follow, one cannot ignore the gaps. The first sodomy law, though a relic of English common law, was at times used to target Arkansas's black population by prescribing harsher penalties for black violators. It did not necessarily represent a dividing line of normality and abnormality between hetero- and homosexual acts. Later, to combat rising gay and lesbian visibility, the sodomy law was reintroduced, using language targeting only homosexual acts. The divide between Arkansas's first sodomy law and its last persists because the discourse changed, or noticeably shifted, as legal discourse reflecting social trends shifted from one minority to another. In the post–civil rights era, with the dismantling of Jim Crow–style laws, southern society was no longer in the position to regulate the lives of blacks through distinct legal measures, though nonspecific racism still existed. Instead, state legal bodies, employing a narrower definition of queer transgression, focused on a different and increasingly visible minority.

SEVEN

The Ingredients of Offense

I have pieced together the following two episodes from sparse court and newspaper records. As far as I can tell, it might have happened like this: it was cold in the train station, and two young men quickly grew tired of waiting for the irregular holiday trains. It was New Year's Day 1925, and Sam Jackson, sixteen, and his friend Pete Cash, seventeen, both from the small town of Prescott, Arkansas, were traveling home by train from Graysonia, where they had been celebrating New Year's Eve with friends and relatives. The train stopped in Gurdon, and the boys had about one hour to wait for the connecting train. Bored and cold from waiting around the near-deserted depot, the boys set out for a walk about town to pass time until their transportation arrived.

Returning to the depot by a different route, the youths passed by the home of bachelor John Strum, who, noticing Jackson and Cash, walked to the street and invited them to come in and warm themselves while waiting for the train. The boys agreed but soon discovered that Strum had a broader definition of small-town hospitality. After only a brief while in the front parlor, the three adjourned to Strum's bedroom where he performed fellatio on them. Soon after, the two boys left, apparently satisfied at their act of homosex. But something happened on their way back to the train station. Nearly there, the two boys turned around and walked briskly back to Strum's home, where they dragged him from his living room into the street. Strum broke loose from his attackers and ran down his street with the two boys chasing after him. As it continued, the chase came to the attention of several of Strum's fellow townspeople who, recognizing Strum and not the two boys, intervened on his behalf thinking a robbery was in progress. Sometime during the incident, concerned bystanders had notified the town marshal, R. C. Tyson. Strum told Tyson that the two boys had broken into his home to rob him and he began the chase after he discovered them. When the two boys were interrogated, they told Tyson of the sexual encounter in Strum's bedroom. Tyson then arrested Strum for violating the Arkansas sodomy statute based on the information given by the two boys.[1] According to the law at the time, "everyone convicted of sodomy, or buggery, shall be imprisoned in the penitentiary for a period of not less than five nor more than twenty-one years."[2]

There was a question of evidence. Tyson and the prosecutors knew that the local court would be hard-pressed to convict with only the testimony of the two teenage boys from out-of-town. Jackson and Cash told Tyson that after the act of fellatio had been committed, Strum spit the semen into a spittoon underneath his bed. Hoping to find some sort of physical evidence of the crime, Tyson searched Strum's house for the spittoon but found instead a wooden box beside the bed filled with sawdust and a substance that appeared to be semen. No analysis of the substance was made, and upon trial the presiding judge threw out the box as evidence. However, based on the testimony of the two boys, he convicted Strum of sodomy. After an initial unsuccessful appeal, Strum took his case to the Arkansas Supreme Court who dismissed the testimony of Jackson and Cash and that of Marshal Tyson as "unreasonable" and "too weak to uphold a conviction."[3]

The Strum case is significant insofar it was the first to involve homosex between men. It was, however, not the first sodomy case on the books. Four years earlier, on March 13, 1921, Dixie Smith had her husband, C. V. Smith, arrested. According to the report given to the Sebastian County circuit court in Fort Smith, Smith had violated the "peace and dignity of the state of Arkansas" when he made "an assault upon and did then and there unlawfully, feloniously and diabolically carnally know and abuse" his wife, Dixie.[4] With this, C. V. Smith was arrested for violating the Arkansas sodomy statute.

Once the case went to trial, the proceedings hit a snag, and C. V. Smith was not going down without a fight. He contended that the charge of sodomy was bogus and used the very language of the law to buttress his argument. The Arkansas statute, although prescribing a penalty for the crime of sodomy, did not define exactly what constituted the crime. It was based on this point that Smith and his lawyers, David Partain and G. L. Grant, first attempted to get the charges thrown out. Smith's lawyers argued that their client had penetrated his wife's vagina with his tongue and in no way had he penetrated his wife's anus with his penis. Although the sodomy statute did not state exactly what sodomy or buggery was, Smith's lawyers contended that most Arkansans would regard sodomy as the penetration of the anus by the penis of another.

Judge J. Wood struck down the motion, noting that it was not necessary to dwell on the manner in which the offense was committed. Sodomy, according to Wood, may be committed by the mouth or penis, thus placing cunnilingus, or oral sex, under the growing definition of sodomy. Wood stated that a clear deficit existed in the Arkansas statute in the absence of a specific statutory definition of the "ingredients of the offense."[5] It was at this moment that Wood turned to the common law to find the particulars surrounding sodomy as a criminal offense.

Wood stated that "not alone to protect the public morals, but for other reasons also, sodomy, called sometimes buggery, sometimes the offense against nature, and sometimes the horrible crime not fit to be named among Christians, being a carnal copulation by human beings with each other against nature, or with beast is, though committed in secret, highly criminal in nature."[6] To further support this, Wood read from a sodomy case from a court in New York state, *Lambertson v. People*. In this case the Supreme Court of the State of New York noted that although the sodomy law suffered from vagueness, it did contain all the "words of art required" to uphold an indictment.[7] With this, Wood found Smith guilty.

Smith and his lawyers then took their case to the Arkansas Supreme Court. The court agreed to hear the case, but the justices had little to say, declaring that the evidence against Smith was so "revolting in detail" that it was not necessary to be heard. Although vigorously contradicted, the court held that his wife's testimony alone was enough to support the verdict. With that, the supreme court refused to hear any further arguments by Smith and his lawyers. Smith would go on to serve a five-year prison sentence.

Smith v. State was the first reported sodomy case to appear before Arkansas courts. In that case the supreme court ruled that the testimony of the spouse, though contradicting the other's, was enough to convict. Also, though the courts admitted that the sodomy statute suffered from vagueness, it could now include both anal and oral penetration. The act of language and the creation of law are at the heart of society's discourse. Here, however, the Arkansas sodomy statute in its vagueness could be applied to a host of perpetrators and would-be criminals engaging in sex of any kind.

Sodomy statutes such as Arkansas's were commonplace in the United States at the time of Smith's conviction. Many states inherited or duplicated such laws from one another. When Arkansas was organized into a territory in 1819, it received most of this territorial legislation from Missouri, which in turn received most of its laws from Louisiana. At the time of statehood in 1836, most states in the union had some variation of a sodomy law derived from English common law. In 1837, the year after Arkansas achieved statehood, the government recognized such common law crimes and adopted them into a formal legal code.[8]

The sodomy law was adopted as part of the common-law crimes, and the penalty for violation was set at five to twenty-one years. Ten years after this, in response to the fever pitch of pre–Civil War politics, the sodomy law underwent significant revision. A new sodomy law was adopted specifically for Arkansas's black population, whether slave or free.[9] While the penalty for white offenders remained five to twenty-one years of imprisonment, the penalty for black offenders was much harsher, death by hanging. The statute was further augmented to include a death sentence for any black Arkansan who simply attempted the crime. Interestingly, this portion of the law only concerned the attempted crime against white females, with no mention of white males.[10] This particular version of the sodomy law would remain in effect until the end of the Civil War.

At war's end, and during the period of Reconstruction in Arkansas, the Arkansas legislature authorized a complete overhaul of all the state statutes. During this time the sodomy statute disappeared along with other racially biased elements of the code. The new code of laws resulting in this recompilation in 1873 restored the penalty for an act of sodomy to five to twenty-one years, with no discrimination based on race.[11] Emerging black leaders in Arkansas were well aware of the correlation between self-determination, statewide perception, and political power. They were also quick to recognize just how influential legal discourse can be in shaping the public's perception of growing political influence. In 1869 the state of Arkansas convened its first legislative session with black Arkansans as legislators. Throughout the state, there was a total of 160 black public officials, ranging from county clerks and assessors to more prominent positions in the state assembly. Beginning in 1870, Arkansas's black population was steadily on the rise. Blacks from across the South fled west across the Mississippi. Hearing tales of a sympathetic Republican Reconstruction government that did not hesitate to crack down on Ku Klux Klan intimidation tactics, the African American population in Arkansas grew by 200 percent between 1870 and 1900.[12] Though the exact penalty targeting only African American violators with the penalty of death disappeared following the Civil War, it appears that the African American legislators of the 1871 and 1873 sessions, enjoying a growth in population and therefore a boost in visibility and political power, sought to do away with the race clause in the sodomy statute without officially going on record on matters of sex.[13]

In any case, sex and race were so intertwined in political discourse that it is almost impossible to separate the two in that they both are in constant play with one another and leave not only traces of historical trends but often transparent evidence throughout history. It is clear that Arkansas and its pubic officials manipulated the sodomy law to suit their hierarchical needs. They did so not necessarily to reflect a threat of sexual perversity but to manipulate fluid public perception that for so long kept white and male as normal and black and male as capable of dangerous perversion. Using the sodomy statute alongside laws such as those prohibiting miscegenation, Arkansas legislators sought to uphold a discourse of race along with that of sexuality.[14]

Sodomy laws, their definitions and applications, are constantly in flux but never randomly in flux. In many ways the state, with its style of frontier legality, adopted its version of a sodomy statute directly from its neighbors. Evolving further and fueled by racial bigotry before and during the Civil War, Arkansas legislators sought to further marginalize the black population through the amending of the sodomy statute. Also, as it appeared on the books, the sodomy law was used to regulate indecent acts committed by anyone, same-sex or not. With the Strum and Smith cases, the public and the elected officials operated within the bounds of a much broader definition of what could be seen as abnormal transgressions. This at times could include forbidden interracial sexual activity that threatened the fragile southern color line. The sodomy law would later go through other changes, being declared archaic by Arkansas lawmakers one year and reinstated with decisively homophobic rhetoric the next, with the state narrowly defining queer transgression while greatly increasing its sphere of public influence in contested spaces.

If discourse is anything expressed or said, that which is not said cannot be separated but instead should be treated as a technique within discourse itself. In terms of discourse there can be an exhaustive number of demonstrations and signs of what is being expressed by society. In terms of silence there is much to be said in both its worth as well as its meaning. Philosopher Michel Foucault argues that any given society, in this treatment, pre–civil rights Arkansas, will take "great pains to relate in detail the things it does not say."[15] Whether it is the redefinition of the sodomy statute during the Reconstruction legislature or the treatment received by John Strum, something was not being said. In the use of discourse what is *not* being said is as important as what is being said. The fact that *Strum v. State* made it all the way to the Arkansas Supreme Court is not as noteworthy as the fact that it was never reported on in his hometown newspaper or anywhere else in the county. The absence of an articulation of a sexual desire—in this case same-sex desire—should never suggest the absence of such desires. In the case of Arkansas's first sodomy statute, the silence concerning same-sex desire could be seen as falling somewhere in between general apathy and a public disregard, or perhaps even deliberate avoidance.

EIGHT

Race, Sex, and
Queer Renegotiated

O n an early morning campaign stop, supporters for Democratic
gubernatorial candidate "Justice Jim" Johnson broke out in song.

The rich man from the mountain
With all of his grace,
His boots made of leather and
His panties of lace,
With his greedy grin all over his face,
His hunger for power that's
Held in his paw
Reaches for the state of Arkansas.[1]

Johnson, a strict segregationist and one of the nastier figures to come out
of Arkansas politics, faced a tough fight in the 1966 governor's race. It was
the first governor's race after the Faubus era, a governor's race still well
within the long shadow of Central High. The unthinkable was about to
happen. The man of boots of leather and panties of lace, the rich man
from the mountain, Winthrop Rockefeller, was close to becoming the first
Republican governor since Reconstruction. Arkansas Democrats were
worried; they had, after all, enjoyed what was essentially a one-party state
political system since Reconstruction had ended some eighty years before.

The well-heeled Rockefeller, grandson of John D. Rockefeller, oil
tycoon and one of America's great robber-baron multimillionaires, had
come to Arkansas in the mid-fifties bringing with him no real political
ambitions but hardly escaping his New York playboy image. Rumors of
his possible sub rosa East Coast homosexuality soon followed him.
Rockefeller purchased extensive farm lands and made his home atop scenic

Petit Jean Mountain just outside of tiny Morrilton, Arkansas. Once there, rumors continued to spread. Some hinted that his mountain retreat was in actuality a haven for his rumored alcoholism and his vast stockpiles of pornography.[2] Despite these accusations, it was not long before he was beckoned into the state spotlight by then-governor Faubus. Anxious to use the Rockefeller name and Winthrop's connections for the betterment of Arkansas, Faubus appointed him to the newly created Arkansas Industrial Development Commission. All in all, Rockefeller and the commission prospered from one another. The state, so desperate to industrialize after the Second World War, added almost a hundred thousand new industrial jobs under Rockefeller's leadership, and Rockefeller became increasingly concerned with the state's further economic progress.[3] Along the way Rockefeller developed his own political ambitions.

When Faubus suddenly announced his retirement from public office in 1966, Rockefeller again set his sights on the governor's office. In 1964 he had run for governor and lost, though he did take an impressive 43 percent of the vote, a notable feat for a Republican candidate and an out-of-stater. Rockefeller spent the time after his first campaign shoring up support of state Republicans, who saw their first real chance at a state office in years, and moderate Democrats disenchanted with the Faubus machine and the national embarrassment it engendered. As he had for some time, Rockefeller continued to actively court African American voters, promising increasing access to the political process. A long and vicious battle ensued for the Faubus Democratic heir. From the Democratic primary election emerged "Justice Jim" Johnson, a race-baiter and the man considered by many to have pushed Faubus, whom he deemed Arkansas's "nigger lover," into the national showdown outside of Central High.

Johnson had a formidable opponent in Rockefeller and immediately set out to discredit him on the grounds of his sexuality. Johnson had labeled Rockefeller as the "prissy sissy" and "winsome Winnie" since his days as head of the Industrial Development Commission.[4] In 1955, in *Arkansas Faith,* Johnson's newsletter for his group the White Citizens Council, Johnson's accusations as to Rockefeller's sexuality were extremely subtle but always called to mind the burning and irrevocably linked issues of race and sexuality.

When he moved to Arkansas, Rockefeller brought his trusted aide, a black man named James E. Hudson, to run his ranch operations.

Johnson's publications described Hudson as a "wiry, balding negro who has been Winthrop's right hand man since the two first teamed up as young men in New York City eighteen years ago."[5] The publication states that Hudson was afforded so much respect and responsibility from Rockefeller that locals went along, "granting him a courtesy all too rare in most southern states." The *Arkansas Faith* further reported, "They called him 'Mister.'" From that point Johnson would do more than hint at the nature of their relationship. The rumor that Rockefeller "sodomized black men" was now added to the litany of charges against him.

Now, as the campaign went on, it was becoming more likely that Rockefeller might win. Thus, Johnson's rhetoric heated up beyond his already fiery brand of southern political discourse. Though Johnson was a southern Democrat in the strictest sense, his White Citizens Council began to circulate a publication entitled "Republicans for Better Government." In it, Rockefeller was labeled with every term that might be considered incendiary in southern politics, branding him everything from a socialist to a devout internationalist. On the front page a picture of a "lithe, handsome, and nearly nude valentine" appeared next to a photograph of Rockefeller. In fact, the two were actually at the same function. Rockefeller was judging costumes at a 1949 Valentine's ball benefiting the National Urban League in New York City. The pictures originally appeared in *Life* magazine. Now, some sixteen years later, they were being used to confuse the protected and currently-under-siege boundaries of race by painting Rockefeller as a sexual culprit and big city suspect who could further threaten such delicate boundaries.[6] Johnson continued to campaign vigorously and used what he could to back this idea, but he was no longer subtle in speaking of Rockefeller's supposed sexuality. An article entitled "Winthrop Rockefeller—A Homosexual?" cited various other sources to expose Rockefeller's alleged "homophile nature." The article begins with a source entitled *The Secret Life of Walter Winchell* that details Rockefeller's supposed first visit to a New York City brothel in an effort to steer him toward heterosexism. He was sixteen, the source contended, and was sent there to "to be taught that all things could be bought for money and to be kept from the clutches of homosexuals."

Other sources hinted at something improper in the Rockefeller-Hudson relationship. The article featured an excerpt from a source entitled *Rockefeller Public Enemy No. 1.* In it there was a rather dubious quotation from Rockefeller explaining his reasons for relocating to Arkansas. Rockefeller was quoted as stating that "my Army 'boy friend,' Jim Hudson, would not come to New York, so I went to Arkansas to be with him."[7] The article went on to use another source, *Those Rockefeller Brothers*, to allege that Hudson and Rockefeller had spent months touring the country by car and that "Winthrop calls Hudson his 'assistant' because he says he has never been able to think of any other title for the Negro."[8]

Johnson's political discourse was already quite sexual even before he turned his attention toward defeating Rockefeller. Miscegenation and segregation were high atop the Johnson agenda. In *Arkansas Faith* white women were often seen as the target of sexually charged blacks and their sympathetic white political supporters. In one political cartoon appearing in the newsletter, a tornado deemed "mongrelization" was bearing down on a hapless white mother and her baby. In another a blonde woman, completely nude except for a cloth named "southern civilization" covering her lower torso, was crucified on a cross. The nail in her right hand was labeled "White (?) Politicians." The nail in her left hand read "NAACP" while the one in her feet was labeled "Supreme Court Ruling."[9]

Despite Johnson's efforts, voters narrowly awarded Rockefeller the governor's office in the 1966 election. Rockefeller would go on to serve a difficult second term, finding it increasingly cumbersome to deal with the large Democratic majority in the state government. Adding to his misery were the rumors of alcoholism that had dogged him most of his life. To unseat him in the 1970 election it took the young Dale Bumpers, who had no ties to the past Democratic machine represented by the segregationist Faubus and race-baiter Johnson.

Though not successful in his bid for governor, "Justice Jim" Johnson had succeeded in creating a political discourse that combined race and sexuality and bringing that discourse into the mainstream. Rockefeller never responded either publicly or privately to the accusations during the election, and Johnson, when I spoke to him in the fall of 2005, still maintained that the rumors surrounding Rockefeller's sexuality were a "minor part of the overall campaign."[10]

This politics of skin—its color, its exposure, its usage—worked to specifically define the *other*, the *queer*, as the deviant outsider working to unseat the status quo in Arkansas. The New Yorker Rockefeller with his trusted black companion Hudson at his side was the perfect target and personification of fears unsuccessfully exploited by Johnson. Though Johnson's incendiary rhetoric proved unsuccessful, it did succeed in introducing a queer discourse of race and sexuality, two analytical rubrics that truly cannot be separated, into mainstream Arkansas.

The Johnson campaign's attempt to combine both racial fears and those of the homosexual, the queer outsider from the city jungle, capitalized on new fears of the queer corrupter and older fears of maintaining racial and sexual order and white supremacy in the South. The discourse surrounding the latter had been in place for some time, as illustrated by the Arkansas legislature's manipulation of the sodomy statute in the nineteenth century to target specifically the black minority within the state. The queer outsider was a new concoction, however. During periods of sexual panic and political upheaval, erotic life is renegotiated in the United States.[11] In the American South this also occurred during periods of racial upheaval. The politics of race and sexuality clearly came to a dramatic intersection in Arkansas. Johnson saw his chance, accusing Rockefeller not only of the crime of sodomy, but sodomy with a black male. The campaign attempted to capitalize on the recent struggle and social upheaval involving Central High and that of Rockefeller's big-city and perhaps-sinful past.[12] This combination was potentially volatile but never produced the results intended. Most Arkansans paid little attention to the rumors of interracial homosexual affairs, just as Rockefeller had done. Johnson, in an effort to exploit the old political lightning rods of race and deviant sexuality, concocted a new formula for queer. Though Johnson's gubernatorial bid was unsuccessful, Arkansans nonetheless were introduced to a new social deviant and only five years after the results of Dorothy Van Rippey's prison physical were splashed across statewide headlines. The sexual queer would join and soon replace the often queered black male as Arkansas's predominant and increasingly politicized social fear.

NINE

Redefinition

March 10, 1977

Dear Governor,

I urge you not to sign House Bill 117 into law. I moved to
Arkansas three months ago and have finally found my home. I do
not wish to leave but cannot see living in a state where people are
prosecuted for their sexual preferences. I am not gay yet I strongly
feel this. Please keep Arkansas a humane place to live.

Sincerely,
Patti Holmes
Pocahontas, Arkansas[1]

Seven days after receiving the above letter, Arkansas governor David
Pryor was told that representatives of the American Civil Liberties Union
were outside his office. This was expected. However, the Quakers, representatives from the Society of Friends, were a bit unexpected.[2] In fact, both
groups were part of a long parade of visitors who were concerned about
the future of House Bill 117.

House Bill 117 had been sitting on the governor's desk for just a few
hours. If he signed it, the new law would prohibit sodomy in Arkansas
but only between members of the same sex. Most states had sodomy
laws. Arkansas had been without one since its legislators scrapped the
old sodomy law with little debate in 1976 while revising the entire criminal code. In less than a year Pryor saw the debate reopened with enthu-
siasm and the Quakers at his door insisting that he veto it. Both the
Quakers and representatives from the ACLU met with Governor Pryor's
legal advisor Larry Yancey urging him to oppose the bill. After all, he
could have let it become law without his signature.

Besides his visitors opposed to the bill, the office phones were constantly ringing with calls from people with similar views. Governor Jerry Brown called from California with his concerns. Milton Shapp, governor of Pennsylvania, also phoned, following up a letter from his office urging Pryor not to sign the legislation into law. In this letter, Milton Berkes, Shapp's special assistant for human services, pointed out that his state had taken a progressive stance toward the protection of gays and lesbians within the state. Months earlier, Shapp had issued two executive orders outlawing discrimination against persons due to their "affectional or sexual preferences."[3] Governor Shapp went on to mention that his office had also formed the State Council for Sexual Minorities, with the primary goal of "obtaining equal rights for all persons" regardless of sexual orientation. In closing, Berkes also pointed out that since 1961 there had been a "clear trend" of repealing sodomy laws, with eighteen states including Arkansas striking them from the books. Berke stated that he was sure that Governor Pryor would agree "that law enforcement funds can be better used for serious crimes against person and property rather than for this type of consenting conduct."[4]

Oregon legislators also wrote to the governor urging him not to sign the bill. The state of Oregon had removed its sodomy legislation in 1971. The legislators who wrote to Pryor argued that his signing the new bill would hinder the progressive momentum that had seen so many sodomy laws repealed across the country. They also noted that the main reason that such laws were repealed was that they never really decreased sexual activity but only made criminals out of otherwise law-abiding citizens.[5]

Other than these groups and lawmakers from outside the state, the governor's office was inundated with letters from ordinary Americans both within and outside the state delivering the same message as that from concerned Arkansan Patti Holmes. Of the dozens of letters received by the governor's office, all were against his signing the bill. Some letters warned that the state could face "undisclosed ramifications" if the bill became law. They spoke of costly civil suits and the funds needed to enforce such legislation. Many constituents also expressed the concern that a new sodomy law could invite blackmail of Arkansans. Beyond the possible legal ramifications, one correspondent warned that the bill, once signed, would "jail our major American playwrights, many of our ballet stars, singers, writers, not to mention the many professional doctors, and teachers, etc." Other letters were far more poignant than this.

March 12, 1977

Dear Governor Pryor,

The state which I viewed with pride in 1975 and 1976 as one of the most progressive states in the union, I now view with utter shame and disgust. I am gay, but I am still a citizen of the United States. This entitles me to certain constitutional rights, such as the pursuit of happiness. I cannot see how the pursuit of happiness in this manner adversely affects the general public if it is done in private. I am not sick; I simply prefer to have sexual relations with members of my own sex. Do I have to give up my so-called inalienable rights simply because legislators cannot understand my desires and therefore fear them? I pose no threat to the public. I do not molest children or press myself on unwilling heterosexual males. All I ask is the right for two *consenting adults* to do as they wish with their *private* lives. I cannot see that this right should be subject to the whim of a bunch of homophobic legislators.

Sincerely,
Patrick Simmons
Stuttgart, Arkansas[6]

What was this progressive wave that Arkansas had seemed to be riding up until House Bill 117 appeared in the spring of 1977? Arkansas had, after all, repealed its sodomy statute a year earlier and in doing so joined a national trend of legal reform, completely overhauling its entire penal code. Across the country the debate concerning state criminal-code reform had been going on for several years. It was clear to many that the American legal system was in grave condition, the Arkansas penal code being no exception. State legal codes across the nation struggled to operate within antiquated legal systems, with many laws written in the colonial period, they themselves remainders of English common law. In response to this crisis the American Law Institute developed the Model Penal Code, a guide to help states modernize their existing penal codes by removing unnecessary laws from the books. This institute, an independent group of judges, lawyers, and law professors, sought to "modernize American law in almost all aspects."[7]

In following this nationwide wave of reform, the Arkansas legislature formed the Arkansas Criminal Code Revision Commission. Consisting of Arkansas lawyers, lawmakers, law professors, and law enforcers, as well as ministers and Catholic priests, the commission drafted the 1976 Arkansas Criminal Code to be considered by the legislature, with practically every offense undergoing at least minor definitional revision. Borrowing directly from the Model Penal Code, the decision by the revision commission was that any sexual activity committed by consenting adults in private would be considered legal behavior. The proposed code contained statutes forbidding sexual activities with minors, activities in public spaces or in the view of the public, and activities with nonconsenting parties. The new criminal code suffered little scrutiny and with even less debate easily passed both houses of the Arkansas legislature and was signed by Governor Pryor to go into effect on January 1, 1976.[8]

The old sodomy statute that had always been on the books in Arkansas in one form or another had not been removed simply by happenstance. When drafting the new criminal code, revision commission members saw its removal not necessarily as a progressive move but as simply common sense. Then something happened that year that brought sex offenses, particularly sodomy, back to the forefront: two men were arrested in a contested space but had apparently committed no real crime.

It was a strange case from the beginning. The facts were simple, but for Little Rock law enforcement officers they were also infuriating. Officer Hugh Gentry found himself sitting in court testifying on behalf of Arkansas officials and attorneys that the Little Rock City Jail, and indeed all jails within the state, should be considered public space. With this, inmates found engaging in sexual intercourse could be charged with public sexual indecency.

On February 12, 1976, Little Rock police, after several complaints from neighbors about noise and nuisance, proceeded downtown to 1113 West Fifteenth Street where they arrested James Black ("Sammy" to his friends), forty years of age, on a charge of public drunkenness. Black was placed in the drunk tank at the Little Rock City Jail around 3:30 p.m.. An hour later and across town, police noticed Willie Henderson weaving in and out of the lanes of the new freeway, and he was subsequently arrested for driving under the influence of alcohol. He soon joined Black in the drunk tank. The two men had never met, nor were they alone in their confines. They were now waiting to sober up in the drunk tank with about fifteen other detainees. Besides these inmates, jailers and officers periodically patrolled the drunk tank and the surrounding cells.

Hugh Gentry was on duty that afternoon. An hour after Henderson joined Black, Gentry observed the two engaging in oral sex.[9]

Gentry and other officers were furious when they were told that Henderson and Black, beyond their transgressions involving alcohol, had apparently committed no crime in their act of homosex. After all, a sodomy statute had been absent from the new, now one-month-old, criminal code; their behavior was perfectly legal, or at least no longer illegal, in Arkansas. The two men could not be charged with sodomy, as they could have been before January 1.

Those in charge of Little Rock's correction facilities were furious. They found their ability to police such acts usurped by outside forces. In place of sodomy some hoped a charge of indecency would stick. With their influence, the case found its way in front of Little Rock municipal judge Jack Holt, long regarded as one of the more liberal to sit on the city's benches. Holt ruled that the city jail was a private space, and therefore, Henderson and Black could not even face prosecution on a charge of public indecency.[10] Holt reasoned that if someone had "slipped a bottle of liquor to a prisoner and he got drunk, you couldn't charge him with public drunkenness."[11] Thus the two men could not be charged with any sex crime.

No one at the Little Rock prosecutor's office took issue publicly with the ruling, though many privately expressed dissatisfaction. Chief deputy prosecuting attorney Wilbur C. "Dub" Bentley remarked to his colleagues that the city jail would soon "turn into a gay bar."[12] After Holt's decision the case went unnoticed for several weeks. Many within the prosecutor's office simply wished to ignore the matter and let the deadline for appeal pass. After all, many prosecutors took little issue with the decision. However, there were some who did.

After Holt ruled, the state had one year to again file charges of public sexual indecency against Black and Henderson, which is what deputy prosecuting attorney John Hall Jr. did. When he got the same result—a dismissal—Hall appealed to Circuit judge William J. Kirby and put Hugh Gentry on the stand to testify that the jail should be considered a public place. Judge Kirby asked Gentry if a private citizen could enter the jail without being on some sort of official tour. "It's not like going to the library," Kirby quipped.[13]

After declaring the jail a private space, Hall filed notice of an interlocutory appeal to the Arkansas Supreme Court. The case, for those who wished to pursue it, was becoming an embarrassment. After the case reached the supreme court, almost one year after Black and Henderson found themselves in the act, the state prosecutors finally received a decision that pleased them. Despite the lower courts' decisions, the Arkansas Supreme Court declared the jail to be a public space. The court heard from state prosecutors that besides the staff and inmates and their visiting friends and families, tours through the Little Rock city jails were frequent, and though these tours were always guided by detention personnel, this was only to prevent weapons from being smuggled in or citizens harming prisoners and not to illustrate a jailer's control of an otherwise public space. Prosecutors argued that it was not the fact that there was no tour but the fact that there could have been that led them to question the lower court's ruling. The supreme court agreed, and the charge of public sexual indecency against Willie Henderson and Sammy Black had been affirmed.[14]

April 10, 1977

Dear Governor Pryor:

The Executive Board of the Independence Baptist Association, in session March 29, 1977, passed a resolution commending Anita Bryant for her firm Christian stand against the immoral practices of homosexuality and similar atrocities and extending to her our assurance of prayerful support.

The same resolution lends our prayerful support to you, Governor Pryor, and to the Honorable Jimmy Carter, President of our country, that as you deal with these groups, you might uphold always the Biblical teachings concerning these immoral practices.

Through your examples, others all over our country may be encouraged to speak out against what is wrong in our world today, seeking to preserve for our children, and others to follow, the moral and spiritual purity God intends.

Be assured of our prayers and our support as you seek His will in your strategic position as Governor of our fine state.

May God bless you,
The Executive Board,
Independence Baptist Association,
Mrs. S. D. Hacker, Clerk[15]

This letter received no reply from the Governor's office.

In September 1977 the cover of the *Arkansas Times,* a popular alternative magazine in the state, featured an article entitled "'The Arkansas of the '70s: The Good Ole Boy Ain't Whut He Used to Be." The author, Jim Ranchino, a native of Arkadelphia, Arkansas, wrote that "premarital sex, the use of marijuana, and unfaithfulness to marriage vows are now becoming more the rule than the exception."[16] These particular departures from traditional institutions such as marriage and family were not altogether lost on Arkansans. In fact, state legislators had been anxious about the growing trend for some time.

Early in 1977 the *Arkansas Gazette* reported that the Arkansas House of Representatives "discovered sex" and "intends to do something about it."[17] During the first seven days of the session, legislators introduced four bills dealing with sexual conduct. Rep. Arlo Tyer of Pocahontas took credit for the first two bills: House Bill 237 sought to prohibit "R" and "X" rated movies within the state and House Bill 238 would levy a tax of $1,500 on men and women living together without being married. This latter bill sought, according to the *Gazette,* to make the point that while "such cohabitation is now common in many communities," it was not to be condoned by the state of Arkansas. Besides paying the tax, the couple also would be required to undergo blood tests and obtain a permit from a chancery judge to continue cohabitation. The judge could only issue the "living together permit" if the couple were able to show "good cause."[18] A third measure, House Bill 191, introduced by Rep. Earl Jones of Texarkana, sought to censor sexually explicit material in the state. The "comprehensive obscenity bill" would outlaw books and magazines that had no redeeming social or artistic value. The fourth bill, which would recriminalize sodomy in Arkansas, was introduced by High school football coach and state representative Bill Stancil of Fort Smith who claimed that he had been hoodwinked into voting for the revised criminal code that excluded sodomy.

Stancil soon took action to rectify the situation. In haste he drafted House Bill 117 that would define sodomy as any deviate sexual behavior and make it a class C felony punishable by as many as ten years in prison. The bill and its author soon drew criticism from legislative colleagues. Rep. Art Givens of Sherwood noted that the new criminal code had decriminalized sodomy because it was a "victimless" crime. He argued before the house judiciary committee that Stancil's bill would potentially make criminals out of many husbands and wives in the state and warned that "everything except what is done strictly for reproduction may be criminal in nature."[19] Givens suggested that Stancil consult the Arkansas attorney general's office for its opinion, but Stancil responded that he was not particularly interested in the attorney general's opinion. Nevertheless, Stancil agreed to amend the bill to define sodomy more precisely and to reduce the penalties with which it could be punished. As amended, House Bill 117 made bestiality and sodomy class D felonies, carrying prison terms of as long as five years, and defined sodomy as an act between two members of the same sex.[20]

Despite the questions raised by Givens while the bill was in committee, it seemed that few legislators took it seriously. During the committee's proceedings, the room often exploded with laughter. Committee vice-chairman N. B. "Nap" Murphy of Hamburg, who was presiding, continually pleaded for dignity. The giggles continued and, at one point, the hilarity was so intense that the course of business became difficult to follow. Murphy, repeatedly striking his gavel, pleaded, "Gentlemen, I do not know what is going on at this time."[21] Despite this recklessness, Givens was able to convince many house members that the bill required further revision. In a compromise Stancil agreed to change the proposed statute to define sodomy as a misdemeanor rather than a felony. This would carry a maximum penalty of up to a year in prison and a thousand-dollar fine. The judiciary committee adopted the amended bill and sent it to the floor with a "do pass" recommendation.[22]

The young Bill Clinton, then attorney general of Arkansas, described Bill Stancil as a "muscular, square-headed, broken-nosed guy." Clinton had taken notice of the sex bills the minute they were introduced. Together with his colleague Jim Guy Tucker, who had worked tirelessly to put through the criminal code revision and would replace Clinton as governor once he won the White House in 1992, Clinton worked behind the scenes to defeat the measures. However, as attorney general he could only offer his official opinion on the constitutionality of House Bill 117 if a public official requested it. A few young liberal Democrats in the house worried about the bill's chances as it made its way to the floor. Instead of delaying the bill, they sought to make a mockery of it during debate. Bill Clinton watched his colleagues from the public viewing gallery, knowing that something was up.

A young legislator stood up and praised Stancil for his forthright stand on morality in the state but said that the bill did not go far enough. To strengthen it, he offered an amendment making it a class D felony for any member of the Arkansas legislature to commit adultery while the general assembly was in session. As Clinton and his colleagues erupted with laughter in the visitors' viewing gallery, silence fell on the floor. Clinton knew, as everyone did, that for many of the lawmakers from small towns and districts, two months in Little Rock were comparable to "two months in Paris."[23] Not amused by the amendment, the legislators refused to act on any further house business until the amendment was withdrawn.

Stancil had a few floor theatrics of his own in store for his colleagues. To convince his fellow lawmakers, he went to the well of the house and produced from his briefcase copies of the King James Bible and the Arkansas Constitution. Stancil paced the floor waving the two works and shouting, "One of these can be amended, but the other can't." The bill passed the Arkansas House of Representatives on a vote of sixty-six to two.[24]

Again working privately, Clinton sought to delay the bill until the legislature adjourned, letting Stancil's work die of natural causes when it reached the senate. A political ally of Clinton, Sen. Nick Wilson of Pocahontas, stalled the bill in committee until just hours before the senate and the rest of the general assembly was to adjourn until the 1979 session. However, Sen. Milt Earnhart of Fort Smith, the bill's sponsor in the senate, apologizing to his colleagues for not "having any live demonstrations" to accompany his explanation of the bill, got it to a vote by promising Wilson funding for a new vocational school in his district if he would stand aside.[25] Hours before adjournment, the senate passed House Bill 117 with little debate on a vote of twenty-five to zero. The next day, despite the numerous pleas for him not to, Governor Pryor signed House Bill 117 into law.[26]

From the beginning, Arkansas's original sodomy statute suffered from a great deal of vagueness. Perhaps it was meant to do so. The language that was used to define sodomy in Arkansas, and indeed all over the American South, used such phrases as "a crime unfit to be named" or an "unnatural crime against nature." Now, in the political atmosphere in Arkansas that preceded and predicted in many ways the coming of such things as the Moral Majority and the beginnings of the religious right, these terms were deliberately and exclusively used as synonyms for homosexual conduct.[27]

In the new law Stancil even grouped homosexual acts with bestiality to further queer the subject in the eyes of Arkansans. But this was relatively new. Indeed, given the cases presented earlier (*Smith* and *Strum v. State*), it seems Arkansas was only marginally interested in regulating homosexual sex, though courts were willing for the act to fall under the sodomy umbrella, a category constantly in flux and acting as a barometer for prevailing social and political discourse.

When examining Arkansas's original sodomy statute, it is important to remember that the statute, at one time, prescribed a much harsher penalty for the black offender: death. With this, it is clear that the sodomy statute changes with societal discourse or reflects whatever the dominant society, in this case the white, increasingly heteronormative South, deems queer behavior at the time. Clearly, in post–Civil War Arkansas and even until the beginnings of the civil rights era, Arkansas would have been more concerned with interracial sex than any sort of same-sex sexual activity, the former seen as far queerer and more worthy of regulation than the latter, with the earlier version of the Arkansas sodomy statute acting more as a miscegenation law than anything else.[28] And though in both cases we see that erotic life becomes renegotiated politically, sexual deviants were still, as historian Jeffrey Weeks calls them, the "omnipresent scapegoats" for whatever a predominant society fears at that time.[29] Some tweaking was involved, but a suitable language was already in place for a reproduction of difference. By using the older sodomy statute as a foundation, the Arkansas legislators sought now to exclude the new queer Arkansan from the state constitution, casting homosex and the homosexual as a perverse and rural and backward living contrary to social norms.

The new law's inclusion of bestiality and a narrower definition of homosex not only wove a greater web of abnormality around same-sex desire but also cast homosex and the larger identity around homosexuality into the rural sphere. Bestiality was always considered a backward and indeed backwoods practice, and it is often found there in popular media representations of rural areas, especially that of the Deep South and Appalachia where one had everyday contact with beasts and fowl, master/beast relationships that could easily slide from the practical to the intimate. To link homosex with sex with animals helps conjure an image of the uneducated, the perverse, the slack-jawed, boondocks yokels unable to place their desire within appropriate places or acceptable faces. Bestiality is considered almost a common practice in rural areas where so much of day-to-day life and indeed survival of the person in a campestral setting has to do to with the upkeep and survival of the animal. Young men on the farm, perhaps in a reaction to the lack of women in their surroundings, vented sexual desires with what was at hand: the cows, the stallions, or each other.[30] In the rural we see both the absence of people and close contact with an abundance of farm animals, leaving conditions ripe for fornication with what was at hand. The utterly confused category of sodomy as an umbrella term for perverse desires now saw its boundaries tightened by limiting its terms to homosex. The twist of bestiality was added as the state of Arkansas found itself at the rural/urban crossroads and moving to a more respectable national position where success was seen in the growth of cities and the abandonment of rural life.

With the repeal of the old sodomy statute came the ever-poignant matter of queer space and the distinction of public and private spaces. Henderson and Black unwittingly found themselves and their case at the forefront of this debate. However, Stancil and other representatives were not concerned by this distinction and sought to regulate homosex in all spaces. Though the city of Little Rock had difficulty charging Henderson and Black with any crime, the 1977 general assembly fashioned a definition of sodomy that made no distinction between public and private. Soon legislators and particularly law enforcement officers sought to increase what was known in the public sphere as regulation of homosexual sex was an increasing concern of the state.[31] Law enforcers would have more in store.

April 6, 1977

Dear Ms. Holmes,

Thank you for your recent letter regarding HB 117, the so-called Sodomy Bill. As you know, I have signed the bill into law.

This was a very difficult decision for me to make, and I was grateful to have your thoughtful comments during the deliberations on this issue. Please feel free to contact me in the future about matters of concern for you.

Sincerely,
David Pryor

"Every governor bows to political pressure," Larry Yancey explained years later, "and no one, including the governor, wanted a 'nay' vote on their record, especially when it came to sodomy."[32] Though many had made light of the bill, all but two legislators fell prey to the same pressures as Pryor. Yancey recalled that legislators would complain that "preachers back home" were giving them the "what for about sodomy."[33] A national backlash against gay and lesbian visibility led the state legislature to outlaw homosex in all spaces, public or private.

Earlier in the same month that the sodomy bill became law, the Arkansas House of Representatives considered House Resolution 32. Introduced by Rep. Albert "Tom" Collier, the legislation applauded Anita Bryant for her opposition to equal housing and employment legislation for homosexuals in the Sunshine State. It drew attention even from a White House aide who, after receiving dozens of letters and phone calls from gays and lesbians, called Collier, according to his own account, to ask what the resolution had to say. Collier also noted that in response to his legislation, he received "a real nice letter" from Bryant thanking him and the Arkansas House of Representatives for the resolution, which easily cleared the legislature.[34]

While the Arkansas legislature was debating the sodomy law, Bryant was making national headlines in her campaign against gay rights. Bryant had long been a popular performer in the American South, making a name by singing at conventions and state fairs and wooing audiences with patriotic numbers such as the "Battle Hymn of the Republic" and "God Bless America." However, by 1977 the native of Barnsdall, Oklahoma, had become most recognizable as the spokeswoman for the Florida Citrus Commission. Most memorably, she appeared in television commercials singing, "Come to Florida, sunshine tree! Come, sunshine, naturally."[35] At the urging of the citrus commission, she had made Miami, Florida, her home. Once there she became alarmed upon learning from her local pastor that the Dade County Metro Commission, the legislative body for the city of Miami, was planning to add "affectional or sexual preference" to the city's civil rights ordinance. Adding this phrase would protect homosexuals from discrimination in housing, public accommodations, and employment. Enraged, Bryant became determined to defeat the measure. However, time was short, and Bryant and her allies were able only to sway a few votes on the commission before the proposal passed on a vote of five to three. In response, Bryant created the "Save Our Children" campaign aimed at toppling the legislation. In the campaign literature Bryant stated, "I don't hate homosexuals! But as a mother, I must protect my children from their evil influence. . . . They want to recruit your children and teach them the virtues of becoming homosexual."[36] This rhetoric proved highly effective. Bryant convinced many voters in the Miami area that the law would allow homosexuals employed in the county's public schools to freely advertise their sexuality. Bryant and her "Save Our Children" campaign pressed for a referendum to decide if the ordinance forbidding discrimination against lesbian and gays should be allowed to stand. She got it, and 70 percent of voters supported the repeal in a special referendum on June 9, 1977. Bryant pledged to continue her crusade. "We will now carry our fight against similar laws throughout the nation that attempt to legitimize a lifestyle that is both perverse and dangerous to the sanctity of the family, dangerous to our children, dangerous to our freedom of religion and freedom of choice, dangerous to our survival as a nation."[37]

It was apparent that few were willing to have a vote against an antisodomy ordinance on their legislative record and were proud to praise Bryant for her antigay stance. An episode in southeast Arkansas suggested what might have awaited a legislator who dared to take a stand against the homophobic tide swelled by Bryant. On January 5, 1978, the *Lincoln Ledger*, the only newspaper in rural Lincoln County and Star City, Arkansas, published an editorial by Ross Dennis. It urged Bryant to "sit down and shut up," insisting that she had no right to save the world from what she considered to be sin. The editorial set off a small firestorm. The small paper and its editors were bombarded with phone calls and visits from local pastors who threatened a boycott if the editorial was not retracted. In the next issue the *Ledger's* general manager and owner, Thomas Roark, apologized, stating that he was "very wrong in letting this material be published." In the same issue Dennis published "An

Open Letter to the Readers" in which he apologized for having caused offense by his editorial. He explained that he chose Bryant simply "because she is such a controversial figure and he needed someone to point a finger at" and admitted that he "chose the wrong person for this part of the country." Despite his apology, Dennis was fired from the *Lincoln Ledger* one month later.[38]

Ironically, for all of her crusade's seeming efficacy, Bryant paid a high price for her outspokenness. Under pressure from a gay-organized boycott, she lost her lucrative orange juice contract. Bryant suddenly found it hard to find venues for her concerts. In its July 1977 issue the *Ladies' Home Journal* published results of a survey that asked high school students to identify the man and woman who have "done the most damage to the world." The man ranking first was Adolf Hitler. The woman was Anita Bryant.[39]

By late the following year, Bryant could not even draw a crowd in Little Rock. Wearing a red-and-white dress with a long, flowing cape and carrying a red velvet–covered Bible, Bryant arrived in the state capital on Saturday, October 21, 1978. Considering the state's recriminalization of sodomy and the house of representatives' passage of a resolution applauding her, Bryant probably assumed Arkansas would welcome her. She may have been surprised then to find only three hundred in attendance for her performance at the three-thousand-seat Robinson Center auditorium. Despite the rather poor turn out, Bryant continued with the show, entertaining the faithful few with such songs as "How Great Thou Art," "God Bless America," and "This is My Country."[40]

It might have seemed that Bryant's influence in Arkansas and across the nation was fading fast. Yet the die had been cast, and Arkansas's sodomy law and similar antigay laws elsewhere remained in force. Perhaps many lawmakers, unwilling to take a stand on the issue, thought they could simply wait for a court to declare the laws unconstitutional, sparing them legislative hardship and political complications. Or, perhaps most agreed with the laws and were satisfied.

TEN

Public and Private Prejudice

*At shortly after five o'clock on a weekday evening, four
men enter a public restroom in the city park. One wears a
well-tailored business suit; another wears tennis shoes,
shorts, and a tee-shirt; the third man is still clad in the
khaki uniform of his filling station; the last, a salesman,
has loosened his tie and left his sports coat in the car.
What has caused these men to leave the company of other
homeward-bound commuters on the freeway? What common interest brings these men, with their divergent back-
grounds, to this public facility?[1]*

—LAUD HUMPHREYS

Begun in the 1950s, the interstate highway system, the great victory of the automotive lobby, soon symbolized the postwar economic boom, connecting far-flung cities and the citizens therein,
and so began the American love affair with the automobile and leisure
in general.[2] The highway rest area offered travelers services to aid them
in their journey, including toilets, picnic facilities, and tourist information. The Morgan rest area was opened in October of 1973 at a cost of
almost half a million dollars. It sat near mile marker 146 on Interstate
40, meaning it was 146 miles from the Oklahoma border to the west.
From that point it was 138 miles east to Memphis on Interstate 40, which
now runs coast to coast. The Morgan rest area was at that time one of
thirty-six rest areas in the state.[3]

In 1991 Robert Howard found himself on the road again, almost
thirty years after he had hitchhiked to New Orleans passing as a little
blonde girl, but this time he was making his regular commute from Little

Rock to the smaller bedroom communities surrounding the city. He now ran his own business, Self Image, Inc., a licensed massage and beauty service that offered in-home services to clients, some in Conway about thirty miles northwest of his home in Little Rock. He usually worked late to accommodate clients after their workday. By the time he left his last client on February 1, 1991, it was almost 11:30 p.m. Howard stopped off to use the public toilets at the Morgan rest area, sitting roughly halfway between Conway and Little Rock.

The rest area already had a reputation. The fact that a great many men used the space for anonymous sexual encounters was not lost on Howard, nor was it lost on local law enforcement officers. Howard parked his car and entered the men's toilets. He had noticed a few men loitering around the building and in the nearby woods that surrounded the rest area on one side. He paid little attention although he knew of the men's intentions. Robert Howard is a gay man, but he did differ from the loitering individuals in that his intention was only to use the toilet for its intended purpose. Afterward, as he was walking back to his automobile, an attractive young man in his late twenties stopped him. Intrigued though not necessarily interested, Howard felt sympathy for the young cruiser and obliged him with idle chitchat.[4] The small talk took the usual route of first conversing about the weather, and then rather abruptly, as Howard remembers, the young man propositioned him for oral sex. A bit put off, Howard told the young man that "cruising an interstate rest stop for sex was no way for a gay man to meet people."[5] The man persisted, asking Howard to join him in his car, although Howard kept declining and walked briskly away. At this point the young man produced a badge from under his shirt, revealing himself to be a Pulaski County sheriff's deputy. Robert Howard was under arrest for loitering for deviant sexual activity, a misdemeanor.[6]

Howard was not the only man arrested during the two-hour sheriff's-office sting that night. A total of eight men were arrested on various charges, including two for violation of the Arkansas sodomy statute. For many, especially those arrested on sodomy charges, the raid would seem peculiarly well timed.

On Thursday, January 17, 1991, two weeks prior to Howard's arrest, Arkansas state senator Vic Snyder introduced a bill into the legislature that quickly sparked opposition from his fellow legislators as well as various religious groups. Snyder, a Democrat representing among other places Pulaski County, introduced Senate Bill 125 aimed at removing homosexual activity between consenting adults from the state's sodomy statute.

Snyder's bill would have left intact the bestiality portion of the law. Snyder, a Little Rock physician, noted that the law was contradictory to Arkansas's efforts to contain the AIDS virus. Snyder stated that, on the one hand, the state wished to stop the spread of AIDS by encouraging both homosexuals and heterosexuals to undergo blood tests and confide in their doctors, who promised confidentiality. On the other hand, Snyder pointed out, the activity that prompted their testing was deemed illegal by the state.[7] Essentially, sodomy's illegality would drive both it and testing for HIV/AIDS underground, thereby creating a severe public health dilemma for which Snyder contended the state was simply unprepared. To have yourself tested would be tantamount to turning yourself in. An imposed silence on the gay community would equal death for many.

Arkansas religious groups were quick to respond to Snyder's proposed legislation. Mark Lowery, executive director of the Christian Coalition of Arkansas promised his organization's opposition to it despite not having seen the bill. Lowery stated that Snyder's reasoning for the removal of homosexual activity from the sodomy statute was unsound, since there were no laws requiring doctors to report to the police when they discovered someone to be homosexual.[8]

Senate Bill 125 was first discussed by the senate judiciary committee, where emotions ran high. Snyder pleaded with the committee not to "incorporate one moral perspective or one religious view" when considering the bill.[9] Political opponents to Snyder were quick to argue that the state had a duty to take a stand against homosexual behavior as destructive and unnatural. Beyond this, the committee members offered no other discussion or defense of their position. They did, however, extend an invitation to citizens to testify for or against Snyder's proposed changes to the sodomy statute. John Miles, senior pastor of St. James United Methodist Church in Little Rock, offered testimony agreeing with Snyder's position that the present sodomy statute might discourage gay men from being tested for AIDS. Miles added that he believed that "what goes on between two consenting adults is their private matter."[10]

Offering a counterpoint to this was another Methodist minister,

Norman Carter of the Conway First United Methodist Church (my home church). Carter's testimony attempted to dispute those who argued that homosexuality and, specifically, sodomy was a victimless crime. Carter noted that there was absolutely a need for the law in that it "puts a leash on the aggressive behavior of homosexuals toward innocent people."[11] He added that he himself had been a victim of such behavior; though when asked, he declined to comment on the details of his victimization. During his testimony, Carter produced a copy of the *Gay Community News* and read from what he called the "gay credo," which he quoted as declaring that homosexuals "will sodomize your sons" and, that for homosexuals, the "only gods are handsome young men."[12] Carter's harsh rhetoric was echoed by Lowery, who admitted he had still not read the bill. Both men offered a number of purported statistics indicating that gay men are more likely than heterosexuals to have sex with minors. The two men contended that research had shown that gay men are more likely to have sexual relations with strangers, putting them at a further risk for sexually transmitted diseases. In their rhetoric they continually referred to homosexuals as "unnatural."

After all the testimony was offered, the committee, without further discussion, voted on the bill on January 20, 1991. The next day, the *Arkansas Gazette* ran a bold three-column headline: "Committee Rejects Sodomy Law Repeal." The committee had given Snyder's bill a rare unanimous do-not-pass motion. Snyder had no illusions concerning the chances of Senate Bill 125. Nevertheless, he felt it necessary to introduce the measure, hoping that subsequent attempts would prove successful.[14] Later, as committee members were approached by *Gazette* reporters, many stated that they were simply following the wishes of their constituents, though they may have personally agreed with Snyder and his rationale for removing homosexuality from the sodomy law. Sen. Wayne

Also opposing the bill in the committee hearing was Larry Page, attorney for the Arkansas Baptist Association. Page stated that while he did not hate homosexuals, he abhorred homosexual behavior. He testified that such "destructive" and "harmful" activity mainly occurs in public spaces such as parks and restrooms.[13] Page, a former Little Rock city prosecutor, also said that he had never prosecuted anyone for violating the sodomy statute. He suggested that those who oppose the law should see it as innocuous in that it constituted no real danger to gays and lesbians in Arkansas.

Dowd of Texarkana, who offered the do-not-pass motion in the committee, explained with surprising candor that "what it comes down to is I guess I have a lack of backbone."[15] Dowd, an attorney in Texarkana, stated that as a lawyer and lawmaker, he felt that any legal challenge to the sodomy law would most likely see it declared unconstitutional by Arkansas courts. However, Dowd noted that he "had so many communications from constituents opposed to the bill that, trying to represent the people that elected me, I voted against it."[16]

On Friday, February 1, the day after the *Gazette* ran its front-page story, Robert Howard was on his way to the Pulaski County jail. Both in the cramped confines of the back of a state trooper's patrol car and within the holding cell, Howard was bombarded with antagonistic and homophobic remarks from the arresting officers who called him "worthless" and "faggot."[17] He was released later on bond posted by his partner. To say that Howard and the other men arrested that night were in the wrong place at the wrong time would not begin to describe their predicament.

On that Friday, the sting lasted a little more than two hours. It was led by Sgt. Jay Campbell who later told the *Gazette* that the sheriff's office had received a number of complaints from citizens concerning the "misuse" of the rest area. Campbell claimed that in their misuse of the facilities, local gay men had "gotten pretty bold" and were attempting to "take the park over."[18] Campbell was also quoted as saying that the rest area had become a popular gathering place for gay men looking for "one-night stands," adding that "they need to rent a motel room or something," although that would not necessarily make the act any less illegal.[19] In the sheriff's office raid twenty-year-old Bryan Blystone of Orange, California, and thirty-six-year-old Ronald Simmons of North Little Rock were charged with sodomy after officers observed the two men in an act of fellatio in the back seat of Simmons's parked automobile. The other six men, not actually caught in a sexual act, were all charged with loitering for the purpose of deviant sexual activity, a misdemeanor. Campbell explained that he preferred to arrest the men rather than to simply issue citations on the scene so that they would have to appear in court instead of paying their fines without a public appearance.

The sheriff's office also claimed that two of the individuals that had been arrested had tested positive for acquired immune deficiency syndrome in blood tests performed by state physicians. As a result of this information, the sheriff's office announced its intention to ask the arraigning judge to require the arrested men to submit statements during their arraignment showing that they had been tested for the AIDS virus. Campbell said that he would ask for the AIDS test in the interest of public health and to discourage men from coming to the rest area.

It was not long before questions arose as to the connection between the legislative debate and the raid that netted two sodomy arrests. Campbell told *Gazette* reporters that it was "merely coincidence" that the two events happened within forty-eight hours of each other.[20] The Arkansas Gay and Lesbian Task Force did not accept this explanation. Although small in number, members of the task force were quick to voice their outrage concerning the arrests and the subsequent treatment of gay men at the hands of Pulaski County and Little Rock law enforcement. A small group of men and women assembled on the corner of Capitol Avenue and Main Street in view of the state capitol to protest. Jan Hodges, head of the task force, said that the sodomy arrests followed too closely after the debate on Snyder's bill. He condemned the Pulaski County sheriff's office, which he suggested was attempting to illustrate to the public through the raids that there was still a need for a state sodomy statute. Hodges read from a prepared statement condemning the arrests and the media coverage of them, which he deemed sensational. He argued to a meager assembly of local journalists that the reports concerning the Morgan rest area only perpetuated society's stereotypes of gay men. Responding to testimony in the legislative hearing contending that most homosexual activity occurs in public places, Hodges countered that, in fact, "the overwhelming majority of gay male sexual activity is at home between two consenting adults."[21] Hodges condemned the media for doing little to dispel the myths that stigmatize gays and lesbians, noting that "rarely is there something positive in the media" concerning homosexuals.[22] Hodges said that as a gay man, he was not embarrassed that so many were arrested at the Morgan rest area. However, he expressed his sadness that "people like us are rounded up, arrested, and dehumanized because anonymous sexual activity is the only way these men can keep their secret."[23] Also, Hodges hoped that the two sodomy arrests might prove to be good test cases for removing the sodomy law through a judicial challenge.

Regarding the allegation that two of those arrested had tested positive for HIV/AIDS, Sergeant Campbell said he had misunderstood the question asked by a *Gazette* reporter. Two men had tested positive for

AIDS, but those individuals had not been apprehended during the initial raid at the Morgan rest area but rather in a separate rest area months prior. However, despite this correction, Pulaski County municipal judge David Hale agreed with the sheriff's office request. Upon their appearance for plea and arraignment, Hale would order that all men arrested at the rest stop submit to an AIDS test. Hale justified his decision by citing precedent in previous sex-related cases. Hale told reporters he had followed the same procedure in a case where arresting officers were scratched by women arrested on prostitution charges.[24]

In the early stages of the Morgan operation, the sheriff's office installed hidden cameras inside the building that housed the public toilets. Their use of the hidden cameras came to light only when the sheriff's office offered taped scenes as evidence against various men arrested at the rest area. Tapes were then passed on to local media outlets and broadcast nightly on television. Campbell defended his use of the cameras by contending that Arkansas Supreme Court rulings allowed for the use of hidden cameras in public restrooms in the course of criminal investigations. He said that the cameras were only in the men's restrooms and were only turned on when undercover officers believed someone was breaking the law inside. When *Gazette* reporters inquired about this at the Arkansas Attorney General's office, a spokesman said that they could find neither a U.S. Supreme Court case nor an Arkansas Supreme Court case that supported the use of hidden cameras in public restrooms.[25] However, he said that in a situation like the Morgan sting, courts generally would admit video surveillance as evidence because "there's not an expectation of privacy in a public place." [26]

Some felt differently. Though he declined to file a motion to suppress the video-taped evidence since his clients were not among those who were captured using the hidden cameras, Ike Allen Laws, a Russellville attorney, disagreed with the sheriff's department. Laws stated that the issue had never been appealed to the Arkansas Supreme Court but that several states had established that evidence gathered by law enforcement officers in public places where there is "an expectation of privacy," such as a toilet stall, is not admissible.[27] Though Laws conceded that "public restrooms certainly are not the place to have sex," he did question Sergeant Campbell's use of manpower and equipment only to collect small fines on misdemeanor charges.[28]

It was not long before attorneys for the American Civil Liberties

Union voiced their concern over the matter of cameras inside the Morgan rest area. Jay Jacobson, the state director of the ACLU, argued that their use was an "outrageous violation of the people's right to privacy" and illustrated "bias and bigotry against homosexuals."[29] Jacobson also argued that if the state would simply legalize sodomy between consenting adults, there would be no need for the sheriff's office raids. Jacobson went on to say that "if there was not a sodomy law, if homosexuals were not evicted from apartments and if they were not beaten up . . . then you wouldn't have clandestine activity because there is no place for them to meet."[30] In defense of the cameras the sheriff's office stated that they were not operational at all times. Sheriff Carroll Gravett also mentioned that the camera served a dual purpose, looking for those violating Arkansas's statutes prohibiting public sexual encounters and those using the rest area for illegal narcotics dealings.[31]

The *Arkansas Gazette* disagreed and ran an editorial questioning the use of cameras by the sheriff's office. "They are called 'public restrooms' because they are installed for the public's convenience," the editorial argued, "but most people would consider what they do in a public restroom to be private."[32] Like Laws, the editorial questioned the officers' tactics during the operations at the rest area. The *Gazette* went on to say that, "had the deputies quit their peeping and instead posted even one of their uniformed number where he could be seen, at the door of the restroom, say, no illegal activity would have occurred."[33] The editorial closed by saying that "the right of privacy is real, though its boundaries are not so plainly marked as others."[34]

The cameras mounted at the rest area and the continuing arrests that took place there added to unwanted attention not only for the Pulaski County sheriff's office but for the Arkansas Highway Department as well, since the rest area was ultimately the property and responsibility of the department. In October 1992, almost a year after the raids began, the highway department announced its decision to close the Morgan rest area with no plans to reopen it or to create a similar facility at another site. In reaching this decision the highway department hardly mentioned the homosexual activity for which the space had become almost notorious. Instead, the department focused on maintenance issues and repair costs that exceeded its departmental budget, claiming that an additional $300,000 would be needed over the annual budget of $84,000 for the rest area to repair structural damage in the brick-and-concrete building that housed the public toilets. Also, citing the recent passage of the Americans with Disabilities Act, the department concluded that the cost to comply with the act, specifically modifying existing buildings, walkways, and drives to provide access to the handicapped, would be too great.[35]

One employee, however, was willing to connect the closure of the rest area with the recent homosexual activity that had become heavily publicized in the past year. In an interview with the *Arkansas Democrat,* an employee with the highway department who wished to remain anonymous for fear of losing his job claimed that sexual encounters coupled with related vandalism and the high cost of repairs had become the greatest problems at Morgan. According to this employee, the various acts of vandalism included replacing the stalls in the men's toilets, either because "glory holes" had been cut into the metal or they had been torn down altogether. Also, the employee said that the amount of graffiti in the men's toilets advertising various willing participants for sexual activity required that the restrooms be repainted frequently. The employee's statement appeared at odds with the satisfactory reviews filed after all recent inspections.[36] The employee went on to mention that due to the high volume of traffic through the Morgan rest area, citing up to ten thousand a day in the busier summer months, the rest area had become particularly attractive to gay men seeking anonymous sexual encounters.[37] Given the news article and the information given by the employee, the Arkansas Highway Department was quick to comment. Randall Ort, public affairs officer for the department, said that "vandalism is going to be a problem at any rest area."[38]

In October 1992, the highway department sought approval of the Federal Highway Administration to close the rest area effective immediately following the Thanksgiving holiday weekend, citing both the condition and the "misuse" of the facilities as the reasons. The Federal Highway Department agreed but refused to fund the actual demolition of the rest area.[39] On the morning of Monday, November 30, 1992, department crews erected concrete barriers at the entrance of the rest area. The picnic tables were removed from beneath the family pavilions and transported to other rest areas around the state. Everything else—the charcoal grills, the restroom mirrors, the water fountains—was sold as surplus at a state auction. Above the picnic and parking areas, demolition teams began razing the structure that had housed the public toilets and so many anonymous sexual encounters.

Vic Snyder tried again in 1993 and 1995 to topple the Arkansas sodomy law. With these attempts, Snyder was more optimistic. Bill Clinton, former Arkansas attorney general and governor, had been elected president in 1992 on a pro–gay rights platform. Also making Snyder more hopeful was that Sen. Mike Everett of Marked Tree, Arkansas, had joined him in the effort.

During discussion of the bill in 1993, Everett noted that he was forced to confront his own prejudices when his only son revealed to him that he was gay. Since then, Everett had decided that no one could choose to be a homosexual because no one would "choose to engage in a lifestyle that would generate as much prejudice as this does." He went on to say that the Arkansas sodomy law was tantamount to "state-sanctioned prejudice."[40] Despite his emotional plea to his fellow committee members, the bill was defeated. Snyder and Everett tried again two years later with the same result. Snyder now, however, used more direct language than in previous attempts. He told the committee that "every heterosexual in the state can engage in sexual activity in the privacy of their own home and the state doesn't get in their face, but if you are gay and lesbian, the state has the right to go into your home and arrest you."

This was the essence of the argument made by seven gay and lesbian Arkansans who gathered in the rotunda of the state capitol on Wednesday, January 28, 1998, to announce a lawsuit seeking to have the state's sodomy law declared to be in violation of the Arkansas Constitution. Though the plaintiffs acknowledged that there had not been a single instance of anyone being arrested for violating Arkansas's sodomy law in a private place, one of them, Vernon Stokay, argued that the law "is always an overriding threat. . . . You never know what kind of regime will come around. . . . It's always hanging over your head." The seven—Elena Picado, Robin White, George Townsand, Bryan Manire, Randy McCain, Vernon Stokey, and Charlotte Downey—all residing in different locations throughout the state, were backed by Little Rock attorney David Ivers and the Lambda Legal Defense and Education Fund, a national gay-rights organization. They believed that any future efforts to topple the sodomy law through the state legislature would fail just as Snyder's had done. The challenge would have to come through the courts.[41]

There followed four years of legal jousting that saw the plaintiffs win a ruling from Pulaski County circuit judge David Bogard that the law was indeed unconstitutional. On July 5, 2002, the Arkansas Supreme Court in a five-to-two decision affirmed Bogard's ruling. The sodomy law that had been on the books for twenty-five years was declared unconstitutional. The majority opinion, written by associate justice Annabelle Clinton Imber, stated that Arkansas could not use its police powers to "enforce a majority morality on persons whose conduct does not harm others." Citing article II of the state constitution—particularly its guarantees of life, liberty, and the pursuit of happiness and the right of Arkansans to be secure in their persons and homes against unreasonable searches and seizures, as well as numerous laws passed by the state legislature indicating the value it placed on personal privacy—Imber wrote, "It is clear to the court that Arkansas has a rich and compelling tradition of protecting individual privacy and that a fundamental right to privacy is implicit in the Arkansas Constitution." This right extended to "all private, consensual, noncommercial acts of sexual intimacy between adults." The court also ruled that the 1977 sodomy law violated the state constitution's guarantees of equal protection in that it criminalized sexual acts between homosexuals that would be perfectly legal if engaged in by heterosexuals.[42]

The Arkansas Supreme Court had thus found more expansive guarantees of liberty, privacy, and equality in the state's constitution than the U.S. Supreme Court had been willing to find in the federal Constitution in the now infamous case of *Bowers v. Hardwick*. Shortly after the decision, one of the seven who had challenged the law, Randy McCain, declared, "I'm proud of the Supreme Court. I've always been proud to be an Arkansan, but I'm even more proud today."[43] After the court had ruled, Attorney General Mark Pryor, the son of the governor who had signed the sodomy bill into law, issued a statement that he would not seek a review of the case by the U.S. Supreme Court. His spokesman noted simply, "The issue is settled."[44]

The issue, though, was hardly settled nationally. Arkansas had found its sodomy law in violation of the state's constitution. However, it would be a full year before the nation would follow suit. Mimicking closely the circumstances in which Michael Hardwick found himself, two Houston men were arrested for violation of the Texas sodomy statute. For John Geddes Lawrence and Tyron Garner, one man white and the other black, the details of their case were eerily close to that of *Hardwick*. On

September 17, 1998, Harris County sheriff's deputies entered the home of Lawrence on suspicion of a weapons violation (a charge later found to be false). Instead, deputies found the two men engaged in anal sex and arrested them.

Seeing their chance to overturn the now infamous *Hardwick* ruling that had come down fourteen years prior, civil liberties groups championed the two men as their case was taken through the appellate system. Once at the Supreme Court, the two men, now represented by the national gay and lesbian rights advocate group Lambda Legal, were joined by a curious assembly of amicus curiae ("friend of the court") briefs with varied interests in seeing the *Hardwick* decision reversed.

In further testimony to the power of historical analysis, Justice Anthony Kennedy continually referenced an amicus brief submitted by a group of academics.[45] Echoed in this chapter, Kennedy's main arguments built upon recent scholarship on sexual practice and community identity, specifically the argument concerning the creation or invention of hetero- and homosexuality and the subsequent articulations of distinctions between the two sexual identities. The creation of the original sodomy statutes in the United States preceded the creation of the concept of homosexuality by some two centuries, and the enforcement of sodomy statutes from the founding never solely targeted homosex. It was recently that they were wrongly interpreted to be designed to curb both homosex and homosexuality. For Kennedy, the "rationale behind *Bowers* does not withstand careful analysis" because it does not take into account the contextual histories found in sodomy law creation and application. In short, the historical debate surrounding *Hardwick* was not simply faulty; it did not exist.

Lawrence et al. v. Texas thus overturned the notorious *Hardwick* ruling. The Arkansas Supreme Court was ahead of the curve by declaring its sodomy law unconstitutional a year before. Given the statutes history, homosexuals as a community and homosexuality as an identity in Arkansas responded and changed according to the creation and implications of the sodomy statute just as the sodomy statute responded to the development and growing visibility of Arkansas queers. This would have its most poignant articulation on the Arkansas highway, the great connector and facilitator of queer communities.

ELEVEN

Constructing a Gay Life

A ccording to sociologist Laud Humphreys in his work *Tearoom Trade: Impersonal Sex in Public Places,* the Morgan rest area would easily qualify as a tearoom. A tearoom, used here in the context of what Humpheys calls "a homosexual subculture," is a place forged by reputation and facilitated by gay men seeking anonymous sexual encounters without further involvement emotionally. Functioning tearooms can be found in a number of settings. Usually, they are found in spaces where the line between public and private is less distinguishable, that is, public spaces that can afford a great deal of privacy for an individual: a created space where one could remain for hours at a time without being asked to leave. They can be, for example, a dark movie theater, deep within the stacks of a public library, or the steamy corners of a public sauna or bathhouse.

Indeed, of all the places, public toilets—particularly roadside rest areas—are the most desirable locations for those wishing to engage in anonymous sex. They remain so for three reasons. First, in keeping with the American fascination with the automobile and the resulting drive-through craze, not to mention the freedom of movement and the desire for community by gay men in Arkansas, public rest areas are easily accessible to those with cars. The Morgan rest area, though only serving eastbound Interstate 40 traffic, was merely twelve miles from Little Rock, the state's largest urban center. Also, the rest area offered ample parking spaces, many that were connected to private picnic pavilions in remote settings throughout the grounds of the rest area. Second, rest areas are easily recognizable to any passing motorist. Signs are posted in numerous and highly visible locations telling interstate travelers not only where a particular rest area is located but also how much farther one can expect to travel before finding it. For those who lived near rest areas, their intended and unintended functions would also be somewhat obvious. The third and perhaps most important reason for the popularity of rest areas and their public toilets for private sexual encounters is that though they are considered public space, they often offer little public visibility. Cruising the tearoom offered a chance for the man to shed his known identity, to travel beyond the prying eyes of his neighbors, the watchful eyes of his family, to a public place that afforded him more privacy.[1]

The Morgan rest area not only was surrounded by dense woods and overgrown brush but also lay a few yards from endangered wetland protected by environmental law. This isolated the still-accessible rest area, and indeed the tearoom forged there, from any other space. There was no chance of little-leaguers wandering off from a baseball diamond, no chance of a family spotting sexual activity from an area playground. The Morgan rest area offered none of these things. More than that, the space only succeeded in confusing public and private. Families could choose far-removed and secluded picnic areas, affording them an amount of privacy within a public space.

Also worth mentioning, the rest area was set off of the interstate an irregular distance for facilities of that type. The building that housed the public toilets was high atop a hill that overlooked the busy thoroughfare. One could observe passing automobiles whizzing by, but there was little chance of a passing motorist spotting anyone or for that matter recognizing any particular automobile as at that of a neighbor or coworker.

Unbeknownst to the Arkansas Highway Department, they had constructed a space ideal for someone to engage in impersonal homoerotic activity. However, the same reasons that led to the creation of the tearoom for those who wished to use it for sex also attracted those who wished to close it down. Given the statutes regarding sodomy and loitering for sexual purposes, the Pulaski County sheriff's office had a full range of laws with which to arrest possible offenders. Humphreys offers three possible avenues for police involvement in tearoom activity. The first is spying, used at the Morgan rest area in the form of hidden cameras. Given the unfavorable publicity surrounding their use, hidden cameras are no longer used in public toilets by either local law enforcement or the highway department. However, all rest areas in Arkansas, down from thirty-six to thirty-two, are now equipped with cameras mounted *outside* the buildings housing public toilets to monitor criminal behavior on the grounds of rest areas. The second opportunity of involvement by law enforcement officers is the use of decoys, that is, undercover officers, as Robert Howard could tell you. According to Humphreys, the use of decoys remains the most popular means of capturing men in the act of anonymous public sex.

Lastly, police detection seeks to hamper tearoom activity through raids and sting operations. Raids, like those played out at the Morgan rest area, are mainly a result of reactionary purposes. Though the sheriff's office often stated that they had received several complaints, they failed to mention how many complaints were taken. The timing of the initial raid, especially to those arrested and local gay and lesbian rights groups, seemed peculiar at best. Perhaps in light of Vic Snyder's failed attempt at toppling the sodomy statute, local law enforcement agencies wished to demonstrate to the community the need for keeping on the books a sodomy statute that regulates homosex. Perhaps more importantly, Snyder's main argument for removing the sodomy statute was not that it threatened civil liberties for gays and lesbian Arkansans but that it stood contradictory to the state's attempt at containing the AIDS virus.

On November 30, 1990, the *Arkansas Gazette* reported that Arkansas had jumped from ranking fortieth to twenty-eighth nationally in the number of reported AIDS cases per capita. The first reported case of AIDS in Arkansas was in 1983, but since records regarding AIDS and HIV infection began to be kept in 1985, health department officials noted that cases of AIDS had jumped 111% in Arkansas. In 1990 the Arkansas Department of Health had a total of 490 AIDS cases on record. Officials estimated that an additional three to five thousand Arkansans were HIV positive. In 1990 Pulaski County, where the Morgan rest area was located, had the highest number of cases by county with 112 reported.[2]

Though Snyder argues that the sodomy statute worked against the state's efforts to contain the virus, many took the opposite view. It is a regrettable fact that the AIDS virus hit the gay community with particular ferocity. Though the *Gazette* in 1990 stated plainly that the majority of new cases in Arkansas were heterosexual, particularly in women and children, perhaps many regarded abandoning the sodomy law an open opportunity for an even further dramatic rise in AIDS cases. Perhaps the raids at the Morgan rest area and the opposition to Snyder's attempt at repeating the sodomy law was a conscious (or perhaps unconscious) reaction to this development.[3] However, despite the great number of deaths caused by AIDS and the social reaction to it, the virus energized gay activism and helped solidify a national gay identity.[4]

There are certain risks to the game, as Humphreys calls them. Many of the men arrested at the rest area, totaling thirty-five by the time the raids finished and the rest area was demolished, lost their jobs and their families. Robert Howard was able to beat his charges. He lost very little and kept his name. Others were not so lucky. The *Arkansas Gazette* ran only the names of those men arrested for violating the sodomy statute. The *Arkansas Democrat,* its far more conservative rival newspaper, went further by publishing the names and addresses of all the men arrested, regardless of the charges. This was a common practice for the *Democrat.* When a popular local weatherman was arrested for soliciting sex from an undercover police officer in North Little Rock's Burns Park in 1996, his predicament was heavily reported on by the paper. When the man's grandmother died some three months later, his public torment was augmented by his arrest being mentioned in her obituary. When a university professor was arrested the same year in a local department store for loitering with the purpose of deviant activity, he committed suicide out of fear of public humiliation. "Goodbye, it's all in the paper," his suicide note to his partner read.[5] At each arraignment for the men arrested at the Morgan rest area, Hale suspended the sentence if the individual produced the results of a recent AIDS test.[6] Those who did not provide the court with their test results were ordered to pay hundred-dollar fines and serve ten days in the local jail.

Despite themselves, the press and the sheriff's office both were perhaps unwitting accomplices in forming a gay and lesbian Arkansas identity. Arresting gay men, running the stories, publishing their names and addresses—all of this only succeeded in illustrating to gays and lesbians all over the state, to small towns spread across a rural landscape and to people like me, that there were indeed others like us to be found. If anything, I owe these public officials, so intent on erasing gay men from public view, for introducing me to gay discourse within my temporal sphere. The *Gazette* and the *Democrat* not only told you who these gay men were but, if you were so inclined, where you might want to go to meet them.

CONSTRUCTING A GAY LIFE

To meet was, after all, the goal. The public toilet, especially those located in the rural environment, as a queer social space is a deeply complicated one. Of the eight men arrested in the initial raid on the Morgan facilities, only two were actually arrested for violation of the sodomy law. So what of the other six? Had they simply not had time to meet anyone? Truly, when does enjoyment of state-created space become loitering, a state-law violation? Although Humphreys is quick to define public facilities such as these as ideal places for anonymous sexual encounters, in the rural setting they could represent much more than that. With two arrested within the actual toilets and six elsewhere, the data suggest that the grounds play a more important role than the actual building itself. With gay men coming from both Little Rock to the south as well as small towns and hamlets now connected by the interstate, the rest area served to forge community among men who simply came to talk and to meet with the possibility of engaging in sex there or going off to another location, to someone's home, or to a downtown restaurant for coffee and conversation. The construction of a rest stop had the possibility to foster all these things. A casual encounter had the possibility to become much more as gay men increasingly used the rest area as an avenue for discovering queer community in Arkansas. This arrangement differed from an urban tearoom setting as gay men from the surrounding rural environs and the big city of Little Rock met and mingled with each other, some looking for that fleeting erotic encounter, others not. So too were they enticed to return, perhaps the next month or in a night or two, whenever they might be able to get away to Morgan where they could recognize fellow queers, acquaintances, friends. Altogether then and well after the actual demolition of the rest area and the erasure of a queer space by the state, these men left their markings and unique rural and urban footprints on a site that is not only largely representative of queer Arkansas but also entirely influential in forming an identity around what it means to be a queer Arkansan.

In his unique study of Oscar Wilde, *Who Was That Man?*, queer theorist Neil Bartlett attempts to answer, through urban traces and sexual geography, to what degree his life and personal identity are connected to gay men who lived in London though well before him. He explains in his introduction to the study,

What I've done, I suppose, is to connect my life to other lives, even buildings and streets, that had an existence prior to mine. This is in itself remarkable, because for the longest time imaginable I experienced my gayness in complete isolation, just like any other gay child in a small town. And now, gradually, I've come to understand that I am connected to other men's lives. . . . That's the story.[7]

Bartlett adds, "Some of my most basic ideas about myself as a homosexual man were invented not by me but other men, in another time, in another city."[8] These traces left behind, like those of a demolished and dilapidated rest area, are the cultural production and urban clues that one must begin to locate in order to fully document and understand particular queer histories. In this act of recovery, seeking brief and seemingly minute episodes of sexual deviance, one also places them into a proper context of broad social trends that enable us to investigate the past as a rightful and needed intrusion into the present.[9]

Though I was only thirteen years old when the events described above took place, I do remember them. I grew up in Conway, Arkansas, with the rest area in question only twenty miles down Interstate 40 to Little Rock. When the arrests began to happen, they commanded headlines across the state of Arkansas. The battle that began was not only over the use and misuse of a public place but about the creation and facilitation of a gay identity and space in the thick of the American South.

Growing up gay in the American South is never easy, though at times easier. For many it requires a duplicitous existence, constantly juggling different lives for different people, for parents and for those at church and at school. Robert Howard likened it to walking a tightrope. I was fourteen years old when the highway department began to demolish the Morgan rest area. Numerous news reports, rumors, and accusations flew. Sitting in study halls in the nefarious space of junior high, boys would bring their father's discarded sports page—and sometimes the front page with them. With them, gay discourse was able to seep into my red brick public-school education. I sat and listened to their jokes, slandering, and hinting at who among them might be queer, all the while trying to mask my feelings of absolute horror and sheer fascination. Gay men were no longer the just characters that I, a boy just beginning to come to terms with his sexuality, watched with intense scrutiny on television shows such as *The Golden Girls* and *Miami Vice*, both of which my parents deemed too indecent to be watched. (My grandmother was less discerning and I watched with her.) Now for me, gay men were no longer confined to a soundstage hundreds of miles away. They were here, with me, in Conway, Arkansas, essentially just down the road at a rest area that had previously just been a blur on a car ride to Little Rock.

Not only was the story run throughout the state's newspapers, but also the work to raze the rest area was visible to all who passed by it. I remember traveling down the interstate toward Little Rock with my father in his oversized pickup truck, which now was doing its share of damage to the ailing American interstate infrastructure. We passed the busy workmen at the rest stop. He took it upon himself to explain why the state was flattening the rest area though I already knew. "It turned into a gay bar all of a sudden," he said.

I visited the Morgan rest area for the first time almost twelve years after the public toilets were bulldozed and the grounds closed to the public. I parked my father's dark blue pickup truck by the side of road. Ignoring signs forbidding trespassers, I scaled the concrete barricades. The roofs of the picnic pavilions were caving in, the picnic tables themselves long since carted off. Rusted parking lights, fallen tree,s and overgrown brush now decorated the grounds. I made my way up to the now sun-baked brittle concrete foundation that was once the public toilets building, now punctured in places by sapling pines. The recording here of the Arkansas sodomy law was done more than to simply construct a narrative that might have been lost or forgotten some time. The toppled rest area and its noticeable absence sitting along a hillside on a stretch of busy highway still contributes its own discourse. What is written here will, I hope, add to it. For those who read this chapter who had no idea of its history and the role a now-razed rest area and those men who frequented it played in shaping rural queer lives, their lives are now in conversation with those who came before, in an effort to continually forge the dynamics of what it means to be a queer Arkansan.

PART THREE

The Land of Opportunity

TWELVE

Creating Space,
Separating the Self

Y ou couldn't miss it: two men walking down the winding streets of Eureka Springs, Arkansas, holding hands and nary a cross word or disapproving glance thrown in their direction. In fact, any negative comment or gesture toward them would have been seen not only as rude but as out of place in this quaint mountain village. What provided for such an understanding and acceptance of subtle queer acts and displays of affection in a small Arkansas town tucked away in the Ozark Mountains? It was the summer of 2004 when I sat down with Charlotte Downey, defendant in the successful *Picado v. Jegley* lawsuit, in the renovated cellar of the Mud Street Cafe in downtown Eureka Springs. There she told me the narrative of her life so far. I thought her story an extraordinary answer to the question of how a small mountain community became such a defined queer space outside of the urban.

She told me this: she shot him. Just outside of a lesbian bar in downtown Tulsa, he charged and she fired. Almost twenty years before Charlotte Downey had found herself standing in the rotunda of the state capitol in Little Rock with her compatriots announcing their challenge to the Arkansas sodomy statute, she was on trial for her life. The charge was murder.[1]

Before finding herself in Tulsa, Downey and her family had moved around middle America from one military base to the next, never staying anywhere for more than a year. Thanks to a father in the military, she was always the new kid in public schools, something that she now credits for her strong, independent nature. The moving stopped at Tinker Air Force Base in Oklahoma, a place Downey described as typically "midwest." In 1964, by the time she was eighteen and attending Central Oklahoma

College, Downey actively sought a queer social network among her coeds. She found three other women who told her of The Black Cat, a bar in Tulsa they knew little about except that it had a reputation locally for being a queer bar. Wondering exactly what *queer* meant or what indeed was so queer about this particular space, the four women entered in the midafternoon only to find the bar completely empty. They ordered sodas and waited as factories began to let out at the four o'clock whistle, reckoning that soon the bar would begin to fill with working-class lesbians from all over Tulsa's industrial park, an area that sat alongside the Arkansas River on the blue-collar west side of town.[2] The bar filled quickly, and Downey began to feel more comfortable, more and more at home with each casual smile, each effortless nod in her direction, as she sat in a space that grew more and more queer with each push of the door. She worked up the nerve to return by herself two weeks later. Soon, she was a regular, sitting at the bar at The Black Cat three and four nights a week. The eighteen-year-old Downey soon found herself "looked after" by the older lesbians who had been frequenting the bar for years.

It was necessary. Across the street sat what Downey described as the area "redneck beer bar," another blue-collar bar for factory workers but a space that was heterosexual male. Brawls at The Black Cat were commonplace as drunken men stumbled from across the street, from their space to the space of others, to pick fights with the queers, no matter that they were women. In a fierce defense of their own space, Black Cat lesbians tucked young Downey safely under the bar and took to rednecks with fists, pool queues, and bottles, whatever impromptu weapons they could find, to drive the belligerent men out of their bar.

In 1965, less then a year after Downey had discovered The Black Cat, the bar closed its doors. At the same time, Downey moved to Oklahoma State University in Stillwater. Higher education never really caught on with Downey. Using her family connections in the service, she left school and took a job at the air force base, working there until 1968 when she was asked to vacate her job so that a "family man" who had children to support could have it. Downey obliged her superiors at the base and took work as a clerk with the post office. By that time, though The Black Cat had closed, the Tulsa lesbian community formed around other bars and city league softball teams so common in the American South and Midwest.[3] It was while playing for such a team that Downey suffered a

Charlotte Downey and one of Tulsa's all-women softball teams. Downey is the tallest in the back row. *Courtesy of Charlotte Downey.*

knee injury. Following surgery and the necessary period of convalescence, Downey was fired from her job as a postal worker. She sued for unfair dismissal and won.

She took the money awarded in her lawsuit and opened "Our Place" in 1970, a lesbian beer bar on the model of her beloved Black Cat on the outskirts of Tulsa. To keep out undesirables—that is, anyone who was not a lesbian—Downey charged them seventy-five cents a glass for a draft beer instead of the normal twenty-five cents a glass for "sisters." She opened at noon everyday except Sundays, and the bar soon proved as popular with the working-class lesbians much as The Black Cat had been. Like The Black Cat, Our Place was often a magnet for prying eyes and violent trespassers. Also, being but three blocks from a Tulsa police station, the bar would often attract unwanted attention from law enforcement. Downey recalls what she saw as superficial visits from the Tulsa Department of Health that would disrupt business for hours.

Downey was philosophical, seeing these intrusions as normal and expected. Downey responded as best she could. Rowdy straight men like those who taunted and fought with the customers of The Black Cat would occasionally enter looking for trouble, and one such disturbance in 1972 proved fatal for one man. Two brothers entered Our Place, dragged two lesbians out, and began assaulting them in the street. As others rushed to help, Downey reached for the small twenty-five-caliber handgun she kept hidden under the bar, a commonplace feature in small town bars across America. She ran outside and fired three shots into the air hoping to stop the assault. The fighting stopped, but one of the men stood and charged toward Downey. She then put a bullet in his stomach. He lingered for a few days in the hospital before dying from an infection of the gunshot wound.

After first charging her with attempted manslaughter, the prosecutors then upped the charge to first-degree murder, a capital offense in Oklahoma. Downey was in complete shock. Thinking from the beginning that it was a case of self-defense, she offered her statement freely without a lawyer. The police took everything down in what they regarded as Downey's confession. Downey endured three trials. The first was declared a mistrial. In the second Downey was convicted of first-degree manslaughter and given a forty-year sentence, but this was later overturned on appeal. By the time of the third trial, Downey, although mentally weary from what had turned out to be an extended nightmare, still refused to plead guilty. The verdict was returned as manslaughter with a four-year suspended sentence.

Though it was the last trial she would face as a result of the shooting, Downey had enough. The trials were at the end of a long list of instances and episodes of injustice that pushed Downey out of Oklahoma and into nearby Arkansas. She was sick of Oklahoma and the seemingly constant harassment she faced as an out lesbian there. She had left by 1983, looking for a peaceful, outdoor space, a rural area where she could be left alone, a place to enjoy fishing, swimming, and canoeing. She found a home just off Beaver Lake a few hours away from Tulsa in the Arkansas Ozarks. She purchased a bait-and-tackle shop near the Beaver Lake dam just outside Eureka Springs, an Ozark tourist hotspot. She had no idea of the town's past or its running reputation as the "San Francisco of the Ozarks," though it did not take her long to find out. She found Eureka Springs to be a community of all sorts of people who had flocked to the town from the countryside surrounding it, for various reasons. Locals frequented her bait shop, if not for the bait, then for the beer. Downey took tourists on canoe and fishing trips. She became a visible member of not only a mountain community but also a queer community created by those wishing to separate and form new queer identities outside the urban. According to Downey, to say that the population of Eureka Springs and the surrounding areas was 30 percent gay and lesbian was too conservative an estimate.[4]

Downey's story dramatically outlines larger trends of urban-to-rural queer migrations that had been going on for some time. Just as Downey sought to create space for herself and other lesbians in Tulsa, so had many like her sought to create their own similar spaces in the Ozark Mountains in northwest Arkansas. Beginning a decade before Downey's arrival, lesbians, and later gay men, had been settling around Eureka Springs and Fayetteville to create queer spaces that delivered certain aspects of living that the urban could not. Queer spaces, as always, are self-created and at times remain volatile, reflecting the growing pains of larger and increasingly nascent queer communities. The desire to create space from scratch, by queers from both within and outside Arkansas, led to the formation of lesbian communes and communities, later spilling over into an entire mountain town that reflected larger political trends of feminism and separatism so prevalent at the time. These spaces, unique in their creation and function, provided rural and urban lesbians with new alternative settings from which to foster exceptional queer identities.

Downey epitomizes those seeking greater opportunity elsewhere—economic, sexual, and otherwise—in a similar drive that brought other women to the region. The narratives in the following chapters represent problems faced by the larger lesbian movement that yielded the ideas of relocation and separation as a solution. If this work relies heavily on such personal narratives, this particular section does so even more, and its very nature—rural queer living, queer lives in the hills—brings me as a writer and researcher to nontraditional and less tangible sources of historical inquiry. Here, I will depend heavily on oral history and build on often colloquial but highly revealing personal histories. These women's narratives not only represent the problems of the early communes and communities, many now gone from the Arkansas mountain landscape, but also their extraordinary solutions to these problems. These remedies, dealing with such matters as financial stability and basic rural know-how, race, and sexual politics as well as deeply personal problems such as privacy and loneliness, represent the drive and determination of creating space and identity for the self. Thus far this work illustrates the various cultural and social circumstances found in Arkansas, the social and cultural circumstances and complex contradictions that produce a distinct queer populace and alternate modernity. In the stories that follow are the lesbian women and gay men who sought with their own tactics and devices to reverse this order, to create and adjust their social surroundings given their own political agenda in a desire for affinity with others like them and the land on which they found themselves.

THIRTEEN

Losing Space, Separating Identities

G ay men could claim a variety of spaces reserved for them in and around Little Rock. Few such spaces in Arkansas were reserved for lesbians. The exception lay in the mountains of northwest Arkansas. Settling around the then liberal college town of Fayetteville, a short drive from Eureka Springs, lesbians took advantage of a rise in feminist visibility among women attending the University of Arkansas. In many ways Fayetteville was the epicenter of the feminist movement in Arkansas. During the 1970s feminists in Fayetteville, through a combination of university funding and private donations, were able to secure a separate space from which to serve women's needs in the area. The group had been operating out of various locations since 1972, but in the fall of 1978 the Fayetteville Women's Center opened its doors at a new facility, a small converted house provided by the university just across from the football stadium.

In creating a campus and community home for feminist politics, the university had given them an actual house. The address of the small converted home purchased by the growing university a year before was 207 Razorback Road. Speaking of their space, the members of the women's center proudly described its new home as complete with "a large, sunny living room with a fireplace, plus three other smaller rooms that can be used for meetings and other activities. There is a large kitchen, a garage, and a backyard with some playground equipment for children."[1]

The new women's center was advertised as "a space where women of the campus and community of Fayetteville can come together and relate to one another as women."[2] The center offered a rape crisis and pregnancy hotline, a battered-women's shelter, a health collective, a women's sports collective, a women's coffeehouse, a chorus, and other services. The center also provided space to a lesbian student group, the Lesbian Rap Group, that was advertised as a "group formed to help lesbians deal with social pressures concerning lifestyle and attempts to promote a more accurate image of lesbianism though educational programs."[3]

The University of Arkansas provided the property and the bulk of the women's center funds through student-generated accounts and the larger university budget. With university funds came less autonomy, but the women, desperate for funding, were willing to accept this. The group was progressive, and with funds and an allocation of a facility members were most encouraged. However, things quickly soured within the first three months of the center's creation. With the support of the women's center, the Lesbian Rap Group found themselves growing in numbers and visibility on campus early in the fall semester. However, the lesbian student group grew increasingly disenchanted with the politics of the women's center, which concentrated on issues such as abortion access and other feminist legal matters that the rap group deemed largely irrelevant to lesbians. While the center assured them that this was not the case, skepticism as to the motives and goals of the women's center grew among politically involved lesbians on campus.

A rift between the two groups only widened in the fall of 1978 when the Lesbian Rap Group decided to rechristen themselves as the "Razordykes," capitalizing on the popular university razorback mascot, and began promoting lesbian goals on campus. Group leaders thought the name reflected both "gay pride and humor," but for other students it quickly became a name associated "with fear and hatred."[4] The Razordykes sought class time from willing health and psychology faculty to deliver presentations on homosexuality and, using women's center funds, purchased reading materials on gender and sexuality, distributing them around campus.

The increased visibility of the Razordykes brought increased scrutiny by University of Arkansas officials of the rap group and the women's center. Early in the semester the Razordykes announced a potluck dinner at the women's center to be followed by an open forum for discussing lesbian issues on campus.[5] An advertisement for the dinner in the student newspaper, the *Arkansas Traveler*, provoked a string of letters condemning the Razordykes, many of which also criticized the administration of the University of Arkansas for funding a group comprising "degenerates and perverts."[6]

It was not long before the matter came to the attention of state legislators in Little Rock. Already having made their position on homosexuality clear through the reinstatement of the sodomy law the previous year, legislators put subtle pressure on state-appointed university administrators to close the women's center and eliminate funding for the Razordykes. Alumni and university donors also began to raise concerns after an influential alumna, the wife of a wealthy local banker, was sent anonymously an invitation to a lesbian dance hosted by the Razordykes.[7] It is not known whether a friend or foe of the group sent the invitation, but, nonetheless, frustration with the Razordykes and the center grew and put the future of the center in jeopardy. University administrators pleaded with group leaders to at least change their name to something "less volatile."[8] The razorback mascot, in football and basketball, was a cherished and guarded image throughout the entire state, and university officials recognized this. Group leaders, ever obstinate in their politics, refused to even consider a name change. At the root of their stubbornness was an issue of self-determination that went beyond simply wishing to name themselves what they pleased. They felt that to surrender and pick a name not so close to the one cherished by university officials, students, and alumni would be to acknowledge that they did not belong and that certain aspects of university life were entirely off-limits to queer students. In light of the women's refusal, university administrators, stung by the unwanted attention from Little Rock and alumni regarding the Razordykes, acted to "get rid of the women's center."[9] By October, two months after the center opened and two months after the potluck and lesbian forum was announced, the Associated Student Government, the elected student body representatives responsible for doling out public funds to student groups, informed the women's center that their funds for the year were now frozen pending investigation. The student government charged the women's center with using student money to fund a facility providing services to nonstudents. The women's center did not deny that women from the larger community took advantage of their services but were able to show that more than 80 percent of its users were students. However, the fact that 20 percent were not university students was enough for the student government to drastically cut the women's center funding for the 1979–80 academic year. The student government took away the center's facility, the off-campus house the university provided, and relocated the women's center in a single room in the basement of the campus student union. In further discouragement, knowing that the women's center acted as an umbrella organization that then dispersed funds to other groups such as the Razordykes, the student government openly encouraged other campus groups to solicit the women's center for funds, whatever the groups' political leanings. When campus antiabortion groups began to ask for money from the center for their programs, the leaders refused to hear their request. In response, the student government accused the group of being a "feminist clique" and denied its funding for the next academic year altogether.[10] Unable to secure enough funding from outside sources to carry on its programs, the women's center closed its doors.

Many Fayetteville Women's Center advocates privately blamed the Razordykes for the closure, seeing the lesbian group as a lightning rod for unwelcome campus criticism. Many Razordykes considered the center unwilling to support its feminist allies in their time of need as campus pressure continued to mount.[11] For the Razordykes encouraging others to "come out" was at the heart of their political agenda; the very act of coming out, for them, was political. Whatever the reasons, the division between the two groups reflected a national trend in the feminist movement as lesbians felt increasingly disenfranchised by the larger feminist movement.[12] The split of larger feminism and lesbian politics proved dramatic in northwest Arkansas.[13] It was also highly concentrated at the campus of the University of Arkansas at Fayetteville where lesbians sought to further separate themselves from the larger political movement that some regarded as having abandoned them outright during the struggle with the university. Many lesbians in northwest Arkansas who were either active in the Razordykes or nonetheless shared their frustration with the larger feminist movement borrowed ideas and politics from a newly growing back-to-the-land movement by searching for land on which to establish separate lesbian-only communities. Almost a decade before the women's center found itself at the center of controversy, lesbian women had been eyeing the Ozarks as a possible space to organize women's communes and communities. Signs advertising lesbian land and the construction of lesbian communities in the rural were oftentimes subtle.

> *Land for Sale:* 1,000 acres of land located in scenic Johnson County, Arkansas. Panoramic views of beautiful Boston Mountains. Nice retirement area. Write: H. E. Harvey, Rt. 1, Box 259, Stone Hill Rd., Clarksville, Ark. 72830.[14]

The advertisement above was posted by Mr. H. E. Harvey in the classified section of *Ms.* magazine in the winter of 1972, the same year as the founding of the Fayetteville Women's Center and some six years before it disbanded for good.[15] Tucked away in the back pages of a popular feminist magazine lay an invitation to queer Arkansas: land for sale. A woman thumbing through *Ms.* could stumble upon new and subtle possibilities for queer formations in Arkansas. Searching for different outlets to queer identity, perhaps a rural one, women only needed to look at the small print to discover the possibility of establishing queer spaces in the Arkansas Ozarks.[16] Lesbians, especially in rural areas, depended on such small print much more than gay men, who often had larger networks with access to information. Mountain spaces like the one advertised above, secluded and, perhaps more importantly, cheap, had been selling for sometime since the early 1970s to feminist groups and lesbian separatist organizations seeking freedom from the restrictions of an overly masculine world. Lesbians had lost their space at the university, but other spaces were being constructed in the surrounding mountains.

Separatism had long been a cornerstone of gay and lesbian communities. Not only claiming bars and discos, lesbians, and especially gay men in America, had long carved out neighborhoods and districts in larger cities for decades. The back-to-the-land movement and new leftist politics pushed the idea of separating to a new extreme. Owning land had long been a driving force for many and considered a fundamental right of every citizen. Within the rural areas of the South where so much of the economy deals with agriculture and the land, it was seen as simply southern. Now, many lesbians throughout the South, feeling alienated from society and new-wave feminism, sought to purchase pieces of the "Goddess Earth" to "buy her back from the patriarchy."[17] Lesbian feminism that bore ideas of separatism was, according to historian Esther

Newton, "the legitimate offspring of the antiwar movement and radical feminism." Newton went on to describe lesbian feminism and separatism as anticapitalist, rejecting of social order, and downwardly mobile.[18] This separating from the "patriarchal" social order began during the 1970s, and by the 1980s there were over a hundred lesbian separatist communities across the nation, most in rural locations, desirable areas for building new rural queer identities.[19]

Many lesbians pooled their money. Others, who were better off financially, used their savings, dipping into savings or inheritances to purchase land and invited others to join them in communal living. Called "country women," or more precisely lesbian separatists, such women in Arkansas purchased huge tracts of mountain land, unimproved land as it was sometimes advertised, from locals who, excited to have any interest at all, sold it cheap. Advertising in lesbian and feminist publications across the nation, they invited their sisters to follow them. Some placed their land into trust, creating a land haven owned by all who worked it and open to everyone willing to work. The time was right in northwest Arkansas.

Suzanne Pharr was one of those southern queers who became increasingly disenchanted with larger political trends and sought to distance herself from them. Born on a dirt farm on Hog Mountain, Georgia, Pharr spent most of her life in the South. Leaving Hog Mountain as early as she could, she traveled for a time before finding a home in the growing lesbian community in New Orleans, Louisiana. There, she stayed too long and "burnt herself down to a small flame."[20] New Orleans as a city wilted her, and she searched desperately for something else. While she valued the political experience she gained working with lesbian and feminist organizations in New Orleans, her Hog Mountain roots led her to seek a more rural existence.

The idea of returning to the rural was not new to Pharr or her lesbian colleagues in New Orleans. Popular lesbian fiction of the day celebrated the idea of an entirely lesbian utopia, a lesbian nation free from the struggles of the male-dominated society. Northwest Arkansas had been gaining a reputation as a lesbian haven for some time, especially among the lesbian communities in cities such as Atlanta and New Orleans.[21] New Orleans artists escaping long, humid summers in the Big Easy fled to small, inexpensive towns like Eureka Springs for a few months of the year. Word of mouth spread fast in New Orleans of lesbian communes in northwest Arkansas. Seeking a quiet place to write, an exhausted Pharr left New Orleans in her Volkswagen van in 1972 and settled in Huckleberry Farm near Eureka Springs.

The group of lesbian women living at Huckleberry Farm never numbered higher than ten. Nonetheless, Pharr saw it as a lesbian migration. Hearing the same word of mouth that informed Pharr of the lesbian commune's existence, other lesbians came for a weekend, a week, a few days, wanting to camp and share the land, if only for a brief while.

The lesbian communes around Eureka Springs were part of a larger national trend. Pharr remembered that "after Kent State, a lot of us just stopped our political activism and looked for something else."[22] For many, disgruntled as the turbulent 1960s came to an end, the back-to-the-land movement provided a peaceful alternative to frustrating political activism they saw as going nowhere. Pharr's narrative illustrates this trend of growing discomfort with a political system many women found increasingly sexist. Reacting to unchecked growth in urban and industrial culture, the back-to-the-land movement gained momentum as the 1960s came to an end and small groups of counterculture youths departed cities and college campuses for sustainable agrarian living outside the mainstream.[23] The back-to-the-land movement strengthened as it merged with the ideas and politics of the new environmentalism, itself a reaction to the same conditions back-to-the-landers saw as harmful to America, namely decaying urban centers and sprawling suburban peripheries. With this trend, communal farms had been operating in Arkansas since the beginning of the 1970s, though most met with little success.[24] In rural Pope County in central Arkansas, a group of men and women acquired a piece of land for organic farming and went about the community lecturing local farmers on the dangers of pesticides and other chemicals sprayed on their crops of soybeans and wheat. Christened the "Doobie Plantation" by its founding members, the venture was never completely successful.[25] The college students who lived on the land never gained the trust of locals, people who could hardly imagine what must be going on at night at such an operation. In many ways the trend was nothing more than a simple passing idea. The small group of men and women, finding themselves too isolated, soon grew tired of one another, and, as happened to similar farms, inside squabbling put an end to the venture. The tenants of Doobie

Plantation went their separate ways within a year of its founding. Other communal farms in Arkansas suffered the same fate.[26]

Like the hippie communities that preceded them, lesbian separatist communities in northwest Arkansas had similar troubles. Lesbian communes did not let these discouraging tales deter them, and places like Huckleberry Farm continued, but life there was by no means easy. Though the very idea of a back-to-the-land movement suggests that many of the women might have had rural roots, this was not the case for most who began separatist communities. Women like Pharr, who had a rural childhood and were not necessarily adverse to chopping wood or generally improving the unimproved land they had collectively purchased, soon found themselves carrying the weight for women who had no idea how to perform the essential duties of country life.[27] Though the women who created places like Huckleberry Farm craved removal from mainstream society, it was the isolation that often contributed to their falling numbers and eventual closings. As time passed, women became bored and lethargic. As tensions among some women mounted and without outsiders to help mediate, simple arguments often grew into major conflicts, and an egregious quarrel could easily break up a commune.[28]

The Ozark Women on Land

Though the lesbian communes hoped for an ideal utopian existence, the realities of their daily lives filled with hardship, isolation, and doing without certainly proved to be much different. Many of the newsletters and bulletins that filtered out of the lesbian communities in northwest Arkansas's Ozarks suggest growing frustration with detached rural living. Many communes appealed to outside organizations and more established communes for assistance as unforeseen problems began to arise. The Ozark Women on Land, a lesbian separatist group of, at times, eight women who collectively purchased eighty acres near Eureka Springs, appealed directly to the Atlanta Lesbian Feminist Alliance (ALFA) for assistance. In May 1976 in an open letter sent to ALFA, the Ozark women listed such troubles as "how to deal with each other's bad habits like tobacco, beer, communal sloppiness, not listening, not to mention our own sexist, racist, and classist attitudes."[29] The Ozark Women on Land newsletters also suggested that simple "coupling" of lesbians led to factionalism on the farm and pitted women against each other as loyalties lay with sexual and romantic partners who had either formed an attachment on the farm or arrived already bonded.[30]

Money, too, was always an issue, and squabbling over communal funds often led to the folding of farms. Though women from across the nation were encouraged to "flee patriarchal structures of their daily lives" and join the commune, women who arrived with little to no money to contribute quickly proved to be a drain on already fragile commune accounts.[31] Again asking for assistance in dealing with their personal problems in setting up a commune, the Ozark women also pleaded for financial assistance from other communes by using the well established and circulated ALFA publications. Some communes sent what they could. The Oregon Women's Land Trust sent funds, though with an understanding that they would be reimbursed sooner rather than later.[32] Although there was this financial support from other women's groups, undoubtedly facing many of the same tribulations that the Ozark women were facing, money grew increasingly tight as contributions dwindled. Though the Ozark women agreed that "we must first try to heal ourselves with herbs and caring," they also recognized the need to set up crisis funds should a woman need to seek medical attention in town.[33] They realized that a significant health crisis could strain their finances or even bankrupt the community experiment.

Beyond issues of capital and medical needs, the Ozark Women on Land articulated growing discontent with rural living. In many ways privacy was too expensive, and the distance sought by lesbian separatists quickly lost its charm. "We miss our friends back in the cities or farms away from us. We sometimes feel isolated or frustrated with the level of consciousness here."[34] Despite these feelings the Ozark women continued their resolve, closing their August 1976 newsletter by saying, "We know it is important to make this space here in this part of the patriarchy."[35] Over the summer of 1976 the number of lesbians wishing to separate from the mainstream with the Ozark women never exceeded ten. In the same summer bulletin that pleaded for others to join them, the Ozark women advertised for present members who wished to sell their shares and move on. Many who had joined soon wanted to leave, finding themselves lacking the basic skills necessary to sustain rural communal living. Learning had to come quickly, and the hardships often proved too much. Each newsletter closed with a plea for women with carpentry and farming skills, "who would not be afraid of a little hard work."[36]

Early communes were rife with the usual practical problems of rural living, but the Ozark women also struggled with political concerns such as how to define themselves and their communities. They rejected the term *dyke separatist* as a useless label. They wrote:

> The term *dyke separatism* has been floating around for several years. We've been called dyke separatist among other labels and curses. We would like to say what we think we mean: we do not see ourselves as separate from the worldwide revolution against racism/ sexism/classism/imperialism, be it in the form of capitalism, communism, or in the name of "socialism"; for actually all these stem from the same rotten core—patriarchalism.[37]

Attempting a better definition of their community, the Ozark women wrote what they called a "twelve-point Amazonifesto."[38] In it they declared that the "land be left as natural as possible" and "be farmed organically with no chemicals whatsoever."[39] With the ultimate goal of stopping the "cancerous spread of male supremacy," the manifesto barred men from involvement in the commune in any way. This would, at times, prove to be a sore point for lesbian women involved in communes. What of male visitors, guests, and friends? What of the woman who arrived pregnant and later delivered a male child? Though it ultimately drove away those who did not wish to sever their ties with male friends and relatives, the Ozark women were steadfast on the ban of males.

The question of how to fairly allocate work and chores in the community was constantly an issue. Seen as more important to the sustainability and future of the commune and to help "avoid elitism, control, authoritarianism, and specialization, women with the special skills shall share skills with all," according to the Amazonifesto. Furthermore, it stated, labor on the farm "shall be rotated, so all women learn and work at all jobs, as far as physically possible." As many communes did, the Ozark women placed their land in trust to do away with both "legal trips and power trips."[40]

Despite its lofty goals, the Ozark Women on the Land commune did not survive the first harsh mountain winter, a season that only heightened feelings of frustration and isolation. They suffered the same fate as many other earlier communes in Arkansas, samesex and otherwise, though some proved more successful.

The Ozark Land Holders Association

Diana Rivers chose the Arkansas Ozarks for the beauty of the land. She and other women like her looking to form a community sought land that was cheap and plentiful, had a long growing season, and had little to no building codes. The isolated and largely untouched Ozarks supplied all these things in abundance. She had grown up in New Jersey. Then, turning seventeen years old, she moved to the anonymous New York City. She tried her hand at college, though she did not last long at New York's Cooper Union. She quit after her first year when she rationalized her politics would have gotten her thrown out anyway. Afterwards, Rivers tried other communes across the country, moving from her native New Jersey to the Stoneybrook commune in upstate New York. Though it was a successful commune, a bad marriage drove Rivers cross-country, first to various communes in rural Oregon and then, as she came to realize her sexuality, to the Hog Farm, a growing lesbian commune in New Mexico.[41] She had heard of communities in Arkansas and traveled there in the spring of 1970 to see them for herself. She made her way to the Sassafras, a feminist commune in rural Newton County in the lower Ozarks.

Rivers remembers Sassafras being in a constant state of turmoil, people coming and going, few wishing to stay on permanently. "It wasn't pretty," she recalls, remembering that the women there "were in a time of being very, very angry."[42] Those at Sassafras, according to Rivers, were caught up in "very angry feminism as they became aware of how oppressed women could be."[43] The commune would fail as most women there either came out of the closet and left Sassafras or left and came out later. The Sassafras land was abandoned.

Communes proved unsuccessful for various reasons, mainly due to the close proximity to others in which members found themselves. Communes asked their residents to live in the same building, eat together, and share finances, providing a much closer living situation than many had bargained for.[44] An alternative to the commune for those interested in an intentional society was the construction of the *community*.

Though much like a commune in that it depended on attracting those with shared ideas and social politics, there is one important difference between a planned commune and a planned community. A commune offered kindred spirits the sharing of land and ideals but hardly anything else. Communities offered separate homes and enough private space for separate lives. Diana Rivers saw this as a crucial distinction when she went on to form her own community. On land not too far from the failed Sassafras, still in the Ozarks and up the tremendously beautiful White River valley toward Fayetteville, Rivers and other lesbians formed the Ozark Land Holders Association (OLHA), a name made deliberately ambiguous to keep locals in the dark as to their intentions.

It was nearly a decade between the closing of Sassafras and the forming of the OLHA. Money, as in all planned communes and communities, proved to be the most important issue for those involved, but Rivers had this worked out. She had located 140 acres not twenty miles from Fayetteville and a seller not bothered that the buyers were lesbian separatists. Using money from a family inheritance, Rivers made the $30,000 down payment toward the total price of $100,000.[45]

Twenty women including Rivers bought in on the OLHA at a membership fee of $5,000. With the membership, women were given a parcel of five acres of undeveloped land on which to build their home and otherwise do with as they saw fit. They also could host whomever they wanted, regardless of sex. The lesbian women were mainly professionals, school teachers, doctors, and nurses who wished to live in a community close to Fayetteville where they might continue their professional employment. To completely separate would cost too much, financially and perhaps physically.[46] Working with a more flexible idea of separatism, the OLHA found a successful formula for separatist living: private plots within private land where inhabitants could sustain themselves financially with outside employment. [47]

To finance the building of her home and to back the community at large, Rivers found modest commercial success writing lesbian separatist fantasy, "wild women stories" she called them, which proved to be popular in the growing field of queer fiction.[48] In the pages of her five novels Rivers blended personal fantasy while advancing larger separatist politics. Through the series Rivers tells the tale of the Hadra, women with strange powers, chief among them the ability to read the minds of other women. The Hadra, driven out of their villages and ostracized by their families, created separate communities far away from the larger, poisonous "patriarchal" society. Out of the pages pour stories of women communicating with each other without words, sharing land and labor, and depending on each other for their basic needs for survival, comfort, and companionship. In Rivers's lesbian fantasies the message was clear: any woman facing exclusion from a larger society had a fantastic option in separatism. Rivers's narrative and her extraordinary solution, helping finance a separatist community through writing lesbian fantasies, employ the unique tactics and sheer determination to form space and identity.

The name, the Ozark Land Holders Association, offered them a bit more privacy, though locals quickly figured them out. Still, the women were surprised by the lack of grief they encountered as word spread. The mountain folk they encountered, who themselves often felt queered by the larger urban society, proved to be gracious, helpful neighbors.[49]

Arco Iris

When the Sassafras land was abandoned a decade before the OLHA's, it was not the end. The land, though vacant, was placed in trust, waiting for another group of women willing to give rural living a go. Two women did take up the land and rechristened it Arco Iris, or "rainbow," a symbol of the gay and lesbian movement. They corresponded regularly with other lesbian communes, just as the Ozark Women on Land had done, and learned from the mistakes and lessons provided by neighboring communes and communities. Also, they wrote regularly to *Maize Magazine,* a publication out of Wisconsin for and by rural lesbians.[50] Contributing frequently to the "On the Land" portion of the magazine, a section where letters and updates from communes were printed, the women of Arco Iris wrote of situations similar to those faced by their communal counterparts.

Arco Iris was nestled between protected national forests on 120 acres of land that once hosted the failed Sassafras commune. When the first women—Maria Chistina Moroles DeColores and her partner, Miguela

Borges DeColores—arrived, they found only a couple of shabby cabins used by hunters during the fall deer-hunting season. Practically nothing of the old Sassafras commune was left. The tract was only accessible by an old overgrown logging road, but once there the women found a creek and cold springs as well as many "cliffs and bluffs and many natural wonders to enjoy."[51] It was the same natural beauty that attracted the two city-born women in the first place. Maria, later changing her name to Sunhawk, hailed from Dallas, Texas, and had been living on the streets after leaving an abusive home life when she was thirteen. She never completed an education at the seventh-grade level, but that was enough to secure her a GED from the state of Texas.[52] Both Sunhawk and Miguela grew up in large government housing projects, Miguela's in New York City. They had met while hitchhiking across the midwestern states seeking jobs. Along the way they picked up skills in carpentry and construction and a particular deftness and strong will that would prove invaluable to the sustainability of the commune. Also, though growing up in urban Dallas, Sunhawk roots in poverty gave her nonetheless a rural edge. Despite living in the city, Sunhawk knew chickens. Her family had always kept them.

In the autumn of 1984 the women of Arco Iris found that their spring had run dry. They had founded their commune in 1978, two years after the Ozark Women on Landhad disbanded, and through determination, hard work, and often sheer luck, the women of Arco Iris had endured almost six years of rural life. Now they had only 250 gallons of usable water stored, hardly enough to last them the winter. Being less rigid in their politics than those who had come before, these women had no qualms about seeking the assistance of a neighbor they saw as an asset to them for his knowledge in having dealt with similar situations many times before. Together with the neighbor the women constructed a cistern capable of holding more than a thousand gallons of water. This successful venture encouraged the women of Arco Iris to stay the course.

As in all these groups, there were always the money issues, and the women of Arco Iris found that bartering for goods and services produced few of the materials needed to sustain them. During the startup, they also relied on government welfare programs. Combining feminist politics, ecology, and the rural capitalism of selling homemade goods to the wider community as well as Eureka Springs's past as a place for healing, the women of Arco Iris touted their goods in publications such as *Maize Magazine,* hoping to profit from like-minded women who shared in their common goals of ecological and political sustainability. Among their products they offered "rainbow medicines and women's tonics" with formulas to treat anything from arthritis to the common cold.[53] Also, to be "more in harmony with the earth," the women of Arco Iris offered reusable "Red River 100% Cotton Menstrual Pads" using no synthetics or dyes and offering "much more absorbency than the commercial disposables."[54] As this narrative reveals, with these products not only had the women of Arco Iris been able to combine the political agendas of the groups they drew inspiration from in forming their commune but these cottage industries of rural remedies for feminine matters also helped in creating a self-sufficiency that was essential for the success of communes.

Despite their ingenuity, times were still hard. The goods sold by the women helped to provide for the monthly cost of the commune, but progress on improving the land was slow. Nonetheless, the women remained steadfast. Upon request from the readers of *Maize,* the women sent in a rural wish list of items needed for their commune: saddles, chainsaws, bows and arrows, used filing cabinets, and, naturally, money.[55] As with earlier communes, other women sent what they could. With these pleas came invitations, and women from across the nation visited Arco Iris to take part in what was going on there.

The situation at Arco Iris seemed only to improve for Miguela and Sunhawk and the women who would visit them. By the summer of 1988 Arco Iris boasted a large fruit orchard and a flower and vegetable garden. The produce helped to feed those involved with improving the land while the surplus was sold at farmers' markets with money going back into the commune. All the while, production continued on the tonics and environmentally friendly menstrual pads, a cottage industry that was by no means lucrative, but every cent mattered.

Sunhawk and Miguela often wrote of the growing frustration with loneliness and isolation. For them, the demands and needs of the land and commune made for "less time to travel and connect with sisters."[56] Also, both women were first-generation American citizens whose families had emigrated from Mexico, and they sought to bring other women of color to the commune to free them from the strains of urban life.

The Arco Iris women work to erect permanent structures on their land. *Files of author.*

They advertised in publications for others to join and published a statement in *Maize Magazine* that read,

> All people of color in this country are descendants from native people who have been uprooted from their native lands and traditional ways. Most of these native people no longer have the advantage of access to or availability of the rewards and health of country living. The original ways that their ancestors had of living off the land in harmony with the Earth have been lost to them.[57]

To reconcile this, they opened Arco Iris for women interested in "weekly stays, for workshops, conferences, hikes, and expeditions."[58]

Clary Perez-Carrera

Besides the hardships discovered once communes were established, lesbian separatism drew harsh criticism from outside lesbian communities.

Reflected in the advertisement above, lesbian activists began to cite separatism as problematic in that it often denied minority access and, if they
were admitted, then denied them access to minority men and their ability to ally themselves with those who share common circumstances.[59]
Many lesbian separatist communes were quick to recognize these concerns and ultimately recruited minority women to their spaces. Some

minority women responded to the advertisements posted by the Arco Iris commune. Clary Perez Carrera's story that illustrates queer migration to the city then back to the land and sheds light on some of the problems of minority women in lesbian spaces.

Born in Panama in 1948 to a wealthy family, Perez-Carrera went to Roman Catholic schools. When a family dispute disrupted her life, nuns suggested that her father send her to the United States for further Catholic education. With the help of the local diocese, they randomly chose Cullman, Alabama. By that time it was 1961, and Cullman found itself in the thick of the civil rights movement. The young Panamanian Perez-Carrera, with her broken English, was too dark to pass as a white Southerner and too light skinned to be accepted by local blacks. Suddenly, she found herself discriminated against and turned away from institutions for the first time in her life.

She endured, though she would carry the experiences for the rest of life. After graduation she made the move to the city, like so many gays and lesbians who had grown up in the South and later sought out the urban. She settled in New York in the late 1960s and immersed herself in the hippie movement that embraced her regardless of color. Finding a home in Greenwich Village, she frequented the infamous Stonewall Bar, a space she saw as friendly to lesbians of color.[60] Finding others there and at other underground queer bars, she became involved in the city's gay and lesbian movement. She stayed until 1978 when she returned to the place of her southern upbringing, like so many gays and lesbians from the South who became disenchanted with what they found in the city. Though she did not consider the South her home, she did feel the need to go south after responding to an advertisement similar to the one posted by Arco Iris in a feminist newsletter pleading for women of color to join the lesbian communes around Eureka Springs. Remembering the hardships she faced during her time in Alabama, she became eager to return and fight against racism in the rural South.

She made her way to Newton County, Arkansas, and joined the "country women" at Arco Iris and eagerly assisted in the work of the farm. Some like Perez-Carrera stayed on through the hot summers and long winters, working and maintaining the land. The women constantly struggled with money matters. Wishing to contribute monetarily as best she could, Perez-Carrera sought part-time work in nearby Eureka

Springs. Though in the seasonal tourist town, good steady jobs were difficult to come by; Perez-Carrera found work waiting tables at the local Pizza Hut.

By the 1990s most of the lesbian separatist communities around Eureka Springs had folded for various reasons. Some women like those at Arco Iris hung on, though most, like Perez-Carrera, had moved to town or away altogether. Perez-Carrera met her partner, K. J. Zumwalt, in town. Together they opened a bar in the rejuvenated downtown that would serve for some time as Eureka Springs's only real gay and lesbian bar. In *Ms.* magazine announcements for gay- and lesbian-owned businesses soon replaced those of people wishing to begin or augment separatist communities that had laid a foundation for increasing visibility in Eureka Springs. The separatist communities, seeking to remove themselves from a larger patriarchal order also sought economic independence, which proved difficult to achieve. As lesbians removed themselves from economic oppression, so too were they able to construct a personal and group identity based on their ability to create space and generate a wealth so closely linked to their identities. Before this, other foundations, other formulas would have to be laid and tested in Eureka Springs before queer sensibilities and economics could take hold.[61] And these would come from the most unlikely of places.

At the heart of lesbian separatism was the concept of creating autonomy based on feminist politics and basic feminine characteristics that many considered part of their biological makeup. Rejecting the idea of gender as a social construct, women who came to the hills saw men as biologically wired to be gruff and disruptive. In contrast they laid claim to compassion, purity, and other values as feminine traits upon which they could create a space separate from the male-dominated world. They found value in being women and value in joining together as women.[62] As seen here, the reasons for the closure of many of the communes were numerous and varied, but most succumbed to highly concentrated problems of personality, economics, and the particular challenges of the generally isolated rural landscape.

It is not that this essentialism was flawed or that separatism failed, but, as many of the women involved saw it, the autonomy sought and the desire to determine their space and their surroundings rather than letting their surroundings determine them would survive. While this lesbian separatist movement existed, there was a conscious desire to reverse the order of things so that the lives of queer people could dictate social circumstances. This is perhaps the most conscious and deliberate construction of an alternative modernity we have seen thus far. Though many of the communes and communities recorded here would not survive, the desire to carefully select and build personal surroundings more closely attached to identity would. In many ways this desire was already in place, from drag bars and rest stops to the private homes of queer Arkansans. The lesbian women who came to the Ozarks pushed the desire for greater self-determination out of the hills and into the streets of Eureka Springs. Many women packed up and moved out of state. Many, bitter with their experiences, carried with them the depression and anxiety of failed ventures. Others went to town, carrying with them courage, experience, and notions of independence, and there they became successful capitalists without turning their backs on community.

FOURTEEN

The Mansion on the Hill

The Ozarks never offered land of great value. Rocky, hilly, unsuitable for farming, the Ozarks had a reputation as a sanctuary for the hillbilly, the subversive, the outlaw—a place where polite, educated people dare not tread. Then something of value was discovered and with it the possibility of generating wealth. In what would become Eureka Springs, settlers found dozens of natural springs that bore waters that, according to local legend, carried great medicinal properties. From these waters the town of Eureka Springs sprang. Founded in 1879, hilly Eureka Springs, a town still without a single ninety-degree intersection, quickly became known as a place where the misfits fit as colorful individuals flocked to the town for the baths, joining the mountain folk who now found themselves with a trade to sell and a lucrative new industry found in the water.[1]

At first they came by the hundreds, and then the thousands, for the healing waters. After the Civil War, high-dollar hotels and resorts began popping up around the natural springs offering spa treatment and healing waters that could cure anything from paralysis to insomnia, scrofula to rheumatism.[2] The town hit its first boom in the 1890s, a period that local residents still refer to as the "Gay 90s." The town hosted hundreds of Civil War veterans, mainly from the North, traveling to eccentric Eureka Springs to treat old wounds and new ills. So many came, in fact, that Eureka Springs is perhaps the only town in the South whose square boasts a statue honoring a Union solider rather than a Confederate one. Entrepreneurs, catering to those too ill to travel, bottled numerous supposedly healing tonics from the springs and shipped them across the country, helping make the name "Eureka Springs" a nationally known place and tourist destination.[3]

Business dried up after the First World War as healing springs and folk cures were replaced by profound strides in modern medicine. As science, chemical prescriptions, and rational explanations took hold, the curious powers of healing waters began to be seen as more hokey than healthy. The town soon became deserted, altogether a hollow version of its former grandeur. The old hotels downtown closed for what the owners hoped would only be a short lull in the tourist trade. As the 1920s were roaring elsewhere, the buildings of downtown Eureka Springs had been boarded up, and many owners had moved on. The Crescent, the crown jewel of the high-end hotel in town, filled its beds by becoming a hospital. Businesses, restaurants, and general tourist services that depended on the hotels closed just as quickly. The quaint Victorian and Queen Anne cottages that made the town so attractive to visitors were abandoned. The charming and winding mountain streets once lined with specialty shops now were all but a ghost town. The town that had boasted a population of over fourteen thousand at the turn of the century saw its numbers slip to just under fourteen hundred by the time the Second World War had come to a close.[4]

Things finally began to turn around twenty years after the Second World War had ended. During the early 1960s, as the population of Eureka Springs was at rock bottom, the demographics included the elderly from the heyday, mixed with poets and painters and assorted hippies who sought out Eureka as a quiet, almost private space to work, nestled in a serene mountain landscape. With this serenity came cheap real estate. Enter Gerald Lyman Kenneth Smith, a man who would transform the tired mountain town and construct an economy based on an identity expression that would later provide inspiration for the town's queer economy.[5]

An American fascist and ardent anti-Semite, Smith, without his ventures in the Eureka Springs tourist industry, would have easily found his way into the history books. Close to the infamous Louisiana politician Huey Long, Smith was the national organizer of Long's "Share Our Wealth" campaign and ran the entire operation after Long's assassination in 1935. He soon abandoned this national role due to pressure from within and outside the organization. As the Second World War began, having strongly declared his fascist sympathies for some time, Smith found himself the subject of an FBI investigation. Having been pushed out of the ailing "Share Our Wealth" program, Smith went on to found such anti-Semitic organizations as the Committee of One Million and the Christian Nationalist Crusade.[6] A fierce critic of Roosevelt, Smith ran three times for the presidency or the Christian Nationalist Party ticket. After the Second World War and the defeat of fascism abroad, Smith was no longer the giant of the far right. He found himself drifting into obscurity, a laughable figure to most, which was not a comfortable position for a man who once drew praise from such figures as his fellow anti-Semite Henry Ford and staunch isolationist Charles Lindbergh.[7] His current social position and historical legacy were not flattering, and Smith sought to redeem his image and leave a lasting impact, a movement he could leave behind that reflected his personal beliefs and perhaps make some money along the way. But he was approaching old age, and Smith also sought peace and serenity far from the scrutiny that his unpopular politics attracted. He found an opportunity in economically distraught Eureka Springs. Smith purchased one of the many run-down Victorian homes in Eureka Springs and made the town, now one of the many examples of rural southern poverty, his home in 1964.[8]

Telling locals of his vision of a giant statue of Jesus Christ in the Ozark Mountains, he set to work on his new crusade, one he saw as a tribute to true Christianity, *his* Christianity. Smith, now sixty-six years old, told reporters, "Nothing could bring us more joy during the sunset days of our lives than to pay tribute to our lord and savior, Jesus Christ."[9] Local businessmen and town leaders were delighted because, beyond Smith's dubious past and religious fundamentalism, his presence and his new plans for their town meant the possibility of the returning tourist, an absence felt by almost everyone.[10]

Ground was broken in June 1965 for what he began to refer to as his "sacred project."[11] For the construction Smith brought in the talented Emmett Sullivan who had served as an assistant sculptor on Mt. Rushmore. After it was completed in the spring of 1966, the statue was illuminated at night with violet lights accompanied by loud speakers playing inspirational music by such American gospel greats as Tennessee Ernie Ford and Kate Smith. It measured 1,500 feet in height, an imposing presence on the mountain landscape to say the least. Smith boasted that his statue could be seen from four states, though that was hardly the case. The commanding Christ proved to be just the beginning for Smith and his ministry.

Critics denounced it as a monstrosity, ugly, self-serving, a giant milk carton with arms.[12] Smith dismissed them. Town leaders, some initially hesitant to support Smith's controversial plans, now found themselves eager as tourists began to trickle then flood back to Eureka Springs to marvel at the sight of what was now being referred to as *Christ of the Ozarks*. With the new tourists came new precious dollars that the town had been starved of for so long. With that, Smith saw only greater opportunity. The typical Ozark valley below the Christ statue, Smith noticed, provided for a natural amphitheatre, an ideal setting to stage biblical productions, namely what would become Eureka Springs's *The Great Passion Play*. Branson, Missouri, which would be his main competitor, had its *Shepherd of the Hills* production, a play dealing with a man who fled the corrupt city life to live in the peace and purity of the Ozarks where he competed with a "dandified snob" from the city for the heart of a young girl. The play had been popular for years and drew crowds of thousands from across the Midwest.[13] To be successful, Smith would have to dwarf Branson's established performance in both size and production. He did. Smith hollowed out a space equivalent to two football fields with an elaborate system of tunnels so that actors above could move about the set with greater ease. Atop, a massive team of construction workers toiled to recreate old Jerusalem, complete with Herod's palace, the Temple, Pilate's palace, and a marketplace dotted with scores of animals. The seats constructed on the hillside could accommodate up to 4,100 tourists.[14]

With costs skyrocketing, Smith found himself needing to cut corners as loans became due. He had already saved money by choosing a site for the statue and play just yards from the city limits of Eureka Springs, thereby making his new business and his tourist dollars exempt from city taxes, though he demanded, and got, the use of city water.[15] Ever careful and often clever, Smith was quick to have his ministries and ventures deemed nonprofit, thereby making them exempt from state and federal income taxes.[16] The actors who would perform the production also went unpaid. Of all those who performed at the passion play, at times numbering almost three hundred for a single production, cast members selected a local church to which Smith would donate a portion of the profits given in the name of the actor in place of a paycheck. It would be several years before cast members actually received a paycheck from Smith's ministries for their performance.[17] Also, the identities of cast members were hidden from those in attendance in order to further remove the actors from their biblical characters, though it was not difficult for locals in the audience to pick out their neighbors. Smith, in a personal greeting in his seventy-five-cent souvenir program, wrote that "due to the sacred nature of the production and because they are aware of their frailties in relation to the divine personage of their portrayals, all cast members wish to remain anonymous."[18] And Smith hardly left his anti-Semitic proclivities in the past. He insisted that his performers have Christian features and voices, denying auditions to actors who did not fit his dubious requirements. Smith included in the script the stark and controversial scripture verse reading, "His blood be upon us and our children," a passage from the Gospel of Matthew delivered at the time of Christ's crucifixion that many Jewish American groups denounce as antagonistic toward Jews. Also, Jewish groups who were onto Smith from the beginning of his ventures in Eureka Springs were quick to point out that his script departed heavily from scripture at other points in the production. Contrary to scripture, the Smith production had Jesus whipped at Herod's palace, not at that of Pilate, who would later deliver a monologue stating that the execution of Christ was at the hands of the entire Jewish people.[19]

Despite the controversies, the play and the entire venture were a complete success. Townspeople, though benefiting in part from Smith's religious schemes through the tourist revenue it had brought in, never saw the town rejuvenation they had been promised by Smith. Moribund historic buildings that had sat abandoned and in disrepair remained so. Townspeople that had at least hoped for summer jobs in the enormous cast were told that, as true Christians, they would not receive a paycheck. Other outside entrepreneurs swooped in with their own capital. Wishing to benefit from *The Great Passion Play,* they built strip motels and buffet restaurants close to Smith's project. Motels were constructed to sleep exactly fifty-five people, or the precise seating for one Christian tour bus.[20] Lodges proudly displayed Christian emblems on their signs, next to postings stating, "No bikers, please." Yet, historic Eureka Springs, the old downtown, was still in desperate need of renewal. Its once superior and posh hotels were in an increasing state of disrepair. The historic downtown found itself surrounded on the hilltop above, along Arkansas Highway 67, by cut-rate motels catering to the Christian tourists who wandered downtown only to marvel at what once was and to purchase the occasional T-shirt from the souvenir stands that appeared almost overnight. Nevertheless, a tense relationship of "downtown people" versus "the highway crowd" began to develop.

Still, despite his initial success, Smith was not satisfied. Beyond the statue and the successful play, Smith was determined to import the actual holy land to northwest Arkansas. Just across from *The Great Passion Play* on the extensive grounds that now included 360 acres in total, Smith constructed the New Holy Land on fifty acres, complete with full-scale replicas of the Great Eastern Gate of Jerusalem's Old City, the Garden of Gethsemane, Moses's tabernacle, and the Bethlehem Inn. Christian tourists could now walk freely about the holy sites that Smith had provided for them. Actors and volunteers in historical costume dotted the landscape and notable figures such as Simon Peter told biblical stories to visitors.[21]

The Eureka Springs tourist industry grew somewhat, though it in no way resembled what it once was. The wealthy tourists who flooded Eureka Springs at the turn of the century for its luxury hotels and healing spas were replaced by Christian tourists who did not spend as lavishly. Smith brought them in during the 1960s, but others came as well, and not for the spiritual needs fulfilled by such undertakings as *The Great Passion Play* and the New Holy Land tour.

In 1972 in the same edition of the Eureka Springs newspaper, the *Times-Echo*, that announced the fiftieth wedding anniversary of Gerald L. K. Smith and his wife, Elna, a birth announcement appeared for a baby boy born to a popular couple in the growing "freak" community.[22] In a bold, unassuming tone, the *Times-Echo* headline read, "Welcome to the World, James Aaron Flatdogtales."[23] The town was becoming a lure for the "hippie" folk, or the "longhairs," to skeptical locals. John Cross, president of Eureka Springs Bank, the institution that served as the "pulse of a good community," noted that the town attracts such people because "they're looking at taxes primarily, and it's an all-white community with no pollution."[24] "I'm not a racist," Cross continued, "but if we don't have blacks, we don't have a problem with them."[25] For Cross, the lack of a black population relieved the town of social problems he believed followed African Americans. Also, in his view, the lack of African Americans in northwest Arkansas was an inherent tourist attraction. The hippies and longhairs were a different problem for Cross. What African American community there was in Eureka Springs had long since dispersed when business turned sour during the Depression era leaving the town entirely homogenous.[26] The longhairs arrived in greater numbers during the tumultuous 1960s with attitudes of free love and relaxed views of self-expression. Some long-established residents, such as Cross, though skeptical of Smith and his past, at least saw the Christian dollar as more respectable than what the longhairs might bring in. Soon, some who shared his views formed vigilante hair-cutting groups, driving around town giving "unsolicited" haircuts to unsuspecting longhairs. Municipal authorities did little to stop them until one vigilante group apprehended and cut the hair of the Christ understudy for the assion play. When the man arrived for the next day's rehearsal noticeably bruised and with considerably shorter hair, Smith saw to it that the attacks subsided after that.[27] Overall, the strife between the town's citizens and the hippies was never a major problem beyond a simple generational issue and that of an increased visibility of the counterculture during the Vietnam War. Cross noted that if it ever became a real issue, "we can always get the sheets out."[28]

Some citizens feared a real attack upon the status quo. The *Times-Echo* exposed what it called a "well-oiled plot" by longhairs to take over the city government. The newspaper pointed out that of 750 registered voters in the town at least 300 were longhairs, making the "deviate set" a considerable voting block. This plot never materialized.[29]

Where Smith failed to fulfill promises to help downtown, others would succeed. Some came in on Smith's coattails while others came with the longhairs, setting up specialty shops as the hippie set started to attract tourists all its own. Shunned by town people like Cross, and those who bought into the local paranoia generated by the *Times' Echo* story, longhairs formed their own business associations and civic groups. Downtown thrived under their care, and the "deviate subculture" was proving to be anything but. As Smith attracted businesses that clamored to be in close proximity to the Christ statue and passion play, downtown, with its historic

architecture and cheap real estate, saw somewhat of a rebirth at the hands
of the longhairs, many of them college-educated younger men and
women who flocked to Eureka Springs. They reopened the hotels and
restaurants. Craftsmen opened specialty shops for pottery, candle making,
and weaving. Others offered lessons in horseback riding, dance, and art.
Soon, downtown Eureka formed an economy independent from what
Smith had created, and the two groups, despite their obvious differences
of education, politics, and class, began to get along unusually well.[30]
Money was forging a truce.

The relationship between Smith and the new, younger set of down-
towners garnered even national attention, attention all too welcome in
a town so desperate for tourist dollars. The New York Times, calling
Eureka Springs a model of coexistence, suggested that if "municipal cor-
porations were eligible for the Nobel Peace Prize, this town, with its two
thousand oddly mismatched residents, would probably win."[31] The
Times reported that while many "straight" people followed Smith to
town to capitalize in his wake, "freaks" also flocked to the town.[32]

Though the so-called freaks were less motivated by money and self-
promotion than were Smith and his cohorts, living in Eureka Springs
took money. A tourist and resort town deep within the Ozark Mountains
is very much a seasonal town, shutting down during the long mountain
winters. The freaks, beyond the services and business they provided,
soon gained the respect of locals when they made it through their first
winters convincing locals that they were there for good. Some of the
freaks even discouraged others from arriving, commonly arguing that
with a shortage of jobs and money those who could not deliver a skill
or a service to the town could not survive a year in Eureka. Even Smith,
who never hid his distaste for the town hippies and even instructed his
driver to speed up to hurry past them when he saw them on the street,
came to regard them as "sincere people who are at peace here."[33] The
town went forward with a sort of cold courtesy on both sides, lending
a general feeling of tolerance in the town as both groups increasingly
viewed Eureka Springs as their town.

The growing counterculture population of longhairs, often college
educated and certainly liberal leaning, led to progressive attitudes toward
sexuality that were attractive to gays and lesbians. Building on the good
nature and accepting attitudes of the hippies and longhairs, they them-

selves often queered by a larger, heteronormative society, gay and lesbian entrepreneurs—though perhaps they would never admit it—borrowed from Smith's successful formula.

At the heart of Christian evangelicalism is the desire to express publicly what is essentially a private religion.[34] This desire was carved into the landscape of northwest Arkansas by Smith. Gays and lesbians seeking business ventures in Eureka, many after leaving failed communes and perhaps drawing inspiration from Smith's endeavors, sought to capitalize by drawing others to display their sexual identity publicly by becoming patrons at businesses that openly catered to gays and lesbians. These businesses depended on gay and lesbian travelers who wished to display their private identities in a new articulation as they spent their dollars. Many would seek out and visit not just the gay bar, but any bar, gallery, sweetshop, or confectionary they knew was gay owned. As the Christian tourist openly congregated around the feet of the *Christ of the Ozarks* statue, so too would queers with the power-wielding tourist dollar in their pocket congregate around reopened downtown bars and bathhouses.

FIFTEEN

Economic Opportunity
and the Queer Community

Travel/Vacation: New Orleans Hotel.
Eureka Springs, Arkansas. Feminist Owned.[1]

The town had an appeal, especially for those seeking independence;
longhairs, hippies, artists and others flocked to Eureka Springs.
An advertisement was posted in *Ms.* magazine to attract this very
set. Barbara Scott fled New Orleans, Louisiana, and a bad marriage. After
coming out as a lesbian, she often traveled to Eureka Springs and eventually moved there in 1972, buying, appropriately, the old New Orleans
Hotel. Having been active in the feminist movement in New Orleans,
she sought to create a space for lesbians and lesbian feminists in Eureka
Springs, but it would eventually become a focal point for gay men as
well as lesbians from across the region. Scott, known by some as "the
first lesbian," brought with her later lesbian feminists from her native
New Orleans, friends and friends of friends seeking quiet getaways in
defined feminist spaces away from the city. As word spread, women from
other cites began to arrive. Many were feminist tourists. Some were not.
Scott remembers that "a lot of women were runaways," leaving abusive
husbands, coming to the hotel "for escape and a change of life."[2]

Scott leased the hotel's downstairs bar to another lesbian woman
and two gay men also from New Orleans—Manny Williams and Vernon
LeBlanc. Both men were familiar with the bar business. In New Orleans,
LeBlanc was a waiter at the popular Fatted Calf cabaret venue.
Downstairs bars were frequently queer in the American South. The
upstairs rooms were let out to the traveler, and the downstairs was let
out to cater to the traveler's needs to meet others like them. Little Rock

167

had two gay spaces operating out of the basements of hotels, as did Jackson, Mississippi, and Mobile, Alabama. The Quarter bar downstairs in the New Orleans Hotel used this trend and the increasing gay and lesbian visibility that came out of the 1970s to create the beginnings of an openly queer community in Eureka Springs. The bar and the hotel were hugely popular as lesbians and gay men began to arrive in droves.[3] Scott remembers there was never any real trouble. The only problem they had was keeping the straights out. "They integrated us," she remembers. "The straights came in because it was the happening place to be."[4]

As gay men and lesbians arrived at the New Orleans Hotel to immerse themselves briefly in the queer community formed there, others came with more permanent goals. Some saw great potential in the land around Eureka Springs. Queer men and women were attracted to Eureka Springs for a variety of reasons. Seeking a break from the city, gay men saw opportunity in Eureka Springs. Purchasing boarded-up homes and run-down businesses in the winding streets of the old downtown, some gay men started businesses in a place that was quickly gaining a reputation as a space that offered much more than simple tolerance. It was a queer space that offered a sense of a larger identity.[5] Though it was hard to find work without the capital needed to cash in on the growing tourist trade, gay men found jobs waiting tables in the increasing number of high-end restaurants in town. Some became gallery attendants, and others found work in the hotels playing piano in the bar or offering concierge services. When all else failed, some gay men with theater training put aside their feelings toward Gerald L. K. Smith and the uptown highway crowd and found work as cast and crew members in *The Great Passion Play,* still one of the area's largest employers.

Steve Roberson came from Houston weary of the city and his life as an accountant. He and his partner looked for a quieter, rural life. They looked at Asheville, North Carolina, but deemed it "too closed." Then they visited Taos, New Mexico, but for them it was "too brown."[6] Then Roberson remembered Eureka Springs. The town was not all that foreign to him; he had visited as a child when his parents took him and his brothers to see *The Great Passion Play.* Roberson returned in 1990, but, aside from the enduring but now ailing Passion Play, he found a town much more inviting than he remembered. Roberson quickly found "a support network" of gay and lesbian business owners.

Roberson and his partner bought an old motor lodge from the 1930s and converted it into a bed and breakfast. They renovated every room and even installed an English garden on the grounds to provide an air of sophistication. They rechristened the motor lodge the "Rock Cottage Gardens." They advertised across the South, offering romantic getaways for couples, "no children, please." Seeing more opportunity for business, Roberson and his now business partner saw further opportunity by advertising their cottages in gay and lesbian newspapers in major southern and midwestern cities such as St. Louis, Tulsa, and Kansas City.

Straight couples made up the majority of Roberson's business, and once they had come, they tended to return for years. Gay couples came as well. With larger disposable incomes than many married couples with families, gay men patronized businesses in Eureka Springs, buying high-end art and antiques from the specialty shops owned by the "longhairs." Other gays and lesbians, like Charlotte Downey, had businesses to provide services and entertainment for gay and lesbian tourists, whose numbers had only increased since the 1990s. Downey offered fishing trips and rafting adventures. Perez-Carrera and her partner opened a restaurant and bar. Even the women of Arco Iris got in on the act, advertising the "Walk in Beauty" land and water adventure for women and children. The package included "private wilderness and river guide service and group trips for hiking, overnight camping, canoeing, caving, and backpacking."

In many ways the increase in gay and lesbian tourism that Eureka Springs benefited from was itself the result of politics and visibility. By advertising in gay magazines and newsletters across the region, these businesses attracted a growing clientele of queer people who found in Eureka Springs the comfort and escape from urban life they sought. As modern queer identities became increasingly intertwined with money, and money was increasingly connected to visibility, choosing a queer holiday destination meant defining not only a sense of personhood but also a sense of self-purpose and identity connected with that space. Those gay and lesbian couples who patronize the bistros and galleries of Eureka Springs, who walk about holding hands, express in a nonverbal but highly visible way a political statement of same-sex desire and a display of personal identities.

As more men like Roberson opened high-end hotels, art galleries, and restaurants, tiny Eureka Springs, although rural, was seen as a distinctly cosmopolitan venue worthy of cosmopolitan dollars. Slowly, rainbow flags began to take the place of Christian symbols on business signs and advertisements, and tourism in the mountain town began to combine travel and politics in an explicit way that allowed for local gay and lesbians to take a backseat in visibility to those from outside the community.[7]

When approached by a *Democrat-Gazette* reporter regarding the growing reputation of Eureka Springs as both a tourist haven and hotspot for gays and lesbians across the country, local gay business owners were reluctant to out themselves. Responses to the reporter's queries ranged from "Being gay has nothing to do with my success" to the more abrupt and succinct "I'd prefer you leave."[8] The *Democrat-Gazette,* in response to these remarks, wrote that "understanding these responses is part understanding the fabric of individual acceptance in Eureka Springs and part understanding the reality of economic success in a rural area."[9]

Though for many the gay and lesbian businesses of Eureka Springs served a community-building function, the people whom it excluded are as important as those it included. These businesses cater to those who can afford the visibility, who have the queer capital needed to travel and spend generously. With this, as queer economist M. V. Lee Badgett writes, a "queer economy is likely to reproduce racial, gender, and class inequality within the gay community."[10] This is quite evident in Eureka Springs. Among the three thousand inhabitants of Eureka Springs, only six are registered by the census bureau as being African American. Northwest Arkansas is sparsely populated by people of color, not to mention queers of color. Although this problem was identified by the lesbian separatist communes at one point, a viable solution was never found, and community focus shifted toward finding spenders rather than identifying groups on whom money could be justly spent. Queer capitalism and tourism sustains these larger attitudes of class and race inequality while merging rural and urban ideas of identity. Money, coupled with identity politics, seemed to be a powerful force.

After all, if one wanted to spend gay tourist dollars, one had plenty of spots to choose from. Queer towns were not unheard of by 1976. There was always San Francisco. Scores of other cities had distinct gay neighborhoods forming well before Eureka Springs garnered its reputation. Queer towns and queer vacation destination besides San Francisco could include

Cherry Grove and Fire Island, New York; Provincetown, Massachusetts; Key West, Florida; and to a lesser degree Rehoboth Beach, Delaware.[11] With these destinations, Eureka Springs would have had something in common. All were tourist spots; all offered beautiful backdrops in ocean or mountain scenery. Eureka, cheaper and more accessible for people across the Midwest and southwest regions, also differed in that all of the aforementioned places were connected to large urban centers with large queer networks. Eureka Springs had no real metropolis to cling to should times get tough. Nevertheless, businesses and lives prospered there as personal politics and economic interests solidified on the mountain landscape.

Virus

Gays and lesbians from across the United States are shaped individually by the social and cultural circumstances that surround them. These social circumstances, beyond the issues of class and race, must now in an increasingly mobile society include those from other geographical areas with whom one comes into contact with, be it for a few hours at a hotel bar or simply with a casual nod or backward glance in passing acknowledgment on the street. These effects are further illustrated through the rural/urban dichotomy as queers from each cross paths in southern tourist destinations. For the gay business owners and the gay tourists they encountered, varied queer identities converged in Eureka Springs.[12] These unfixed and mobile queer identities are formed and continue to be reformed as queer Arkansans shape their sense of self based on personhood, place, and purpose and continue to encounter changing social circumstances.[13] Tourism sustains the blending and re-forming of identities as they are written onto the surrounding hills of the Ozarks; those who separate entirely and those who, with their vacationing dollars, choose to separate only for a long weekend, meet and converge and together continually renegotiate self and group identities.

If tourism aided in the connection of cross-cultural gay and lesbian encounters, it also brought certain elements to the rural space mistakenly thought of as strictly urban. In some ways Roberson and his partner fled death. Living in the popular Montrose neighborhood of Houston, a quarter known by locals as the Gay Ghetto, they had buried too many neighbors and far too many friends during the early days of the

HIV/AIDS epidemic of the mid-1980s. Exhausted from it all, Roberson and his partner found themselves in a situation in which they could no longer mourn. For various reasons they came to Eureka Springs; to escape the virus was one of them. However, Eureka Springs since its inception was always a transient town, a space lending itself to the misfit, the traveler, the one seeking solace from some other life. Gay men came to Eureka Springs from across the country and with them came the virus. Some were already ill. Many had no idea of the virus that sat within. They came and stayed for the weekend and took local boys back to their bed and breakfasts and their rooms at the New Orleans Hotel, and with that the virus made its way into the rural.[14] Of course, the rural would have never been immune to such a virus, but it must be said that it had a greater and much earlier proportional impact on tiny Eureka Springs than the virus would on the rest of Arkansas. In many ways HIV/AIDS came to the South and the rural spaces after it had noticeably changed the urban landscapes of such cities as New York and San Francisco. But Eureka Springs suffered just as badly. Without warning, the virus struck.

Ken Scully, a gay man from Rockford, Illinois, was always fond of the Buffalo River and the hippie communes that could be found alongside it as the river wound through the Ozark Mountains. During the 1970s he and his college friends took canoe trips down the river during school breaks. After graduation in 1976 Scully made the permanent move to Eureka Springs. He was never fond of big cities; Washington DC, San Francisco, and even Key West, he thought, were "too nervous."[15] Eureka Springs for him was simply relaxing. Not long after he moved to town, he began to date a pharmacist in town whose successful store was popular with uptown and downtown folk alike for his willingness to sell both mainstream medications as well as folk herbal remedies. As tourists came in from the cities, some of them told what could only seem as tall tales of mysterious cancers that only gay men seemed to catch. For Scully the stories seemed too ridiculous to believe; his pharmacist partner did not dismiss them so easily. As new terms like *retrovirus* and *immune deficiency* entered mainstream vocabulary, he quickly realized that it was not fiction.

All along they wanted to believe that AIDS was a "big city problem." Sculley recalls that it was those "big city boys" who came to stay at the

New Orleans Hotel and "trick with the locals."[16] The federal Centers for Disease Control reported in 1990 that the Ozarks, along with other rural mountain areas such as the Appalachians, represented spaces with the lowest AIDS rates in the United States.[17] However, Eureka Springs never could afford such a statistical luxury. The virus surfaced there long before it did in the rest of the Ozark region as gay men came into the region at a disproportionate rate by gay tourism. This spilling out of the virus over interconnected highways and airways carried the virus along winding mountain passes and back-country roads that connected Eureka Springs to cities such as Houston and New Orleans.[18] Of Arkansas's seventy-five counties, rural Carroll County, home to Eureka Springs, ranked seventh in infection rates from 1985 to 2005 with nearly twenty-three known cases per 100,000 people. Compare this to Carroll County's neighbor to the west, Madison Country, and to the east, Boone County, with a zero rate of infection per 100,000, or to that of more populous Pulaski County, home to Little Rock, with twenty-nine infected per 100,000 people.[19]

It was the gay traveler who was more willing to take certain sexual risk while on vacation. Reading of Eureka Springs in gay magazines and hearing of the charming mountain retreat from friends, gay men saw the opportunity to take sexual risks in the Eureka Springs as they felt a certain degree of comfort and safety brought on by a greater sense of anonymity and reprieve from routine. In the early days of the epidemic, small-town doctors in Eureka Springs and the surrounding areas had no idea what they were seeing when men came in complaining of strange symptoms and pointing to lesions on their feet and legs. For this reason many infected gay men were wrongly diagnosed with leukemia and were given any number of pills and treatment that only succeeding in worsening their already fragile condition. Chemotherapy meant to kill the lesions that were now spreading all over their chests, arms, and necks wiped out whatever precious virus-fighting T cells they had left in their frail bodies. Besides those in town who fell ill, there were the gay men living outside the state that simply wanted to come home to Eureka Springs, to the Ozarks, or elsewhere in Arkansas. They had contracted the virus in the city, and they came back to Arkansas from places like Houston, Dallas, and New Orleans to die at home, some with blood family at their side, others just because the sense of a homecoming helped put them at greater ease. Just as lesbians sought out Eureka Springs to carve out of the mountain landscape a place where they could live with each other and live by and with themselves, AIDS was somehow solidifying the area as a place where one might come, ill or healthy, in response to outside forces. These outside influences not only pushed those suffering from AIDS from rural spaces to an urban ones but also saw those infected, as well as those scared of possible infection, driven out of urban centers to rural spaces where the stereotypical "good ole boy" was now the compassionate neighbor.[20]

As his friends began to "look more and more like skeletons," Scully and others did not sit idly as their friends and neighbors fell increasingly ill.[21] The impact of AIDS in the urban is credited with the greater solidification of gay and lesbian rights movements; in the rural it created a greater need for a viable community and a network of social services. Gay men and lesbians in Eureka Springs were quick to recognize this, and the "affectional community" that had been created there was more than willing to respond. Scully and others formed the Ozark AIDS Resources and Services and ultimately turned to the larger community of Eureka Springs for assistance.

The hippies and longhairs who in many instances preceded the movement of gay men to Eureka Springs joined in the effort. Established Eureka artists donated paintings, sculptures, often anything they could for charity auctions and offered services like dance and guitar instruction, painting, and pottery lessons. Steve Roberson and his partner offered romantic weekend getaways for lucky couples. The auctions were held often and more often than not raised tens of thousands of dollars for AIDS victims. Some saw this approach as a more personal one than what the city could provide.[22] They were raising funds for a specific person, a face they all knew, rather than a larger cause.

To say that AIDS had and continues to have an extremely evident impact on urban settings would be a gross understatement. However, in many instances, its impact on the rural is overlooked. Per capita, Eureka Springs suffered as badly as San Francisco, but it suffered differently. As the virus devastated gay neighborhoods in urban spaces, the citizens of small-town Eureka Springs could not help but to see a more conspicuous effect as their neighbors appeared more like shadows; it was everywhere and there was no escaping it.

If bars served as community spaces for gays and lesbians in Arkansas, then Eureka Springs needed one badly. AIDS had claimed both the proprietors of Quarter Bar, Manny Williams and Vernon LeBlanc, and the once-prominent focal point of queer Eureka Springs all at once ceased to be. As citizens, gay and straight alike, scrambled to counter the effect of AIDS on their tiny mountain community, Perez-Carrera and her partner offered a space where those hurt most might forget for a night what was happening to their community. Together they started Center Street downtown. In 1994 the twenty-fifth anniversary of the Stonewall Inn riots, the pivotal demonstration Perez-Carrera had participated in, Center Street held its first "gay only" night, beginning a trend that would continue once a month from then on. The nights were an immediate success. Perez-Carrera posted on the door a sign reading "Private Party." The events had a disco theme, and the bar was open later than usual. To add to the festive mood, Perez-Carrera and her partner brought drag queens from nearby Fayetteville or as far away as Joplin, Missouri. Drag queens were paid fifty dollars, given a free hotel room downtown, and given all the drinks they could handle. Attendance averaged two hundred, mostly gays and lesbians with a few of their straight friends. You had to know someone to enter. Perez-Carrera had the occasional trash can thrown through the window, though trespassers were always prosecuted by local authorities. Crime against the gay community was imported from elsewhere, often nearby Berryville or Cave City, never from Eureka Springs itself.

Though there were the occasional complaints from outside the queer community, the bulk of resistance to the gay-only night was from the gay and lesbian townspeople. Some thought it wrong to have a night that was exclusive to queers. They argued that given a town that was so welcoming to them from the start, it would be wrong to exclude the larger community. Others argued that it gave the gay and lesbian community of Eureka Springs unwanted visibility that could cause problems. Perez-Carrera paid these arguments little mind. Later, she and others began Eureka Springs "Diversity Weekend," a celebration complete with a gay-pride parade that weaved through the winding roads of the downtown. For the first parade in 1996 there were sixty cars and countless participants. During that weekend, in a ritual that has been repeated many times since, the then-mayor of Eureka Springs married gay and lesbian couples at Center Street in half-mocking, half-truth ceremonies. The ceremonies proved so popular that *Our World* magazine, a gay and lesbian travel magazine based in Florida, advertised Eureka Springs as "the predominant 'wedding capital' for gay men and lesbians."[23] The bar closed in 2002 when Perez-Carrera died of cancer.

AIDS, in its own peculiar way, helped define and solidify the community boundaries of Eureka Springs. The virus also helped to close the gender differences in settlements—lesbians in communes, gay men downtown—by bringing people together to care for others. As historian Meredith Raimondo writes, "as long as its 'spread' remained imminent, not here, not yet, then the borders of community remain to be defined, as if epidemiological surveillance was a form of neighborhood watch."[24] The movement of the virus also deconstructs the notion that gay men only grow up to come out and flee to the city, or vice versa. Gay men do flee to the city. Many come home. Many never could or would leave in the first place because it was unaffordable and out of reach. Those who remained and later met those coming home dealt with AIDS as best they could and increased their determination that the queer community of Eureka Springs was there to stay.

SIXTEEN

And Then *She* Came

D espite how AIDS had changed the landscape of Eureka Springs, gay and lesbian tourists, many unaware of what had happened there, still flocked to the mountain town for weekend getaways. Queer tourists wanted desperately to take advantage of what *People* magazine dubbed "the gay capital of the Ozarks."[1] Even for those gays and lesbians who were not tourists, gay spaces, though only operating for one night out of the month, gave them a stable sense of community from which to operate. A town government friendlier toward the growing gay and lesbian population and greater favor with the locals gave the town a welcoming feel despite Smith's evangelical enterprises along the highway.

The mountains, any mountains, had long been regarded as a place of seclusion, an environment that afforded opportunities to hide out, lie low. Clearly such spaces had the ability to attract those from both sides of the social spectrum. And then, in 1991, *she* came. Anita Bryant had long personified homophobia and intolerance for many Americans, gay and straight alike. Since she fell out of favor with her fans and lost her orange juice spokeswoman deal following her "Save Our Children" campaign, Bryant had become somewhat of a national joke, a symbol of the kind of ignorance and backwardness that many business owners in Eureka Springs, in an effort now to attract upscale tourists, were trying desperately to abandon. Gays and lesbians saw her arrival as a slap in the face to them and the community they had built. Bryant arrived in May of 1991 and received significant financial backing from the Gerald L. K. Smith Foundation. The foundation, attempting to turn the tide of gay and lesbian tourism, chose not to place Bryant's show safely along the uptown highway and close to Smith's New Holy Land but squarely downtown in the Fore Runners Hotel's Grand Duchess Ballroom, not a hundred yards from the New Orleans Hotel and the Quarter bar. The marquee outside the hotel read simply, "Anita Bryant: America's Sweetheart."[2]

For a home, Bryant and her husband, through a large amount of borrowed funds from local investors, bought a fifty-nine-acre farm in nearby and more rural Berryville, thinking that even tiny Eureka Springs had too many "big city temptations" in which to raise a Christian family.[3] Plus, they were both "country bodies," a reason that made Berryville most attractive to them. As to the success of the show, Bryant was optimistic. For her, despite the gay and lesbian population growing in both size and visibility, her old, loyal fan base would surely show and tickets would sell. Bryant did have a reason to believe. Almost a quarter of Eureka Spring's 1.2 million yearly tourists were from her native Oklahoma. Also, of those tourists almost 30 percent were between the ages of fifty-five and sixty-five, Bryant's key demographic, the same demographic that the passion play depended on to sell seats.

Despite the promising numbers, Bryant was still weary. She and her new husband, former astronaut Charlie Dry, were well aware of the town's growing reputation as a queer tourist destination. She told reporters of her fears that members of the local gay and lesbian community, mocking her past status as a national orange-juice huckster, would show up to "orange her" as she entered the theater. To Bryant's relief, protesters never showed, having opted to ignore her and her operation. Ken Scully planned a new route to and from work so that he would not have to drive past her theater. To Bryant's embarrassment and disappointment, everyone else seemed to be ignoring her as well. Tickets sales never materialized as the older, more conservative tourists from nearby Oklahoma and Missouri never showed. Her production did not last the year before she packed up and moved to Eureka Springs's main competitor, Branson, Missouri. Bryant and her husband left behind debts totaling almost two million dollars. To the passion play and the Smith Foundation, Bryant owed almost $200,000 in borrowed funds. The foundation took the couple to court but was only able to secure a small portion of the money owed from the now bankrupt couple.[4] It was a tremendous blow to *The Great Passion Play* and the Smith Foundation that had been declining for some time and that expected Bryant's show to increase their sales from crossover tourists.

Despite the Foundation's best efforts, *The Great Passion Play* could never exorcise the ghost of Gerald L. K. Smith. Despite the show's endurance, critics of Smith's anti-Semitic tendencies were never quieted. Smith died in April of 1976 and was buried at the base of the controversial *Christ of the Ozarks* statue, causing some to remark that the entire statue was always meant to be Smith's own monument. For many, the play had grown stale. The production had not changed a single line or stage direction since its first performance in 1968.

As criticism of *The Great Passion Play* never dissipated, attendance continued to drop, and board members scrambled to think of ways to attract new visitors. Hope was resurrected when Mel Gibson's controversial *The Passion of the Christ* hit cinemas in the winter of 2004.[5] Having garnered much criticism of its own for anti-Semitic tones and fundamentalist views, as well as violence that some denounced as near pornographic, the Smith Foundation board members and the cast and crew of the play hoped that it would at least attract new visitors to their version of the last days of Jesus. In preparation for this new crowd the technical crew was ordered to add greater amounts of blood to the production.[6]

Still, despite the box office success of Gibson's film, ticket sales for *The Great Passion Play* continued to slip. People were "just passioned out," according to directors. Despite pleas from the mayor and other city officials to update the script and the performance, or to rent out their large outdoor amphitheater to other types of acts to attract new, younger tourists, board members, seeing the script as untouchable, refused to alter it in any way. Instead, the Smith Foundation sought to bring back older visitors and their children by providing new attractions. In the summer of 2005, complete with actual fossils, Dinosaur World opened on the grounds of *The Great Passion Play* and New Holy Land.[7] Essentially what the Smith Foundation was going to provide was a peek at some of the dinosaurs that could not fit on Noah's Ark, this in an effort to reconcile science with fundamentalist creationism to gain a competitive edge in the struggle for the tourist dollar.

Sexuality and sexual identity was locking horns with religion in an increasingly consumer-oriented society. Over time, gays and lesbians appear to be winning on that front. Typically, many gay men and lesbians who can afford to travel have more disposable income than the middle-class Christian tourist. It is these transient sexually-identified tourists who ultimately sustain the downtown space with their spending money and travel guide in hand.

Eureka Springs was always a transient town. If anything, it was in the water. When people came to bathe in it, to drink it, to bottle it up and ship it elsewhere, they saw a profit in Eureka Springs and the lucrative possibility of exporting it elsewhere. That all seemed to change when Smith sought to sell salvation on the bluffs that overlooked the old town, seeing the water as more holy than healthy as the passion play complex sold bottled water, a holier brand of water, to thirsty tourists. Now people come for other things, though more in tune with the older days of relaxation and convalescence. On the whole, lesbians sought the peace and serenity of the Arkansas Ozarks and then laid a foundation for what the town would become. Later, joined by gay men who sought something other than what the fabled cities could give, they constructed a gay space in the mostly unlikely of spaces.[8] But is it right to think of Eureka Springs as a rural space? It is worth noting that of the dozens of gay men and lesbians interviewed for this project, all the oral histories collected, not a single person was actually from Eureka Springs. Hailing from such urban centers as Houston, Atlanta, Dallas, and New York City, gay men and lesbians found value in the land in and around Eureka Springs. Suzanne Pharr suggested that many simply imported what they saw as valuable from the urban to the rural, creating a new Mansion on the Hill, their mansion on their hill. Still, the question remains, how do such opposing forces get along well in such a small space? In drawing from both sides of the spectrum, the town struck a delicate balance that both groups—the queers downtown and Smith uptown—seemed to manage quite well. Ultimately, to not get along, to not coexist within such a small rural space, would be bad for business, the tourist trade that insures the well being of the community, their person, and their larger social groups in the small mountain town two hundred miles away from any big city. Queer Arkansans began to resist straight homogeneity as best they could, allowing themselves at times to break free or allowing others to do so from social constraints that forced them into certain roles in certain spaces.

The misfits did fit in in Eureka Springs, even more so as gays and lesbians from urban centers settled and encouraged others to join them, if only for a brief time. This movement of people across regional boundaries blended the rural setting with an urban one and slowly closed the gap on alternative modernities that differed across space and region. An increasingly global gay and lesbian identity was forming in Arkansas, and greater access to places through travel and exchanges of identities and dollars helped close the door on specific regional identities.

Queer Comes Home

It's always what we don't
fear that happens, always
not now and why are
you people acting this way
(meaning we put in petunias
instead of hydrangeas and reject
ecru as a fashion statement).

—RITA DOVE, "BLACK ON
A SATURDAY NIGHT,"
FROM *ON THE BUS WITH
ROSA PARKS*[1]

On May 18, 1992, Bill Clinton entered the crowded Palace Theater in Los Angeles, California. It was a full month before the crucial California Democratic primary, and Clinton was lagging behind and fighting hard to be the party's presidential nominee. There, in front of an audience of hundreds of gay men and lesbians, mostly gay men, some very ill, Clinton gave what many consider to be the best speech of his campaign and perhaps his career. It was a fundraiser, and one that netted an impressive $100,000 for Clinton's run for the Oval Office.[2] He was not the first presidential contender to court the gay vote. Walter Mondale had done it in 1982 speaking to the newly formed Human Rights Campaign.[3] But something was different about Clinton.

At the podium, Clinton made promises, some later forgotten and some kept. Clinton told the audience that as president he would lift the ban on homosexuals in the U.S. armed forces. He promised the appointment of an AIDS czar to combat the epidemic that too many in the audience knew firsthand. He promised that someone who was HIV-positive would address the Democratic National Convention in July.[4] Standing at the podium, in front of dozens of rolling cameras and flash units, Clinton told the audience, "I have a vision, and you're part of it."[5]

Then in closing, his voice began to crack and Clinton tried to put into words what had happened, what was happening to the gay community in America. He spoke these words:

> If I could, if I could wave my arm for those of you that are HIV-positive and make it go away tomorrow, I would do it, so help me God, I would. If I gave up my race for the White House and everything else, I would do that.[6]

Some could have dismissed it as almost tacky political pandering. But as on-hand *Washington Post* political reporter David Maraniss would later write, judging "from the tone of his voice and the look on his face, many in the audience said they were inclined to believe him."[7]

Clinton's election as the America's forty-second president in the fall of 1992 is where this work ends. It was an election that marked a clear transformation for the nation and gay and lesbian Arkansas. An Arkansas governor was speaking to a group of gay men and lesbians not in Little Rock, Fayetteville, or Eureka Springs but in Los Angeles. Clinton's election would put Arkansas into the national spotlight, under national scrutiny, and with him, gay and lesbian Arkansans were increasingly brought into the fold of a national identity.[8] Any alternative modernities were clashing.

Gay Arkansas would benefit from falling into line with a larger, national identity. After all, with a national identity came national resources. Arkansas plaintiffs seeking to topple the state's sodomy statute found valuable help in their effort from the Lambda Legal Defense Fund, a national gay and lesbian rights group based in Chicago. Arkansas would be ahead of the curve that round, toppling the sodomy law within the state before the U.S. Supreme Court had the chance to eliminate it. The Miss Gay America Pageant flourished under Norman Jones and would be franchised across the nation until finally being sold out of state completely in 2005. It would not go far, relocating just across the Mississippi River to Memphis. Gay men and lesbians across the nation saw advertisements for Eureka

Springs's restaurants and hotels in out-of-state gay publications and came to town spending their dollars freely and openly.

New enemies came as well. The Republican National Committee sent thousand of mailings from outside the state during the 2004 presidential election telling Arkansans they had reason to fear the gays and lesbians who walked among them. The mailer showed a simple black leather Bible with the word BANNED superimposed across it. Next to it, sitting in a white porch swing was a man receiving a wedding ring on his finger from another man kneeling at his feet. Stamped across the two men was the word ALLOWED. The pamphlet warned, "This will be Arkansas if you don't vote." The reverse side of the GOP mailer went on to warn, "Our traditional values are under threat by liberal politicians and hand-picked activist judges. They are using the courts to get around the Constitution and impose their radical agenda," an agenda, the mailer stated, that included "allowing teenagers to get abortions without parental consent" and, above all, "allowing same-sex marriages."[9] The mailer was direct from the Republican National Committee headquarters in Washington DC.

Many bought the message, and 75 percent of the voters approved an amendment to the state constitution in the November 2004 general election that defined marriage as only between a man and a woman and banned any kind of same-sex civil unions.[10] Gay marriage had really never been an issue in Arkansas before. The fact that Eureka Springs business owners had been offering wedding packages to gays and lesbians across the country had attracted little attention outside the city.[11] Arkansas law already included a statute defining marriage as between a man and a woman. On the federal level, Clinton, seeking influence among social conservatives, had signed the Defense of Marriage Act allowing states to refuse to recognize same-sex marriages performed outside its borders. Nevertheless, Arkansan Jerry Cox and the Arkansas Marriage Amendment Committee wanted extra protection against gay marriage. In November of the previous year, the Massachusetts Supreme Judicial Court had handed down a decision legalizing gay marriage in that state. Cities in California, Oregon, and New York also approved like measures. In the summer of 2004 Louisiana and Missouri voters responded by quickly adopting amendments prohibiting gay marriage.

The mailer by the Republican National Committee sent to Arkansas voters during the 2004 election. A similar mailer was sent to West Virginians. I am grateful to Brian Greer for sharing this with me. *Files of author.*

In November Arkansas and eleven other states would adopt similar amendments.[12]

The summer before Arkansas banned same-sex marriage, a gay couple in Conway, Arkansas, my hometown, organized the town's first gay pride parade, scheduled for Sunday, June 27, 2004, a date, a flyer advertised, chosen to honor the thirty-fifth anniversary of New York's Stonewall Riots. The approved parade route would take the pride marchers through the streets of old downtown Conway.

The fact that Conway, a town I always considered small, was going to host a gay-pride parade was big news, perhaps the biggest news to hit the tiny Little Rock bedroom community in some time. It was all anyone could talk about, and the parade was not without opposition. Local churches organized a prayer vigil hosted by the Second Baptist Church of Conway not far from the downtown parade route. Conway alderman Sandy Brewer planned to introduce a resolution to the city council condemning the parade. The resolution stated that "Conway, Arkansas, is a community which encourages the promotion of traditional family-oriented values and activities" and that a pride parade is a "potentially divisive and disruptive activity."[13] The resolution was up for a vote before the city council a week before the pride parade was to take place. In the tiny courtroom where the council would meet, hundreds of Conway citizens and many from surrounding communities piled in to have their voices heard on the matter.

Fresh off the airplane from a year of graduate school in London, England, I learned that the city council was to meet the next day to consider the parade. I was going to spend the summer months in Conway doing research for this project. My parents told me, reluctantly, about the controversy. Practically begging, they asked me not to attend the meeting, fearing that something drastic might happen when hot tempers combined with even hotter southern temperatures. I assured them that my wanting to go was entirely out of anthropological and historical interest, no more. But I too was nervous. I was not sure what to expect out of the meeting but braced myself, knowing that at least some very hurtful things might be said. Walking into the courtroom almost half an hour early to find it already packed, I spied one empty chair. Sitting next to it was my parents' Southern Baptist minister. He and I had a long-standing agreement that was tantamount to cold courtesy toward one another. I quietly sat down next to him and said hello. He said nothing. Instead he shifted uncomfortably in his seat and arranged himself so that his back was to me.

The aldermen filed solemnly into the room. Then, the mayor stood in front of their long meeting table and led the entire room in prayer, asking the lord to protect those in attendance as well as the civic interest. The council moved the pride parade resolution to the top of the agenda; Sandy Brewer read his resolution aloud to applause and amens from the crowd. He then moved for its approval. Silence. The aldermen sat there, some twisting in swivel chairs, others staring blankly at the papers in front of them. No one would second the resolution and, after a few moments of anxious silence, the mayor declared the resolution dead and moved on to other town matters.

A man shouted from the back of the room, "All of these people and you aren't going to let us talk."[14] The mayor reminded those in attendance that a city council meeting was a public meeting, not a public forum. At that point Alderman Brewer moved that the meeting be opened to a public discussion. That found no second either. A woman behind me barked at the council members, "Y'all are as limp wristed as they are." She was ignored too.

It all was over in less than five minutes and most left after that, perhaps not wanting to be bored to tears over issues of drainage, road maintenance, and sanitation. I left the courthouse to surprisingly find my parents circling the block in my father's car. They were that concerned. After hearing of their minister's icy response to my greeting, my mother hardly went to that church again.

I am not sure why the other aldermen balked at Brewer's resolution. I would think, perhaps, it was so that Conway would not find itself the brunt of nasty editorials in national newspapers. In any case the council's silence spoke volumes. I wish I could say to you that the parade went off without a hitch. The following Sunday, the day of the parade, organizers awoke to find the parade route covered in manure, the nasty byproduct of rural living. Police and firemen worked all morning to clear the foul mess from the streets so that the parade might go on as scheduled. The man responsible was caught and fined after police followed the trail of manure all the way back to his home just outside of Conway. About three hundred marchers, many from Little Rock, some carrying signs, some waving from the back of convertibles, made their way down Main Street. Honestly, I do not see why so many townspeople balked at this. Throughout this work we have seen queer displayed in churches, prisons, schools, universities, roadside rest stops, military encampments, homes, bars, cars, deep in the woods, and high in the mountains. I am not sure why the street would have mattered. But this kind of gay being observed was a little different than perhaps people were used to within this space.

At the end of the parade, one organizer gave a quick speech thanking those in attendance for marching. He added, "We want to let people know that gay people don't just live in cities. They live in little towns like Conway."[15] It should not have come as a shock to anyone that not all gay people lived in cities. Those who had just marched down the streets of Conway could certainly have attested to that. But a pride parade, one meant to commemorate the anniversary of the Stonewall Riots, was itself a big-city tactic. During an oral history interview conducted years before the parade, I asked an older gay man in northwest Arkansas what he thought of the Stonewall Riots. He scoffed and quickly reminded me, rightly, that Stonewall had nothing to do with southern queers whatsoever, and indeed vice versa. The riots in June of 1969 at the Stonewall Inn in New York City were so very far away from southern queers in mind and distance that many had not even heard about the riots until years later when they were seen as a cause for nationwide celebration. Nevertheless, even my hometown had entered into a national identity that now included national days of celebration and commemoration. But if not Stonewall, then what? What should we look to if not days of national gay celebration that seemingly bring us together as one community? In the South, a region where so much of a person's lineage and history are passed down by the spoken word, the discovery of life stories and images of those who came before are perhaps the best way to commemorate and see exactly how things have changed in Arkansas. It is Arkansas that provides both the setting and grandest force of personality to this story. In an effort to include all of its aspects and people who shaped it, I have undoubtedly excluded many as well. I have provided a treatment of race and rural life in the realm of sex and sexuality; I would have liked to have delved deeper, to have thoroughly examined the lives of black gay Arkansans more so than I have here, not to mention of course the state's growing Hispanic population. For various reasons, this area of Arkansas life was, in a way, off-limits. Also, I would have liked to have ventured further back into Arkansas's queer past, reaching across time and the limits of historical narrative, but I was able only to provide what available historical sources and time could allow. Building on these omissions, this work also stands as an invitation, a beginning, to anyone wishing to add to the growing discourse about sex and sexuality in Arkansas and the South at large.

Beyond that, I hope this work provides some understanding of how Arkansas offered and operated under specific social and cultural conditions that shaped the lives of its citizens. Often, these conditions were complex and fraught with contradiction. What is clear is that Arkansas's larger heteronormative society not only encouraged but often aided in the construction of enabling spaces for the state's queer populace. These spaces ranged from the rural church hosting a Saturday night drag show and an interstate rest stop, demolished only when categories were questioned, to an hardscrabble Ozark farmer offering up his land in the back pages of a feminist magazine. All of these episodes operated both within and outside southern queer trends.

Now I bring this work to a close by including my own commemoration of a southern queer I consider worthy of celebration. This work begins and ends with my determination to resurrect the memory of a relative long since passed. In the same summer that gays and lesbians marched through the streets of my hometown, my father revealed to me what he and others in my extended family had long suspected about Aunt Opal. Queer had come home. I was determined to find her. It only took an afternoon of phone calls to distant and not-so-distant relatives to learn where Opal was buried. Someone knew someone who could tell me the information I sought. I went there, to Mulberry Cemetery just outside of England, Arkansas. The relative who told me where I might find Opal closed our telephone conversation with a troubling fact: "You know she doesn't have a headstone," she said. Then it occurred to me that in the passing of another generation Opal and who she was would have been lost forever. These pages seek to apply the historical brakes, as it were, on a period of history, Opal and all, who might have slipped away and have light shed on the margins of Arkansas's past. Opal's life supplied me with a map to navigate the margins of Arkansas and, perhaps, the courage to step out.

When I reached Mulberry Cemetery, I found the family Opal was buried among. But, as I feared, Opal's plot remained unmarked. The fragile plastic marker placed there by the funeral parlor had long since vanished.

In lieu of a headstone, this work will have to do for now.

NOTES

INTRODUCTION

1. For the debate over the state nickname, see W. C. Jameson, "Changing Slogan is a Natural Move," *Arkansas Gazette*, 9 April 1987, final edition; "Travel Panel Will Support New Slogan," *Arkansas Gazette*, 22 May 1987, final edition; John Reed, "Car Tags Could Tout 'Natural State,'" *Arkansas Gazette*, 31 July 1988, final edition; Fred Williams, "Does State Nickname Truly Need Updating?," *Arkansas Gazette*, 13 November 1988, final edition; and Dorothy Cox, "Our State is Nicknamed, Naturally," *Arkansas Gazette*, 17 December 1988, final edition.

2. Robert Howard, personal interview, Little Rock, AR, 15 June 2003.

3. James R. Fair Jr., *The North Arkansas Line: The Story of the Missouri and North Arkansas Railroad* (Berkeley, CA: Howell-North Books, 1969), 157, 183.

4. Both French and Spanish explorers of the south and southwest portions of the United States used the term *hermaphrodite* when speaking of homosexuality in the Indian cultures they encountered. Later, the French applied the term *berdache,* from the French for "sodomite." William C. Foster, ed., *The La Salle Expedition to Texas: The Journal of Henri Joutel, 1684–1687,* trans. Johanna S. Warren (Austin: Texas State Historical Association, 1998), 281n23. For the numerous allegations of sodomy levied against La Salle by fellow explorers, see Jean-Baptiste Minet, "Journal of Our Voyage to the Gulf of Mexico," trans. Ann Linda Bell, in Robert S. Weddle, Mary Christine Morkovsky, and Patricia Galloway, eds., *La Salle, the Mississippi, and the Gulf: Three Primary Documents* (College Station: Texas A&M University Press, 1987). For a larger examination of Arkansas Indians and European relations, see Morris S. Arnold, *The Rumble of a Distant Drum: The Quapaws and Old World Newcomers, 1673–1804* (Lawrence: University of Kansas Press, 2000).

5. Of these *berdache,* John D'Emilio and Estelle B. Freedman write that they "disturbed Europeans greatly" in the personal choice in sex and sexuality. However, as seen here with the La Salle expedition, French explorers were not so much "disturbed" but rather intrigued by the social status and mobility enjoyed by queer Indians. John D'Emilio and Estelle B. Freedman, *Intimate Matters: A History of Sexuality in America* (Chicago: University of Chicago Press, 1997), 7, 31.

6. The use of the term *queer,* as well as its theoretical and historical uses, will be discussed at length in the following chapter. Nan Alamilla Boyd, *Wide Open Town: A History of Queer San Francisco* (Berkeley: University of California Press, 2003), 6–7. Also see Michael Warner, *Fear of a Queer Planet: Queer Politics and Social Theory* (Minneapolis: University of Minnesota Press, 1993), 8–14. Concerning the use of *queer* to create transhistorical continuities, historian Graham Robb writes that "early Victorian 'sodomites,' 'mollies,' 'margeries,' and 'poufs' had a great deal in common with the later 'Uranians,' 'inverts,' 'homosexuals,' and 'queers': very similar daily experiences, a shared culture, and of course an ability to fall in love with people of

their own sex." Graham Robb, *Strangers: Homosexual Love in the Nineteenth Century* (New York: Newton, 2003), 12.

7. Martin F. Manalansan IV, *Global Divas: Filipino Gay Men in the Diaspora* (Durham, NC: Duke University Press, 2003), 21. Also see Bruno Latour and Catherine Porter, *We Have Never Been Modern* (Cambridge, MA: Harvard University Press, 2006) and Dilip Parameshwar Gaonkar, *Alternative Modernities* (Durham, NC: Duke University Press, 2001). Also, Samuel R. Delany does well to explain the usage of alternative modernities within specific created spaces in his work, *Times Square Red, Times Square Blue* (New York: New York University Press, 1999).

8. John Howard, *Concentration Camps on the Home Front: Japanese Americans in the House of Jim Crow* (Chicago: University of Chicago Press, 2008), 9.

9. Historian Judith Halberstam calls this trend of confining queer histories to the urban as "metronormativity." Only recently has this trend been questioned and reversed by scholars. See Judith Halberstam, "The Brandon Teena Archive," *Queer Studies: An Interdisciplinary Reader*, ed. Robert J. Corber and Stephen Valocchi (Malden, MA: Blackwell Publishing, 2003), 163.

10. Esther Newton, *Cherry Grove, Fire Island: Sixty Years in America's First Gay and Lesbian Town* (Boston: Beacon Press, 1993), 23. Elizabeth Lapovsky Kennedy and Madeline D. Davis, *Boots of Leather, Slippers of Gold* (Penguin, New York, 1993), 3.

11. John Howard, ed., *Carryin' On in the Lesbian and Gay South* (New York: New York University Press, 1997), 9.

12. John Howard, *Men Like That: A Southern Queer History* (Chicago: University of Chicago Press, 1997), 282.

13. Jeannie M. Whayne et al., *Arkansas: A Narrative History* (Fayetteville: University of Arkansas Press, 2002), 1–19. Ben F. Johnson, *Arkansas and Modern America: 1930–1999* (Fayetteville, University of Arkansas Press, 2000), 182–85.

14. John Howard sums up well the troubles in researching the gay and lesbian South: "Difficulties in researching and uncovering the history of lesbian, gay men, and bisexuals in the United States are compounded when the inquiry is focused on a section that has been particularly hostile to sexual indifference—the American South. Archivists and university administrators often express reservation about the validity of the field; families seeking to preserve the 'good name' of their relatives routinely deny access to materials; and, as in any other part of the country, traditional historical sources remain largely silent with regard to homosexuality prior to the 1960s." John Howard, "Place in Movement in Gay American History: A Case from the Post–World War II South," *Creating a Place for Ourselves: Lesbian, Gay, and Bisexual Histories*, ed. Brett Beemyn (New York: Routledge, 1997), 211.

15. Charles writes that personal exploration of larger social questions "results in the most controversial archival voice . . . an autoethonography, or what I call auto-history. Woven into the fabric of the chronology of legal struggle is the story of my own struggle to tell it, the shifting of my own subject position from a teacher who happens to be gay to a gay teacher who becomes an activist inspired by his research to go out and make some justice of his own." Casey Charles, *The Sharon Kowalski Case: Lesbian and Gay Rights on Trial* (Lawrence: University of Kansas Press, 2003), 3–4. Also illuminating, the Queer@King's series. Robert Mills, "Kiss My Past" (conference paper, Queer@King's, King's College, University of London, 9 February 2004).

TWO

1. "Ad Personnel Present Play, Womanless Wedding," *Rohwer Outpost* (Camp Rohwer, AR), 19 August 1944, final edition. On February 19, 1942, Pres. Franklin Roosevelt signed Order 9066 effectively removing 120,000 persons of Japanese descent from the west coast of the United States to ten incarceration camps. Of those ten, two—Camp Rohwer and Camp Jerome—were built in Arkansas. Camp Rohwer opened on September 18, 1942, and closed on November 30, 1945. At its peak the camp population was 8,475, mostly from Los Angeles and San Joaquin counties. For an excellent treatment of the Japanese American experience during the Second World War, see Roger Daniels, *Prisoners Without Trial: Japanese Americans During World War II* (New York: Hill and Wang, 1993).

2. Jane Xenia Harris Woodside, "The Womanless Wedding: An American Folk Drama" (master's thesis, Univeristy of North Carolina, Chapel Hill, 1997).

3. Hubert Hayes, "A Womanless Wedding," (Camp Rohwer Recreation Center, McGhee, AR, 23 August 1944).

4. Hayes, "A Womanless Wedding," 3.

5. Ibid., 4.

6. This is clearly carnivalesque. Essentially, allowing the subordinates a brief time of misrule and antisocial behavior directed towards authority figures would placate them for the rest of the year. See *Inside the Minstrel Mask: Readings in Nineteenth-Century Blackface Minstrelsy* (Middletown, CT: Wesleyan University Press, 1996).

7. Anne. C. Burson defines folk drama as a "mimetic performance whose text and style of presentation are based on traditional models; it is presented by members of a group to other members of the same reference group. A specific inherited text is not the determining factor that makes an event folk drama; rather, it is the traditional pattern on which the event is based." See "Model and Text in Folk Drama," *Journal of American Folklore* 93 (1980): 305–31.

8. "Wedding Takes Place Tonight," *Rohwer Outpost* (Camp Rohwer, AR), 23 August 1944, final edition.

9. "Ad Personnel Present Play, Womanless Wedding," *Rohwer Outpost,* 19 August 1944. Simon Legree is of course in reference to the most nefarious of all slave drivers and ultimately the character responsible for Uncle Tom's death in Stowe's novel.

10. "Wedding Play a Comedy Hit," *Rohwer Outpost* (Camp Rohwer, AR), 26 August 1944, final edition.

11. "Wedding Play a Comedy Hit," 1.

12. Hayes, "A Womanless Wedding," 5–6.

13. "Womanless Wedding," *Marked Tree Tribune,* 3 May 1918, final edition.

14. *Queer* is used here to describe the productions of womanless weddings and beauty pageants; queer can be seen to signify acts in certain cultures that contradict societal norms, whether by means of sexual, gender, or racial transgression. See Nan Alamilla Boyd, *Wide Open Town: A History of Queer San Francisco* (Berkeley: University of California Press, 2003), 6–7. Also see Michael Warner, *Fear of a Queer Planet: Queer Politics and Social Theory* (Minneapolis: University of Minnesota Press, 1993), 8–14.

15. "Benefit for New Balls." In her rather brilliant work of inverted southern gender and sex, author Fannie Flagg places her characters in a womanless wedding to benefit the local public school in *Fried Green Tomatoes and the Whistle Stop Cafe.* "The

Dill Pickle Club will hold a womanless wedding to benefit the hill school so they can get a set of balls for the football, basketball, and baseball teams this year." In this particular production, the sheriff of the town played the bride. Flagg is clearly playing on the playful symbols of masculinity in the "ball" and the "pickle." Fannie Flagg, *Fried Green Tomatoes and the Whistle Stop Cafe* (New York: Ballantine, 1987), 277.

16. There will always be the exceptions of male cheerleaders and female athletes, though they would hardly enjoy the same social standing and celebratory status as successful male athletes. Certainly, in 1945 Arkansas, athletics for female students were few and far between, as well as the possibilities for male students to enter into classes and social clubs seen traditionally as feminine. Pamela J. Creedon, ed., *Women, Media and Sport: Challenging Gender Values* (New York: SAGE, 1994), 20–23, 65–70. For the importance of school sports in rural areas, though taking place in a more contemporary setting, see what I consider a brilliant and poignant work that touches on many social issues. H. G. Bissinger and Rob Clark Jr., *Friday Night Lights: A Town, a Team, and a Dream* (New York: Da Capo Press, 2000).

17. Elder Fairly, personal interview, Osceola, AR, 29 July 2003After receiving his medical degree, Fairly moved to Wilson to practice in 1945. He often participated in womanless weddings. Also see "Womanless Wedding at Wilson Tonite," *Osceola Times,* March 1935, final edition.

18. Pete Daniel, *Lost Revolutions: The South in the 1950s* (Chapel Hill: University of North Carolina Press, 2000), 158.

19. Jacquleyn Dowd Hall, "The Mind That Burns in Each Body: Women, Rape, and Racial Violence," *Powers of Desire: The Politics of Sexuality,* eds. Ann Sintow, Christine Stansell, and Sharon Thompson (New York: Monthly Review Press, 1983), 329.

20. William J. Mahar, *Behind the Burnt Cork Mask: Early Blackface Minstrelsy and Antebellum American Popular Culture* (Chicago: University of Illinois Press, 1998), 17–29. Also see Eric Lott, *Love and Theft: Blackface Minstrelsy and the American Working Class* (New York: Oxford University Press, 1995).

21. Daniel, *Lost Revolutions,* 159.

22. Eric Lott, "White Like Me: Racial Cross-Dressing and the Construction of American Whiteness," *Cultures of United States Imperialism,* eds. Amy Kaplan and Donald E. Pease, (Durham, NC: Duke University Press, 1993), 474–99. Also see Sioban B. Somerville, *Queering the Color Line: Race and the Invention of Homosexuality in American Culture* (Durham, NC: Duke University Press, 2000).

23. Though having gone out of modern usage, a *flivver* typically refers to a used automobile far past its prime.

24. Hayes, "A Womanless Wedding," 18. According to social historian Robert C. Allen, though burlesque entertainment did not often include racial or ethnic bias, this script with its sexual language and humor depended heavily on the audience's ability to recognize the burlesque tradition the womanless production was both borrowing from and building upon. Robert C. Allen, personal interview, Chapel Hill, NC, 23 November 2004. Also see Robert C. Allen, *Horrible Prettiness: Burlesque and American Culture* (Chapel Hill: University of North Carolina Press, 1991).

25. Ibid., 19.

26. Amelia Jones, "Dis/playing the Phallus: Male Artists Perform Their Masculinities." *Art History* 17, no. 4 (1994): 575–78. Jones states that "the artist has come to epitomize the modern subject upon himself, the construction of the mascu-

line self as a coherent individual at the expense of female masculinity." For a similar treatment of masculine self-humiliation, see Christopher Newfield, "The Politics of Male Suffering: Masochism and Hegemony in the American Renaissance," *differences: A Journal of Feminist Culture Studies* 1, no. 3 (1989): 57–87.

27. "'H' Club Gives Pledges Three Days Intensified Initiation," *Profile* (Hendrix College, Conway, AR), 23 March 1946.. According to the 1910 Hendrix College annual, the *Troubadour*, "No Roman or Spartan warrior prized their crown of laurels or fair lady's smile more than a Hendrix athlete prized their 'H.'" Hendrix College, *Troubadour*, 1910, 106. The University of Arkansas in Fayetteville had a similar tradition. Members of the booster club, whose aim was to "foster pep at all school sports events," put their new members in "girls' hats, makeup, multicolored clothes, unmated shoes, and other accoutrements" in what the yearbook described as the "most original initiation on campus." *Razorback*, University of Arkansas, 1943, 225.

28. Robert Meriwether, telephone interview, 10 July 2003.

29. Alan Berube, *Coming Out Under Fire: The History of Gay Men in and Women in World War Two* (New York: Free Press, 1990), 67–97. Also see John D'Emilio, *Sexual Politics/Sexual Communities: The Making of a Homosexual Minority in the United States, 1940–1970* (Chicago: University of Chicago Press, 1983), 12. D'Emilio borrows from Michel Foucault's notion of discourse in what he calls the "discourse explosion" concerning the mobilization and screening for homosexuality of 16 million men in military recruitment.

30. "Circus Daze." *Camp Robinson News* (Camp Robinson, AR), 2 February 1945, final edition.

31. Ibid.

32. Ibid. One private, Dick Barton, in a production of "Circus Daze" played "Susie Stabberpuss," which a local reporter deemed a "long combination of a Shirley Temple coif and a Veronica Lake bang." "Girlee' Line in Smash 66th Panther Benefit Show," *Military News* (Camp Robinson, AR), 22 October 1943, final edition.

33. "Solider-Actor Trying on Dress for Part in Play, Wows'em in Shop" *Covered Wagon* (Camp Pike, AR), 8 August 1941.

34. Ibid. Perhaps seeing men in women's clothing stores trying on the latest fashion and parading them in the streets outside was not really that particularly shocking.

35. For a detailed look at San Francisco's prewar bar and club scene, see Boyd, *Wide Open Town*, 63–101.

36. Like Goodwin, some southerners operated outside of the drag culture of the period, which consisted mainly of womanless weddings and such drag productions as those noted earlier. The most famous of these performers was Barbette. Famous as a trapeze artist in the pre–Second World War clubs of Paris and London, Barbette would reveal her sex only at the end of her production by removing her wig for the audience. Born in 1904 in Round Rock, Texas, as Vander Clyde, Barbette joined the "World Famous Ariel Queens" on the condition that he appear as a woman, as producers thought female acrobatics were more dramatic. Harvey Lee had the pleasure of meeting Barbette in the spring of 1936 during her production of "Jumbo" in New York City. Of Barbette, Goodwin noted that "she was the best of female impersonators, I think, and gave the profession a decided 'life' in the presentation of his performance, both on the aerial bars, wire and rings. What fantastic costumes and trains and solid feathers from here to eternity he wore!" See F. Michael Moore, *Drag! Male*

and Female Impersonators on Stage, Screen, and Television (Jefferson, NC: MacFarland, 1994), 116–22. Also see Jean Cocteau, *"Barbette": mit dem Essay "Le numero Barbette"* (Berlin: Borderline, 1988).

37. This information was provided by the writings on the back of a photograph, presumably in Goodwin's own hand. Photograph of Goodwin performing at Little Rock Ordinance Plant, Little Rock, AR, 25 September 1942, Harvey Goodwin Collection, A-115, series 4, box 3, file 14, photograph 805. Courtesy University of Arkansas at Little Rock Library, Archives and Special Collections.

38. Such messages are not necessarily seen or portrayed by anyone involved in such productions, nevertheless certain themes are still articulated. Jones, "Dis/playing the Phallus." Though drag culture is more a conscious than an unconscious action, Judith Butler chooses it to illustrate the idea through performativity. Borrowing heavily from anthropologist Esther Newton, Butler argues that drag fully and effectively mocks conventional gender roles and any notion of a true gender identity. She states that "if the inner truth of gender is a fabrication and if true gender is a fantasy instituted and inscribed on the surface of bodies, then it seems that genders can be neither true nor false, but are only produced as the true effects of a discourse of primary and stable identity." This idea of the construction or production of gender and gender identity, and the further notion that any such gender role can be manipulated through performativity, is key to understanding the connection of feminist theory and queer theory. Recent scholarship has suggested that drag performances are highly self-conscious. Leila J. Rupp and Verta Taylor have suggested that drag performers are well aware that they are complicating and challenging traditional roles of gender and sexuality. Also, they suggest that the audience members are not altogether lost on this point either. See Leila J. Rupp and Verta Taylor, *Drag Queens at the 801 Cabaret* (Chicago: University of Chicago Press, 2003). Butler, *Gender Trouble*, 174. Here, Butler borrows from Esther Newton's *Mother Camp: Female Impersonators in America*, particularly the section entitled "Role Models," 102–4.

39. Indeed, beyond the womanless wedding productions and their gender inversions, camps also played host to blackface minstrelsy. John Howard writes that to mark the closure of Camp Jerome, "inmates and keepers, prisoners and guards, together donned special makeup, blackface, to show themselves, to convince each other, what they collectively were not: black. There on stage in Arkansas, the last dance was an 'All-American Minstrel Show.'" John Howard, "The Politics of Dancing under Japanese-American Incarceration," *The History Workshop Journal* (Autumn 2001). Also, for a detailed account, see Howard's *Concentration Camps on the Home Front*.

40. Searching for evidence of womenless weddings and beauty pageants, this fact became increasingly clear to me. Womenless weddings were found at private colleges and universities. Here, before the war's end and the introduction of such progressive measures as the GI Bill, these private institutions housed privileged young men who would later participate in such productions back at home. Well-to-do families who could afford luxuries such as a private collegiate education in a decidedly poor state sent their children away for an education. Having been raised on such spectacles, it would have been only natural for them to bring such productions along to these colleges and universities.

41. For an excellent treatment of the events at Central High School and the civil rights movement in Arkansas, see Sondra Gordy, *Finding the Lost Year: What Happened*

When *Little Rock Closed Its Public Schools* (Fayetteville: University of Arkansas Press, 2009); John A. Kirk, *Redefining the Color Line: Black Activism in Little Rock, Arkansas, 1940–1970* (Gainsville: University of Florida Press, 2002); and David L. Chappell, *Inside Agitators: White Southerners and the Civil Rights Movement* (Baltimore: Johns Hopkins University Press, 1994).

42. Roy Reed, *Faubus: The Life and Times of an American Prodigal* (Fayetteville: University of Arkansas Press, 1997). Commonwealth College was founded in 1925 and, as a result of growing anticommunist sentiment in the Untied States, closed its doors in 1940.

43. Berube, 13–27.

44. According to Daniel, the "Cold War obsession with security often focused on the gay and lesbian community." Specifically in the South, the Johns Committee in Florida, headed by state senator Charley E. Johns, openly linked homosexuals with integrationists and communists. See Daniel, *Lost Revolutions*, 156. Also see James A Schrur, "Closet Crusaders: The John Committee and Homophobia, 1956–1965," *Carryin' On in the Lesbian and Gay South*. For the linking of homosexuality with that of communism during the McCarthy era, see John D'Emilio, *Sexual Politics, Sexual Communities: The Making of a Homosexual Minority in the United States, 1940–1970* (Chicago: University of Chicago Press, 1983), 40–53.

THREE

1. Bill Eddins and Bill Blackshear, "Misunderstanding, Confusion Result as Hazing is Abolished from Orientation," *Profile*, 28 November 1966, final edition. Outside of Arkansas, Harvey Goodwin and his cohorts in the professional drag circuit began fighting new town ordinances that were springing up across the west after the war that banned drag within city limits.

2. Tucker alone had fifty-six different hand-harvested crops. These included seventeen acres of strawberries, fifty acres of cucumbers, seventy acres of sugar cane, a hundred acres of corn and potatoes, and over a thousand acres of rice, Arkansas's most lucrative crop. These crops, not to mention the harvesting of cotton and oats, were first and foremost to make money for the state with hardly any revenues benefiting the prisoners or the prison itself. See Tom Murton and Joe Hyams, *Accomplices to the Crime* (New York: Grove Press, 1969). Tom Murton served as the superintendent of the Arkansas prison system from February 1967 to March 1968.

3. For an excellent detailing of sexuality in the American penal system, see Regina Kunzel, *Criminal Intimacy: Prison and the Uneven History of Modern American Sexuality* (Chicago: University of Chicago Press, 2008).

4. The average age of prisoners at Tucker was twenty-three, with the majority of inmates under twenty years of age. At the time, there was no minimum age of commitment in the Arkansas penal system, and both Tucker and Cummins at this point had boys as young as fourteen. Murton and Hyams, *Accomplices to the Crime*, 90–96. For a study of homosex and homosexuality in American prison from the perspective of the U.S. Justice Department, see Peter C. Buffum, *Homosexuality in Prison* (Los Angeles: University Press of the Pacific, 2004).

5. Murton and Hyams, 90.

6. Joe Wriges, "Held Four Months in State's Jails. He's a Woman, 'Father of 2 Boys,'" *Arkansas Gazette,* 14 December 1961, final edition. For many, homosex and homosexuality was as deviant and threatening as communism. For a detailed look at the linking of homosexuality with socialism and communism, particularly within the federal government, see David K. Johnson, *The Lavender Scare: The Cold War Persecution of Gays and Lesbians in the Federal Government* (Chicago: University of Chicago Press, 2004).

7. The Arkansas criminal code defined bigamy as follows: "Every person having a wife or husband living, who shall marry any other person, whether married or single, except in cases specified in the next section, shall be adjudged guilty of bigamy, and upon convictions shall be imprisoned not less than one year, and be deemed infamous ever afterwards." *Revised Statutes of the State of Arkansas* (Indianapolis, Bobbs-Merrill Co., 47), 1771.

8. "Case of Prisoner Who Turns Out to Be 'She' Up to Courts: Henslee," *Arkansas Democrat,* 14 December 1961, final edition.

9. "Case of Prisoner." The paper reported women's work to be cooking, sewing, and cleaning.

10. Wriges, "Held Four Months."

11. "Prison Learns Real Name of Woman Who Posed as Man," *Arkansas Gazette,* 24 December 1961, final edition.

12. Ibid.

13. *Revised Statutes of the State of Arkansas,* 1771–72.

14. Both stories would have been highly visible. The Van Rippey case appeared on the front page of both state newspapers as well of those of neighboring states, as illustrated by the high school acquaintance recognizing the picture in adjacent Tennessee. The case of Hazel appeared prominently within the memoirs of Tom Murton, who was briefly employed with the Arkansas Department of Corrections. Murton and Hyams, *Accomplices to the Crime,* 90–96.

15. Before the social phenomenon and growing popularity of performing "drag kings," defined by feminist theorist Judith Halberstam as a "female (usually) who dresses up in recognizably male costume and performs theatrically in that costume," and as a person who "makes the exposure of the theatricality of masculinity into the mainstay of her act," there was the theatrical genre of the male impersonator. Halberstam writes that the "male impersonator attempts to produce a plausible performance of maleness as the whole of her act." With this, we can see that Van Rippey would have had a basis from which to perform. The highly visible stage performance of male impersonation would have given Van Rippey inspiration and example from which to build her performance. See Judith Halberstam, *Female Masculinity* (Durham, NC: Duke University Press, 1998), 232–33, 236. Male impersonation would not only have been possible but highly visible on both stage and screen. Two clear examples of this would be Marlene Dietrich's highly sensual performance in *Morocco* (1930) or Greta Garbo's role in *Queen Christina* (1933). For more on the queer heritage in American cinema, see Vito Russo, *The Celluloid Closet: Homosexuality in the Movies* (New York: Harper and Row, 1987), 14–15.

16. See Judith Butler, *Gender Trouble* (New York: Routledge, 1999). Though Butler applies the notion of performance to drag queens and female impersonation only briefly in her text, she is more concerned with the idea of performing the day-to-day

activities surrounding taught gender roles. Van Rippey taught herself these roles as she saw them being performed by men in society and then mimicked them well beyond the point of passing.

17. For an excellent treatment of sexology, see Julia A. Ericksen, *Kiss and Tell: Surveying Sex in the Twentieth Century* (Cambridge, MA: Harvard University Press, 1999). Also noteworthy, Jennifer Terry, *An American Obsession: Science, Medicine, and Homosexuality in Modern Society* (Chicago: University of Chicago Press, 1999).

18. Between 1950 and the late 1960s, hundreds if not thousands of books were printed under the umbrella field of sexology. Listed here are but a few. Anonymous, *My Son, My Lover* (El Cajon, CA: Publishers Export Co., 1965); Dorian Lee, *The Anatomy of a Homosexual* (New York: L. S. Publications Corp., 1965); Martin Hoffman, *The Gay World* (New York: Basic, 1968): Douglas Plummer [pseud.], *Queer People* (New York: Citadel Press, 1965); Irwin Stritch, *The Anal Lovers* (Cleveland, OH: Classics Library, 1968); and Carlson Wade, *Male Homosexuality: A Case Study* (New York: L. S. Publications, 1965).

FOUR

1. The majority of information in this section comes from two oral history interviews with Norman Jones in July and August 2003. Oral histories are vital to this project. However, they can also be problematic. The tale told by Jones follows a clear trajectory of humble beginnings to larger commercial successes, a progressive timeline similar to a Horatio Alger tale of rags to riches.

2. Norman Jones, personal interview, Little Rock, AR, 31 July 2003.

3. Jones, interview.

4. For gay and lesbian life in postwar Washington DC, especially involving gay men cruising city parks and streets, see Brett Beemyn, "A Queer Capital: Race, Class, Gender, and the Changing Social Landscape of Washington's Gay Community, 1940–1955," *Creating a Place for Ourselves: Lesbian, Gay, and Bisexual Community Histories*, ed. Brett Beemyn (New York: Routledge, 1997), 195–200.

5. The USS *Forrestal* was launched on December 11, 1954, and was decommissioned on September 11, 1993. The ship had a crew of just over four thousand.

6. Jones, interview.

7. Jones, interview.

8. During the Second World War, Hot Springs hosted two hospitals geared towards the treatment of venereal disease. Both the U.S. Public Health Service Clinic and nearby Camp Garraday were funded with state and federal dollars and both were open to the public as well as U.S. servicemen. See Edwina Walls, "Hot Springs Waters and Treatment of Venereal Disease: The U.S. Public Health Service Clinic and Camp Garraday," *Journal of the Arkansas Medical Society* 91 (1995): 430–37.

9. John Howard, *Men Like That: A Southern Queer History* (Chicago: University of Chicago Press, 1997), 100.

10. John Leland, *Hip: The History* (New York: HarperCollins, 2004), 348–49. Leland states that "born everywhere, gays and lesbians tend to seek the cover of dense communities, where they are not the only gay person they know." Too often do historians rely on the idea of close queer proximities to establish queer cultures.

Indeed, as seen in the evidence above, gays and lesbians in the rural sought each other out, using distinctive characteristics of the rural, i.e., the departure from the otherwise familiar and the close proximity that often could be coupled with the loss of privacy to their advantage.

11. It is important to mention that not all gay communities operated out of fixed locations such as bars and clubs. With the automobile and the community of friends and partners it helped create, gay and lesbian space was constantly in flux, as friendly space could now shift with greater mobility and ease. See Howard, *Men Like That,* 101. Also see Tim Retzloff, "Cars and Bars: Assembling Gay Men in Postwar Flint: Michigan," *Creating a Place for Ourselves: Lesbian, Gay, and Bisexual Community Histories,* ed. Brett Beemyn (New York: Routledge, 1997), 227–52.

12. John Howard, "Place and Movement in Gay American History: A Case from the Post-War South," *Creating a Place for Ourselves: Lesbian, Gay, and Bisexual Community Histories,* ed. Brett Beemyn (New York: Routledge, 1997), 211–26.

13. The Continental was located next door to The Pit on the corner of Second and Spring streets in downtown Little Rock. This information was provided by a brief and unpublished history of Little Rock gay bars by Jim Norcross. I am grateful to Norman Jones for sharing it with me. Jones, interview.

14. James T. Sears, *Rebels, Rubyfruit, and Rhinestones: Queering Space in the Stonewall South* (Camden: Rutgers University Press, 2001), 80.

15. For a different look at the flight from urban to rural, see Brett William Beemyn, "A Queer Capital: Lesbian, Gay, and Bisexual Life in Washington D.C., 1890–1955." (PhD. Dissertation, University of Iowa, 1997). Here, note the section with the subheading, "Young Pansy, Go North": Attending Drag Balls in and away from the City, 32–35. Again, it is worth noting Tim Retzloff's, "Cars and Bars."

16. Jones, interview. In examining the importance of bar culture in the forming of gay and lesbian communities (and with racism therein) see Elizabeth Lapovsky and Madeline D. Davis, *Boots of Leather, Slippers of Gold: The History of a Lesbian Community* (New York: Penguin, 1993).

17. In many ways black gay males were also excluded from black only spaces during the civil rights movement, a movement that literally preached both masculinity and respectability. Marybeth Hamilton, "Sexual politics and African American Music; or, Placing Little Richard in History," *History Workshop Journal* 46 (1998):161–76.

18. When I speak of *amateur* versus *professional,* this usually refers to paid versus unpaid or career versus noncareer performances.

19. Jones, interview. Of course these are not the judge's words exactly, only what Jones remembers him saying almost thirty years later.

20. "Pageant Draws KKK Protest," *Metro Times,* 1 October 1981, final edition. The *Metro Times* was the gay community newspaper for the Dallas, Texas, metro area.

21. Deborah Gates, "Anti-gays Will Take Pictures," *The Charlotte Observer.* This article was taken from Norman Jones's personal scrapbook. Therefore, no section or page number can be provided.

22. Harvey Goodwin to Ricky Renee, July 27, 1990, Harvey Goodwin Collection, A-115, series 1, subseries 16, box 1, file 15, University of Arkansas at Little Rock, Archives and Special Collections.

23. To what degree this may or may not have changed is an issue for debate. Martin Duberman describes the Stonewall Inn riots as "the emblematic event in

modern gay and lesbian history." However, as Scott Bravmann illustrates, the event can hardly be looked upon by the mainstream gay and lesbian movement as such. Bravmann is critical of Duberman for glazing over key social differences in the demographic mak-up of the Stonewall rioters. Rioters, Bravmann notes, were mainly drag queens, hustlers, and gays and lesbians of color. See Scott Bravmann, *Queer Fictions of the Past: History, Culture, Difference* (Cambridge: Cambridge University Press, 1997). Also see Martin Duberman, *Stonewall* (New York: Dutton, 1993).

FIVE

1. Mark Doty, *My Alexandria: Poems by Mark Doty* (Chicago: University of Illinois Press, 1992), 18–20. Mark Doty is a queer poet writing on themes of post-AIDS society, gender, and the city.

2. David Lee, personal interview, Maumelle, AR, 11 August 2003.

3. Lee, interview.

4. Esther Newton, *Mother Camp: Female Impersonators in America* (Chicago: University of Chicago Press, 1972), 97–111.

5. For AIDS and its impact on southern cities, as well as its role is forging a cohesive gay community, see Meredith Raimondo, "Dateline Atlanta: Place and Social Construction of AIDS," *Carryin' On in the Lesbian and Gay South*, 331–69.

6. Howard, *Men Like That*, 93.

7. Donna Jo Smith, "Queering the South: Constructions of Southern / Queer Identity," *Carryin' On in the Lesbian and Gay South*, 370–85.

8. Ibid., 381.

9. Simon Watney, "AIDS and the Politics of Queer Diaspora," *Negotiating Lesbian and Gay Subjects,* eds. M. Dorenkamp and R. Henke (New York: New York University Press, 1995), 6.

10. *Camp* as a term in the queer community can be difficult to define. I find it best to rely on queer director and icon in his own right John Waters and his rather simple and succinct definition: *camp* is the tragically ludicrous, or the ludicrously tragic. Eve Kosofsky Sedgwick offers perhaps the best treatment of *camp* in terms of audience and viewer recognitions. She writes, "I think it may be true that . . . the typifying gesture of camp is really something amazingly simple: the moment at which a consumer of culture makes the wild surmise, 'What if whoever made this was gay too?' Unlike kitsch-attribution, then, camp-recognition doesn't ask, 'What kind of debased creature could possibly be the right audience of this spectacle?' Instead, it says *what if:* what if the right audience for this were exactly *me?"* Furthermore, according to Sedgwick, it would also depend on others whom you did not know or recognize (you fellow audience members in this case) seeing the performance from the same or similar queer angles as you. Eve Kosofsky Sedgwick, *Epistemology of the Closet* (New York: Penguin, 1990), 154–57. Newton offers this theatrical definition: "*Camp* is style. . . . Importance tends to shift from what a thing *is* to how it *looks,* from *what* is done to *how* it works." For Newton *camp* is also defined by the presence of a performer and an audience and also by the "being as playing a role" and "life as theatre." See Newton, *Mother Camp,* 107. Also, for a detailed treatment of camp and the "work as play" paradigm, consult Matthew Tinkcom, *Working Like a Homosexual: Camp, Capital, Cinema*

(Durham, NC: Duke University Press, 2002), 2, 76. Borrowing on Marxist themes of work and identity, Tinkcom writes that work should regarded as "both the open-ended case, the sense of camp as a form of queer labor that has shaped a way of knowing capital in its lived dimensions with production by queer male intellectuals."

11. A drag queen had to keep performing to be able to keep performing, or find other work to subsidize the high cost of the pageant circuit. To participate in the Miss Gay America Pageant in the year that David Lee did, the costs were considerable. A breakdown: evening gown: $2,000–$3,000, shoes: $50, creative costume: $700, five back-up dancers and their costumes: $300, decorations for talent set: $600, costume for talent number: $700, nails and hair: $400, travel to and from pageant events and host cities, $750. Suzi Parker, *Sex in the South: Unbuckling the Bible Belt* (New York: Justin, Charles and Co., 2003), 49.

12. Martin F. Manalansan IV, *Global Divas: Filipino Gay Men in the Diaspora* (Durham: Duke University Press, 2004) 3, 5.

13. See Newton, *Mother Camp,* 102.

14. While doing the research for this chapter during the summer of 2004, I searched for sometime for a womanless wedding production in the state of Arkansas. They were few and far between. Oddly, and perhaps altogether appropriately, I was able to find a production being performed at Little Rock area nursing home by its inhabitants. I did not attend.

15. Jere Real, "Boys Will Be Girls,' *Southern Exposure* (Fall 1988): 30.

16. "Towering Inferno: Fonda Le Femme," *Girl Talk* 5, no. 5: 44.

17. Ibid.

SIX

1. The law is under Georgia Code Annotated 16–6-2 (a)-(b) (Supp. 1997). The Georgia statute reads: "A Person commits sodomy when he performs or submits to any sexual act involving the sex organs of one person and the mouth or anus of another. B) A person convicted of the offense of sodomy should be punished by imprisonment for not less than one nor more than twenty years."

2. Dudley Clendinen and Adam Nagourney, *Out for Good: The Struggle to Build a Gay Rights Movement in America* (New York: Simon and Schuster, 1999), 536–37.

3. Clendinen and Nagourney, *Out for Good,* 537.

4. "High Court Upholds Georgia Sodomy Law," *Arkansas Democrat,* 1 July 1986, final edition.

5. *Bowers v. Hardwick,* 190. Chief Justice Warren Burger, and Justices Lewis F. Powell, William H. Rehnquist, and Sandra Day O'Connor concurred. Justice Harry Blackmun wrote the dissenting opinion and was joined by Justices William J. Brennan, Thurgood Marshall, and John Paul Stevens.

6. *Bowers v. Hardwick,* 191.

7. Ibid., 197.

8. *Bowers v. Hardwick,* 197.

9. William Raspberry, "Enforcement of Sodomy Law Difficult," *Arkansas Democrat,* 8 July 1986, final edition.

10. "The Sodomy Ruling," *Arkansas Democrat,* 17 July 1986, final edition.

11. Ark. Code Ann. 5–14–122.

12. For a complete list of state sodomy laws, consult Shirley Wiegand and Sara Farr, *Part of the Moving Stream: State Constitutional Law, Sodomy, and Beyond* (Louisville: Harper, 1993). The following excerpt was compiled courtesy of the Lambda Legal Defense Fund of New York. Alabama: "deviate sexual intercourse . . . between persons not married to each other" (ALA. Code 13A-6–65 [a] [3], 60–62 [1994]); Arizona: "the infamous crime against nature with an adult," "in any manner, any lewd or lascivious act with a male or female adult" (ARIZ. REV. STAT. ANN. 13–1411, 1412 [1989]); Massachusetts: "the abominable and detestable crime against nature" (ARIZ. REV. STAT. ANN. 13–1411, 1412 [1989]).

13. In his groundbreaking monograph, *The History of Sexuality,* philosopher Michel Foucault convincingly argues this notion. Michel Foucault, *The History of Sexuality: An Introduction,* (New York: Random, 1990), 1:43, 1:48.

14. Michel Foucault, *The History of Sexuality: The Use of Pleasure,* (New York: Random, 1990), 2:49–51. For a complete analysis of the theories and philosophies of Michel Foucault consult the biography *The Passion of Michel Foucault* (New York: Simon & Schuster, 1993) by James Miller. Also see *Saint Foucault* (New York: Oxford University Press, 1995) by David Halperin.

15. Walter Barnett, *Sexual Freedom and the Constitution: An Inquiry into the Constitutionality of Repressive Sex Laws* (Albuquerque: University of New Mexico Press, 1973), 8–9.

16. Barnett, *Sexual Freedom and the Constitution,* 9.

17. At the University of Arkansas, Fayetteville, for example, in 1983 the student senate denied funding for a gay and lesbian student group seeking money for a series of films and lectures promoting tolerance of homosexuality. Although the gay and lesbian student group met all the criteria for funding, the student senate insisted that it could not fund a group or program that promoted an illegal act. *Northwest Arkansas Times* (Fayetteville), 31 March 1983.

18. Foucault, *The History of Sexuality,* 1:83. Though *The History of Sexuality* deals more with the sexual sciences than with law in general, given Foucault's argument about the relationship between sex and power, unlike law, power can stem from innumerable positions. While Foucault allows that this appearance of power can be embodied in the state apparatus of the law, these were to Foucault simply the *terminal* forms that power can take. With this said, the sodomy law is only a terminal form of exercised state power, the end product of social and legal discourse. However, the discrimination that can come about in society as a result of the law can provide for even greater repercussions and, perhaps, opportunity. Given the argument, we see that power transcends into written law, where it can be applied throughout society. But taken one step further, though Foucault would deem sodomy statutes as "terminal power," power creates the law, and, in turn, power stems from the law. Barnett, *Sexual Freedom and the Consititution,* 9.

19. For many gay men and lesbians in the United States, sodomy laws represent a clear and present danger beyond the possibility of prosecution for the crime. Though many consider the statutes to be antiquated legal codes that still exist, these laws are frequently used to discriminate between gays and lesbians. Numerous pre–*Lawrence v. Texas* examples exists (here provided by the Lamba Legal Defense Fund in New York.) In Alabama, the sodomy law was used to deny funding to a gay-and-lesbian student

group at state-funded universities. Antigay groups noted in their protest that gay student organizations would be using state funds to promote violation of state law. In the state of Minnesota, licensing requirements for state professionals, including public school teachers, include forbidding professionals from engaging in illegal activity. As long as the sodomy law exists, claims the American Civil Liberties Union, jobs held by gays and lesbians remain in jeopardy. In Virginia, a number of parenting cases have hinged on the state sodomy law. Gay and lesbian parents have often lost the right to custody of their children because the state sodomy law in Virginia denotes them as criminals.

SEVEN

1. *Strum v. State,* 168 Ark. 1012, *The Supreme Court of Arkansas* (1925).
2. Ibid., 2.
3. Ibid., 2.
4. *Smith v. State,* 150 Ark. 265, *The Supreme Court of Arkansas* (1921).
5. Ibid, 3.
6. *Smith v. State,* 3. This quotation is from *Bishop's Criminal Law,* an important criminal procedure treatise of the time.
7. Ibid., 3. *Lambertson,* 5 Parker CR 200.
8. *Acts of Arkansas 1838,* 121, "An Act Modifying the Penal Code to Correspond with the Establishment of the State Penitentiary," enacted 17 December 1838.
9. Fixing the penalty as the same is important given Arkansas's free black population, 608 in 1850. The free blacks of antebellum Arkansas faced harsh legal restrictions and deep animosity. Consequently, their numbers never really grew to match that of their neighbors (Louisiana had roughly 19,000) though their presence would remain highly visible. U.S. Bureau of the Census, *Census of 1850 (Population),* 535. Also see Orville Taylor, *Negro Slavery in Arkansas* (Fayetteville, University of Arkansas Press, 1958), 19, 244, 245, 252.
10. *Revised Statutes of the State of Arkansas,* (Little Rock: E. H. English, 1848).
11. *A Digest of the Statutes of Arkansas Embracing All Law of a General and Permanent Character in Force at the Close of the Session of the General Assembly of One Thousand Eight Hundred and Seventy-Three* (Little Rock: Little Rock Printing and Publishing Company, 1874), 1107–8.
12. See *Debates and Proceedings of the Convention which Assembles at Little Rock, January 7th, 1868, Under the Provisions of the Act of Congress of March 23rd and July 19th, 1867, Supplementary Thereto, to Form a Constitution for the State of Arkansas* (Little Rock, 1868), 769–70. Joseph M. St. Hilaine, "The Negro Delegates in the Arkansas Constitutional Convention of 1868: A Group Profile," *Arkansas Historical Quarterly* 23 (Spring 1974): 30–69. Also helpful, Willard Gatewood Jr., "Negro Legislators in Arkansas, 1891: A Document," *Arkansas Historical Quarterly* 21 (Autumn 1972): 220–33. Richard L. Hume, "The 'Black and Tan' Constitutional Conventions of 1867 and 1869 in Ten Former Confederate States: A Study of Their Membership" (dissertation, University of Washington, 1969), 269–70.
13. This too would explain the absence of both political debate and legislative documents.

14. In June 1949 John William Campbell of Fayetteville, Arkansas, was found guilty of sodomy and eventually found insane for having sexual relations with a "negro wench" named Opal Carr. The court considered their behavior as "not plum right," and they both spent time within the state prison system. For a concise treatment of miscegenation and social conditions in the South, see Charles Robinson, *Dangerous Liaisons: Sex and Love in a Segregated South* (Fayetteville: University of Arkansas, 2003).

15. Foucault, *The History of Sexuality*, 1:8.

EIGHT

1. The song was titled "Lest We Forget" and goes on to warn the voter that if he or she splits the vote between the Democratic lieutenant governor and the Republican Rockefeller, they would also be splitting their salaries, as a wealthy Rockefeller governor would raise taxes and would be unsympathetic towards poor Arkansans. "Lest We Forget," Jim Johnson Papers, box 13, file 1, Arkansas History Commission, Little Rock.

2. Ernie Dumas, telephone interview, 2 November 2005. Ernie Dumas covered the Rockefeller campaign for the *Arkansas Gazette.*

3. Diane D. Blair and Jay Barth, *Arkansas Politics and Government* (Lincoln: University of Nebraska Press, 2005), 67–68. The Blair and Barth book remains the best, most complete work concerning Arkansas politics.

4. John Ward, telephone interview, 16 November 2005. During the 1966 campaign, John Ward served as Rockefeller's campaign manager. He also went on to publish two Rockefeller biographies, the most notable being John L. Ward, *The Arkansas Rockefeller* (Baton Rouge: Louisiana State University Press, 1978). In regards to the "prissy sissy" accusations, see Joe Conason and Gene Lyons, *The Hunting of the President: The Ten-Year Campaign to Destroy Bill and Hillary Clinton* (New York: St. Martin's Press, 2000), 67–68. I remain grateful to Gene Lyons and Jay Barth for pointing out these avenues of research to me.

5. "Rockefeller's Right-hand Man," *Arkansas Faith*, (November 1955), Jim Johnson Papers, box 2, file 22, Arkansas History Commission: 11.

6. "The Shocking Facts about Winthrop Rockefeller," Jim Johnson Papers, box 14, file 20, Arkansas History Commission. The fact that Rockefeller was a strong supporter of the Urban League during his New York years was one that he would have to continually explain during his ventures in Arkansas politics. See Ward, *The Arkansas Rockefeller*, 161. The pictures of Rockefeller standing next to the nearly nude valentine originally appeared in *Life* magazine ("Life Goes to a Ball in Harlem," 28 February 1949.)

7. All attempts to find the works cited by "Shocking Facts about Winthrop Rockefeller" proved unsuccessful.

8. Ibid.

9. *Arkansas Faith* (February 1956): back cover. *Arkansas Faith* (November 1955): 21. For more on the sexually charged rhetoric of race and the manipulated fears of rape, see ibid.: 66.

10. Jim Johnson, telephone interview, 2 November 2005. The fact that Rockefeller

never sought to comment on the charges publicly or privately during the campaign was expressed by John Ward. Ward, interview.

11. Gayle S. Rubin, "Thinking Sex: Notes for a Radical Theory of the Politics of Sexuality," *The Lesbian and Gay Studies Reader*, eds. Henry Abelove, Michele Aina Barale, and David M. Halperin (New York: Routledge, 1993), 4. George Chauncey, *Gay New York: Gender, Urban Culture and the Making of the Gay Male World, 1890–1940* (New York: BasicBooks, 1994), 10–11. D'Emilio, *Sexual Politics, Sexual Communities*, 130. D'Emilio writes that "during the 1960s a noticeable shift took place in both the sheer quantity of discourse about homosexuality and lesbianism and the social interpretation of the phenomenon."

12. Not only would the women's rights and the post-Stonewall gay rights movements go on to borrow tactics and draw inspiration from black victories in their struggles for gender and queer equality, the civil rights movement had been quite sexual from the beginning. Prominent black leaders involved with the movement had to preach and defend their own manhood and masculinity against a constant barrage of unscrupulous attacks aimed at discrediting them as community men. Also, some of the more prominent figures at the forefront of the struggle were in fact prominent queers. The most notable of these were Aaron Henry and Bayard Rustin. See John D'Emilio, *Lost Prophet: The Life and Times of Bayard Rustin* (New York: Free Press, 2003); Bayard Rustin et al., *Time on Two Crosses: The Collected Writings of Bayard Rustin* (New York: Cleis Press, 2003). For Aaron Henry, see Howard, *Men Like That*, 158–66, 171–73. For an excellent treatment of the civil rights movement combining race politics and issues of manhood and masculinity, see Steve Estes, *I Am a Man! Race, Manhood, and the Civil Rights Movement* (Chapel Hill: University of North Carolina Press, 2005). On Henry, Rustin, and issues of homosexuality within the movement, see ibid., 68–69, 119, 162–63.

NINE

1. This letter was sent directly to Governor Pryor's office and is now included in the governor's unprocessed gubernatorial papers (Special Collections, University of Arkansas Libraries, Fayetteville.)

2. "Deadline Nears on Sex Bill Veto; Inquiries Made," *Arkansas Gazette*, 28 March 1977, final edition.

3. This letter was dated March 4, 1977, and was signed by Berkes. Along with his correspondence, Berkes included the two executive orders of which he spoke. The first order included gay and lesbian Pennsylvanians in the state civil rights legislation, protecting them from discrimination in employment and housing within the state. The second order established the Governor's Council for Sexual Minorities. This letter is included in Governor Pryor's unprocessed gubernatorial papers (Special Collections, University of Arkansas Libraries, Fayetteville.)

4. Ibid. For a detailed look at queer life in Philadelphia, Pennsylvania, see Mark Stein, *City of Sisterly and Brotherly Loves: Lesbian and Gay Philadelphia, 1945–1972* (Chicago: University of Chicago Press, 2000).

5. This letter was dated March 14, 1977, and was signed by Gretchen Kafoury, state representative of Oregon's thirteenth district. Kafoury wrote that she "cannot in

words express my dismay at this type of legislation." This letter is included in Governor Pyror's unprocessed gubernatorial papers (Special Collections, University of Arkansas Libraries, Fayetteville.)

6. Pryor Papers, Special Collections, University of Arkansas.

7. Rafael Guzman, "1976 Criminal Code: General Principles," *Arkansas Law Review* 30 (1976): 111–13. Guzman, a law professor at the University of Arkansas, Fayetteville, served as a member of the Arkansas Criminal Code Revision Commission. Though the institute did not have any formal control over legislative decisions, its recommendations carried a great deal of weight. While only one state, Illinois, adopted the code as written, many states, including Arkansas, used it as a guide in reforming their criminal statutes. David Frum, *How We Got Here: The 70's, the Decade That Brought You Modern Life (For Better or Worse)* (New York: Basic, 2000), 205–6.

8. Guzman, "1976 Criminal Code: General Principles," 111–13. The most notable and recognizable revision came in legal classification. Each felony was placed in one of four classifications: A, B, C, and D. Each misdemeanor was placed in one of three classifications: A, B, and C. For a complete list of revision as adopted by the legislature, consult the *Arkansas Statutes Annotated,* 41–901–1101 (Criminal Code of 1976).

9. George Bentley, "New Justice Turns Tables for Novel Ruling," *Arkansas Gazette,* 26 March, 1976, final edition.

10. The new criminal code defined public sexual indecency as such: "A person commits public sexual indecency if he engages in any of the following acts in a public place or public view: (a) an act of sexual intercourse; (b) an act of deviant sexual activity; or (c) an act of sexual conduct." George Bentley, "New Code Changes Statutes," *Arkansas Gazette,* 26 March 1976, final edition.

11. Ibid., 6.

12. George Bentley, "Bentley Fears Jail 'Gay Bar,'" *Arkansas Gazette,* 26 March 1976, final edition.

13. Judge Kirby, in his support of the lower court's decision, noted that Arkansas's new criminal code defines *public place* as a "public or privately owned place to which the public or substantial numbers of the public have access." The new criminal code defines *public view* as "observable or likely to be observed by a person in a public space." "Jail Not Public Place, Charges Dismissed," *Arkansas Gazette,* 25 June 1976, final edition.

14. *State of Arkansas v. James R. Black,* 260 Ark. 864, *The Supreme Court of Arkansas* (1977), 1. The opinion was written and presented by Chief Justice Carleton Harris.

15. Pryor Papers, Special Collections, University of Arkansas. The Independence Baptist Association was an organization of Baptist congregations from Independence County, Arkansas. See W. Brock Thompson, "A Crime Unfit to Be Named: Arkansas and Sodomy," *Arkansas Historical Quarterly* 61 (Autumn 2002).

16. Jim Ranchino, "The Arkansas of the '70s: The Good Ole Boy Ain't Whut He Used to Be," *Arkansas Times,* September 1977, 40.

17. "Cohabitation Tax, Other Bills Aimed at 'Deviate Acts,'" *Arkansas Gazette,* 23 January 1977, final edition.

18. Ibid. Speaking of cohabiting couples, Tyer declared, "They may have a desire for each other, physically and maybe even spiritually, but they don't want to conform. This country was built on conformity."

19. Ibid.

20. "Sodomy Bill Amended to Define Restrictions; House Passage Urged," *Arkansas Gazette,* 26 January 1977, final edition.

21. Ibid.

22. Ibid.

23. Bill Clinton, *My Life* (Knopf: New York, 2004), 245–46. The only representatives to vote against the bill in the house were Jodie Mahoney of El Dorado and Henry Wilkins of Pine Bluff. Ted Holder, personal interview, Little Rock, AR, 23 September 2001.

24. "House Supports Abortion Foes With Voice Vote," *Arkansas Gazette,* 11 February 1977, final edition.

25. "Senate Passes Measures in Drive to Adjourn," *Arkansas Gazette,* 17 March 1977, final edition. Speaking of the bill, Earnhart added that it was "aimed at weirdos and queers who live in a fairyland world and are trying to wreck traditional family life." *The Advocate,* April 1977, 7.

26. For a complete narrative concerning Stancil's sodomy statute, see W. Brock Thompson, "A Crime Unfit to Be Named: Arkansas and Sodomy," *Arkansas Historical Quarterly* 61 (Autumn 2002).

27. Joyce Murdoch and Deb Price, *Courting Justice: Gay Men and Lesbians v. the Supreme Court* (New York: Basic, 2001),175.

28. It is important to look beyond Jim Crow legislation, though that of course remains important. Although traditional scholars have typically shied away from the issues of sex and sexuality while dealing with civil rights and the pre–civil rights eras, recent scholarship has connected sodomy with such measures as miscegenation laws in the American South. See Robinson, *Dangerous Liaisons.*

29. Gayle S. Rubin, "Notes for a Radical Theory of the Politics of Sexuality," *The Lesbian and Gay Studies Reader,* eds. Henry Abelove, Michele Aina Barale, and David M. Halperin (New York: Routledge, 1993), 9. Gayle S. Rubin, "Thinking Sex," 35. Though Rubin recognizes the difficulties in establishing a coherent body of radical thought about sex, taking into account the extremely fluid nature of sex and sexuality across time, she sees the almost urgent need for the establishing of a descriptive and conceptual framework for thinking about sex in all its contexts in order to address the need for greater social change. Rubin states that any "radical theory of sex must identify, describe, explain, and denounce erotic injustice and sexual oppression."

30. Perhaps one of the best works to come out recently on sex and sexuality, specifically bestiality, remains Jens Rydstom's *Sinners and Citizens: Bestiality and Homosexuality in Sweden, 1880–1950* (Chicago: University of Chicago Press, 2003), 77–78, 211–33.

31. John Howard, *Men Like That: A Southern Queer History* (Chicago: University of Chicago Press, 1997), 34–36.

32. Lawrence Yancey, telephone interview, 31 January 2002. In an interview Pryor claimed he had no recollection of signing the sodomy bill into law; he declined to comment beyond that. David Pryor, telephone interview, 31 January 2002.

33. Yancey, interview.

34. "Resolution Draws Call from Aide," *Arkansas Gazette,* 30 March 1977, final edition.

35. Dudley Clendinen and Adam Nagourney, *Out for Good: The Struggle to Build a Gay Rights Movement in America* (New York: Simon & Schuster, 1999), 291–338.

36. Tina Fetner, "Working Anita Bryant: The Impact of Christian Anti-Gay Activism on the Lesbian and Gay Movement's Claims," *Social Problems* 48 (2001): 411. The quotation was taken from a direct-mail fundraising letter from Bryant's *Save the Children Campaign,* which existed from 1977 until 1979. The emphasis is in the original.

37. Cleninden and Nagourney, *Out for Good,* 299.

38. Ross Dennis, "We Hold These Truths to be Self Evident . . . ," *Lincoln Ledger* (Star City, AR), 5 January 1978, final edition; Thomas Roark, "I Want to Clear Things Up," *Lincoln Ledger,* 12 January 1978, final edition; Ross Dennis, "An Open Letter to the Readers," *Lincoln Ledger,* 12 January 1978, final edition; Doug Smith, "Orange-juice Horseshoe is Dropped Rapidly," *Arkansas Gazette,* 19 January 1978, final edition.

39. Clendinen and Nagourney, *Out for Good,* 329.

40. "She's Prolife, Not 'Antigay,' Singer Asserts" *Arkansas Gazette,* 22 October 1978, final edition.

TEN

1. Laud Humphreys, "Tearoom Trade: Impersonal Sex in Public Places," *Public Sex/Gay Space,* ed. William L. Leap (New York: Columbia University Press, 1999), 30. Also see Laud Humphreys, *Tearoom Trade: Impersonal Sex in Public Places* (New York: Aldine de Gruyter, 1975), 2–3. Some have criticized both Humphreys's use of language and his seemingly unorthodox research methods, namely his betrayal of research subject anonymity and personal involvement in the acts he was attempting to document. Recently, queer theorists and historians of sex and sexuality have argued its seminal value. See Peter M. Nardi, "Reclaiming the Importance of Laud Humphreys's 'Tearoom Trade: Impersonal Sex in Public Places,'" *Public Sex/Gay Space,* 23–28.

2. Humphreys, "Tearoom Trade," 30–31. Also see John Howard, "The Library, the Park, and the Pervert: Public Space and Homosexual Encounter in Post-World War II Atlanta," *Carryin' On in the Lesbian and Gay South,* 107–31.

3. Ort, Randal (director of public affairs, Arkansas Highway and Transportation Department), personal interview, Little Rock, AR, 20 June 2003. The Morgan rest area offered two dozen private picnic areas as well as parking for recreational vehicles. The cost of the rest stop and its construction date are provided in Dennis Merida (acting division administrator) to Maurice Smith (director of highways and transportation), 28 September 1992, Arkansas State Highway Commission Archives, Little Rock.

4. According to Humphreys, a *cruiser* is someone who seeks impersonal sex without further emotional involvement. Humphreys, *Tearoom Trade,* 2. For specific cruising practices in urban spaces, see Mark Turner, *Backward Glances: Cruising Queer Streets in London and New York* (London: Reaktion Books, 2003).

5. Howard, Robert, personal interview, Little Rock, AR, 15 June 2003.

6. Regarding loitering, the Arkansas criminal code reads "(A) A person commits the offense of loitering if he: (5) Lingers of remains in a public place for the purpose of engaging or soliciting another person to engage in prostitution or deviant sexual activity. (B) Among the circumstances that may be considered in determining whether a person is loitering are that the person: (1) Takes flight upon the appearance of a law enforcement officer; or (2) Refuses to identify himself; or (3) Manifestly endeavors to conceal himself or any object." Loitering is a class C misdemeanor (Ark Code Ann.

5–17–213.)

7. Mike Arbanas, "Snyder's Bills Stirs Opposition," *Arkansas Gazette,* 18 January 1991, final edition. The proposed revision of the sodomy statute was one of three bills proposed by Snyder that day.

8. "Snyder's Bills Stirs Opposition," 1.

9. Mark Oswald, "Committee Rejects Sodomy Law Repeal," *Arkansas Gazette,* 31 January 1991, final edition.

10. Ibid.

11. Ibid.

12. Ibid. All efforts to locate a *Gay Community News* proved unsuccessful.

13. Ibid.

14. Vic Snyder, personal interview, Little Rock, AR, 11 March 2002. During his tenure as state senator, Snyder would try twice more, in 1993 and 1995, to amend or repeal the sodomy statute. Both would prove unsuccessful.

15. Oswald, "Committee Rejects Sodomy Law Repeal.".

16. After Snyder's attempt at modifying the sodomy bill, the *Arkansas Democrat-Gazette* offered his "political obituary." Editorialist John Brummett noted that Snyder's Senate Bill 125 illustrated that Snyder "was the kind of impractical liberal more suitable for San Francisco than Arkansas." Brummett was sure that Snyder would not survive the next election. Eric Camp, "'Snyder to Run Unopposed: Survives Sodomy Repeal Effort," *Triangle Rising,* May 1992, final edition. *Triangle Rising* is the official newspaper of the Arkansas Gay and Lesbian Task Force. Snyder, in fact, was without an opponent for his state Senate seat in the next election. In reference to Brummett's remarks, Snyder noted that "the reports of his political death were greatly exaggerated." Snyder, interview.

17. Howard, interview.

18. John Hoogesteger, "Deputies Acting to Remove Gays from Rest Area," *Arkansas Gazette,* 2 February 1991, final edition.

19. Hoogesteger, "Deputies Acting to Remove Gays from Rest Stop."

20. Peggy Harris, "Sodomy Arrests not Tied to Debate," *Arkansas Gazette,* 7 February 1991, final edition.

21. Valerie Smith, "I-40 Sodomy Arrest Protested," *Arkansas Gazette,* 17 February 1991, final ed., sec A: 2.

22. Ibid.

23. Ibid.

24. Jerry Dean, "14 Sentenced for Sex-Related Activity," *Arkansas Gazette* 20 Mar. 1991, final ed., sec. B: 2.

25. For a detailed account of the use of hidden cameras in public restrooms and the issues surrounding them, see Humphreys, *Tearoom Trade,* 84–86.

26. Peggy Harris, "Sheriff's Office Defends Use of Camera," *Arkansas Gazette* 19 April 1991, final ed., sec B: 1.

27. Peggy Harris, "Attorney Questions Using Rest-Stop Camera," *Arkansas Gazette* 20 April 1991, final ed., sec B: 4.

28. Ibid.

29. Cheryl Waldrip, "ACLU Call Camera in Rest Stop Restroom 'Outrageous,' Bigoted," *Arkansas Gazette* 23 April, 1991, final ed., sec B: 3.

30. "ACLU Calls Cameras in Rest Stop Restrooms 'Outrageous,' Bigoted," 3.

31. Ibid.

32. "No Cameras in the Restrooms," *Arkansas Gazette,* 24 April 1991, final edition.

33. Ibid.

34. Ibid.

35. Dennis L. Merida (facilities management, Arkansas Highway Department) to James C. Williams (acting division administrator, Office of Engineering and Operations), 20 October 1992, Arkansas State Highway and Transportation Archives, Little Rock. The *American* with Disabilities Act of 1990 (ADA) was introduced by Senator Tom Harkins of Iowa and Representative Tony Coelho of California. The act legally freed those with disabilities from discrimination that might accompany their impairments. Section 504 of the ADA guaranteed reasonable accommodation and access to buildings and facilities to those with disabilities. For a detailed discussion of the ADA and its social impact, see Ruth O'Brien, *Crippled Justice: The History of Modern Disability Policy in the Workplace* (Chicago: University of Chicago Press, 2001).

36. Maintenance reports found at the Arkansas Highway Department archives mention nothing of graffiti or frequent repainting. In fact, in one inspection on August 8, 1991, Joseph Young of the highway department gave satisfactory ratings to the rest area and its facilities in all thirty-one categories. In his comments, Young stated that "more attention is needed for clean up of cigarette butts. Otherwise, the park area is well maintained."

37. The traffic through the rest area was far less than ten thousand a day. During the summer months, the rest area averaged 1,025 visitors a day on the weekend and 978 during the weekday, far less than other rest areas in the state. Many motorists simply waited until Little Rock, which offered more services than the Morgan rest area. *Special Traffic Request,* Arkansas Highway Department.

38. John Haman, "State Worker Says Gays Cause Damage to I-40 Rest Area," *Arkansas Democrat,* 19 February 1991, final edition.

39. Permission from the Federal Highway Department was necessary in that federal funding was responsible for the construction of the rest area.

40. Rachel O'Neal, "Senate Panel Rejects Effort to Repeal Sodomy Law," *Arkansas Democrat-Gazette,* 18 March 1993, final edition. At the Arkansas Gay Pride Banquet on June 26, 1993, Senator Mike Everett was awarded the Phoenix Award from the Arkansas Lesbian and Gay Task Force for his efforts on behalf of lesbians and gays in Arkansas. His son, Michael Everett, accepted the award in his father's stead. Mike Everett, personal interview, Marked Tree, AR, 5 October 2002.

41. Seth Blomely, "Seven Sue to Void State Sodomy Law," *Arkansas Democrat-Gazette,* 29 January 1998, final edition. Although many states were successful in toppling their sodomy laws through legislative means, many removed their sodomy laws from the books by providing a court challenge questioning the constitutionality of the law. Kentucky was first, seeing its sodomy law declared unconstitutional in 1992, followed by Tennessee in 1996, Montana in 1997, Georgia in 1998, and Maryland in 1999.

42. *Jegley v. Picado et al.,* 2002 Ark. LEXIS 401.

43. Traci Shurley, "Justices Strike Down Sodomy Law," *Arkansas Democrat-Gazette,* 5 July 2002, final edition.

44. Ibid.

45. *Lawrence et al. v. Texas,* 539 U.S. 558 (2003). Justice Kennedy wrote for the

majority opinion and was joined by Justices John Paul Stevens, David Souter, Ruth Bader Ginsberg, and Steven Breyer. Justice Antonin Scalia wrote the dissenting opinion and was joined by Chief Justice William Rehnquist and Justice Clarence Thomas. In regards to the amicus brief filed by historians, those who contributed were George Chauncey, Nancy F. Scott, John D'Emilio, Estelle B. Freedman, Thomas C. Holt, John Howard, Lynn Hunt, Mark D. Jordan, Elizabeth Lapovsky Kennedy, and Linda P. Kerber.

ELEVEN

1. For a detailed theoretical look at the question of public versus private space, see George Chauncey, *Gay New York: Gender, Urban Culture, and the Making of the Gay Male World, 1890–1940* (New York: Basic, 1994), 179–206.

2. Pulaski County had the highest rate by far. The county with the second highest was Washington County with thirty-one cases, followed by Jefferson County with sixteen. The *Gazette* gave two explanations for the high rate of AIDS cases in Pulaski County. The first, of course, is that Pulaski County is the most densely populated area of the state, with a population of approximately 300,000 in 1990. The second reason is that Little Rock and Pulaski County offered affordable and often times reduced-charge services from the University of Arkansas for Medical Sciences hospital and other charitable Christian hospitals such as St. Vincents, offering care to those that otherwise would not be able to afford it. Pheobe Wall Howard, "AIDS Patients Have Haven," *Arkansas Gazette,* 9 July 1990, final edition.

3. In connecting police raids and crackdowns on prostitution and vice with public fears of disease epidemics, see Howard, *The Library, the Park, and the Pervert,* 118–19. For health department fears concerning gay cruising see, Humphreys, *Tearoom Trade,* 84, 99–101. For a complete and highly useful social history of venereal disease, see Allan M. Brandt, *No Magic Bullet: A Social History of Venereal Disease in the United States since 1880* (Oxford: Oxford University Press, 1987).

4. Meredith Raimondo, "Dateline Atlanta: Place and the Social Construction of AIDS," *Carryin' On in the Lesbian and Gay South,* 331–69. At the time of the rather notorious U.S. Supreme Court ruling in *Bowers v. Hardwick* some were quicker to link sodomy laws to the AIDS epidemic (344–46).

5. "Weatherman Arrested Between Newscast," *The George-Ann* (Georgia Southern University, Statesboro), 16 April 1996, final edition. Jan Cottingham, "Suicide Prompts Protest to *Democrat-Gazette,*" *Arkansas Times,* 20 February 1998, final edition.

6. Judge David Hale was later indicted for embezzlement and fraud. He was removed from the bench in 1992 and served seven months in a federal penitentiary.

7. Neil Bartlett, *Who Was That Man? A Present of Oscar Wilde* (London: Serpent's Tail, 1988), xx.

8. Bartlett, *Who Was That Man?,* 223.

9. Social theorist Scott Bravmann notes that "the importance of history to gay men and lesbians goes beyond the lessons to be learned from the events of the past to include the meanings generated through retellings of those events and the agency those meanings carry in the present." He adds that "lesbians and gay historical representations—queer fictions of the past—help construct, maintain, and contest identi-

ties—queer fictions of the present." Scott Bravmann, *Queer Fictions of the Past: History, Culture, and Difference* (Cambridge: Cambridge University Press, 1997), 4.

TWELVE

1. Charlotte Downey, personal interview, 26 July 2004.
2. In their groundbreaking monograph, *Boots of Leather, Slippers of Gold: A History of a Lesbian Community*, authors Elizabeth Lapovsky Kennedy and Madeline D. Davis write that "working-class lesbians pioneered ways of socializing together and creating intimate sexual relationships without losing the ability to earn a living." Unlike upper- and middle-class lesbian women, working-class lesbians did not necessarily fear loss of social status attached to their sexuality nor did their blue-collar employment depend upon the approval of a larger society. Elizabeth Lapovsky Kennedy and Madeline D. Davis, *Boots of Leather, Slippers of Gold: The History of a Lesbian Community* (New York: Penguin, 1993), 2–3, 63–65.
3. For the importance of city softball leagues in forming lesbian communities, see Daneel Buring, "Softball and Alcohol: The Limits of Lesbian Community in Memphis from the 1940s through the 1960s," *Carryin' On in the Lesbian and Gay South.*
4. Kathy Harrison (mayor of Eureka Springs), personal interview, 24 July 2004. When asked if she would believe the gay and lesbian population of Eureka Springs to be 30 percent of the total population, Harrison dismissed the figure, placing it much higher.

THIRTEEN

1. "The center's space may be scheduled for use (such as meetings, dinners, films, etc.) by phoning ahead." "The Fayetteville Women's Center," *Hard Labor,* October-November-December 1977, final edition.
2. "The Fayetteville Women's Center," *Hard Labor.* An excerpt from the article states, "Who Can Join? All women are welcome to visit the Women's Center, utilize its services, and participate in its activities. There is no formal membership and there are no dues. The center is open weekdays, and there is currently an answering service so that calls may be made 24 hours of the day and messages left." For a detailed account of the feminist organizations in and around Fayetteville, Arkansas, see Anna M. Zajicek, Allyn Lord, and Lori Holyfield, "The Emergence and First Years of a Grassroots Movement in Northwest Arkansas, 1970–1980," *Arkansas Historical Quarterly* 42 (2003): 153–81.
3. Robyn Rogers, "Women's Center Opens," *Arkansas Traveler* (University of Arkansas, Fayetteville), 5 September 1978. Various other programs offered by the women's center included a women's prison project, designed to supply clothing to women in prison. The center also offered a women's committee on the environment, set up to "supply feminist literature and discussion to interested groups upon request." The article continued that "in addition to these groups, the center maintains a library consisting of women-oriented literature."
4. Pam Reich, "Razordykes Continue, Despite Flack," *Arkansas Traveler,* 15 February 1979.

5. "Razordykes," *Arkansas Traveler*..

6. *Arkansas Traveler*, 31 August 1978, 17 October 1978, 26 October 1978. A letter from D. Q. Reynolds Jr., suggested "a new campus organization for heterosexuals to be called *Nuts and Bolts*. The objective would be to match the rapists with the nymphomaniacs, the voyeurs with the exhibitionists, the masochists with the sadists, and the philanderers with the teasers. Further, it would perhaps be considered a noble cause to get the necrophiliacs employment in funeral homes, and child molesters jobs in day care centers. (Of course, the Razordykes could get jobs in the women's prison)." *Arkansas Traveler*, 26 October 1978.

7. Riech, "Razordykes Continue, Despite Flack.".

8. Julie Orman, "Women's Center Controversy: Questions Raised on Razordyke Funding," *Grapevine* (Fayetteville, AR), 15 November 1978.

9. Riech, "Razordykes Continue, Despite Flack.". Also see Zajicek, Lord, and Holyfield, "The Emergence and First Years of a Grassroots Movement in Northwest Arkansas, 1970–1980," 177.

10. Orman, "Women's Center Controversy," 4.

11. Despite the growing pressure from both within and outside the women's center, the group did propose a statement of solidarity for the organization. In it, the women's center stated, "We deplore the university's 'lesbian baiting.' It is a tactic that has often been used against the women's movement, in a attempt to divide women, to dilute our power, and to isolate and ostracize women of vision who get labeled a 'radical.'" The statement went on to say, "We specifically affirm our support of lesbian women, as have the majority of women nationally (for example, in the National Organization of Women and the at the National Women's Conference of 1977). We will not tolerate homophobic threats and scare tactics directed against lesbians and/or the women's center. Lesbian concerns are, and will continue to be, an integral part of every feminist's fight against oppression and therefore an integral part of the women's center." "Proposed Statement of Solidarity for Consideration by General Meeting," 5 November 1978, Fayetteville Women's Library Collection, series 21, sub-series 12, box 42, folder 3, Special Collections, University of Arkansas Libraries, Fayetteville.

12. Lillian Faderman, *Odd Girls and Twilight Lovers: A History of Lesbian Life in Twentieth-Century America* (New York: Penguin, 1991), 236–37. Regarding lesbian separatism, Faderman writes that "borrowing from the example of black separatists who believed that blacks were impeded by any relationship with whites, even the most liberal and beneficent seeming, lesbian separatists argued that the Lesbian Nation would never be established unless lesbian-feminists broke away not only from men but from all heterosexual women as well." Though they could be seen almost as a primary source, see Anna Lee, "For the Love of Separatism," *Lesbian Philosophies and Cultures*, ed. Jeffner Allen (Albany: State University of New York Press, 1990), 143–58; Claudia Card, "Pluralist Lesbian Separatism," *Lesbian Philosophies and Cultures*, 125–42. Also noteworthy is Sarah Lucia Hoagland and Julia Penelope, eds., *For Lesbians Only: A Separatist Anthology* (London: Only Women Press, 1988). Also, it is worth mentioning that separatism was not entirely a lesbian strategy. The clearest example of this is the Radical Faeries organization founded by Mattachine Society founder, and controversial figure in his own right, Harry Hay. Founded in 1979 and operating out of Arizona and other rural areas, the group sought to combine alternative political activism, the

counterculture, and spirituality in creating a separatist society. The Radical Faeries went on to set up communal households in Tennessee, North Carolina, Oregon, and New Mexico. See Stuart Timmons, *The Trouble with Harry Hay: Founder of the Modern Gay Movement* (Boston: Alyson Publications, 1990).

13. The split between lesbian interests and the larger women's movement was highly localized at the University of Arkansas. For an excellent treatment of another highly concentrated rift between lesbian women and larger women's groups, especially dealing with the forging and allocation of space, see Anne Enke, "Smuggling Sex Through the Gates: Race, Sexuality, and the Politics of Space in Second Wave Feminism," *American Quarterly* 93 (2003): 635–67.

14. "Land for Sale," *Ms.*, December 1972, 59.

15. H. E. Harvey to author, 14 June 2005. At the time, Harvey was asking a mere five thousand dollars for the land advertised in *Ms.* magazine. In his letter to me, he characterized the land as "eroded hill lands fit [for] timber and some grass farming." He would eventually sell portions of his land, though not to any lesbian or feminist group. Why he specifically advertised in *Ms.* he does not recall.

16. In his work *Sinners and Citizens: Bestiality and Homosexuality in Sweden: 1880–1950*, historian Jens Rydstrom articulates well the importance for personal advertisements in newspapers and magazines in finding queer communities. Jens Rydstrom, *Sinners and Citizens: Bestiality and Homosexuality in Sweden, 1880–1950* (Chicago: University of Chicago Press, 2003), 237–40, 299.

17. Janelle Lavelle, "Lesbian Land," *Southern Exposure*, Fall 1998: 36. One such woman, known only as Pat, having shed her patriarchal family name, joined the collective on Cedar Ridge Farm in the Ozark Mountains after sustaining a workplace injury during her job as a flight attendant. Having grown up in Florida and attended college in Tennessee, she considered herself a southerner and could not imagine living anywhere else. Like others, Pat simply felt "more comfortable in the South." For her, the "Southern Mountains that are real impressive and dominating and dramatic put me off, but the land in the South that I know, which is from the Smokies to here, feels accessible to me, and feels nurturing to me." Pat had traveled from Kansas City to be a part of the collective. The idea was not entirely new to her. She had been coming to the Ozarks for women's and feminist festivals and gatherings for sometime. Others came from further away, with the appeal of a rural, all-lesbian existence transcending the permeable boundaries of the South.

18. Esther Newton, *Margaret Mead Made Me Gay: Personal Essays, Public Ideas* (Durham, Duke University Press, 2000), 161–62. See Newton's essay "Will the Real Lesbian Community Please Stand Up? (1982/1998)" in this edition.

19. Listed here are but a few, listed in *Lesbian Land*, by Joyce Cheney: Arco Iris (Ponca, AR), Beechtree (Forestburgh, NY), D. W. Outpost (near Ava, MO), Golden and Rootworks (near Sunny Valley, OR), Laughing Rock Farm (Woodstock, NY), Lavender Hill (Medocia, CA), Long Leaf (Melrose, FL), Nourishing Space (Tucson, AZ), Okra Ridge (Luttrell, TN), The Pagoda/Crones Nest (St. Augustine, FL), Silver Circle (Holly Springs, MS), The Wisconsin Womyn's Land Cooperative (near Norwalk, WI), The Web (seventy miles from Minneapolis, MN), Willow Commune (Napa Valley, CA), Willow Two (Galisteo, NM), and Womanshire (Grant Pass, OR). Joyce Chaney, *Lesbian Land* (Word Weavers: Minneapolis, 1985).

20. Suzanne Pharr, personal interview, 9 August 2004.

21. New Orleans was a space itself often queered by southern authors such as Truman Capote and used as a setting for writers such as Tennessee Williams. In his works Capote often employs the term *queer* in his descriptions not only of New Orleans but also of the postwar South in general. For an excellent example of this, see Truman Capote, *Other Voices, Other Rooms* (New York: Vintage, 1994). For Tennessee Williams, see *Suddenly Last Summer* and *A Streetcar Named Desire*, though the former has more of a queer plot than the latter.

22. Pharr, interview.

23. For an in depth analysis of the back-to-the-land movement, see Jeffery Jacobs, *New Pioneers: The Back-to-the-Land Movement and the Search for a Sustainable Future* (University Park: Pennsylvania State University Press, 1997). Also noteworthy, Patrick C. Jobes, *Moving Nearer to Heaven: The Illusions and Disillusions of Migrants to Scenic Rural Places* (Westport, CT: Praeger, 2000). For studies on communes and communal living in the United States, see William Kephart, *Extraordinary Groups: An Examination of Unconventional Life-Styles* (New York: St. Martin's Press, 1987); Timothy Miller, *The 60s Communes: Hippies and Beyond* (Syracuse, NJ: Syracuse University Press, 1999); Ron E. Roberts, *The New Communes: Coming Together in America* (Englewood Cliffs, NJ: Prentice-Hall Press, 1971); and Benjamin Zablocki, *Alienation and Charisma: A Study of Contemporary American Communes* (New York: Free Press, 1980). All works comment only slightly on lesbian communes and gender issues at larger male and female communes. They do, however, provide a useful introduction to the commune and back-to-the-land movement in the United States.

24. According to the *New York Times*, there were an estimated two thousand rural communes and five thousand collectives dotted across the United States by the early 1970s. See Bruce J. Schulman, *The Seventies: The Great Shift in American Culture, Society, and Politics* (New York: Free Press, 2001), 88.

25. Zajicek, Lord, and Holyfield, *The Emergence and First Years of a Grassroots Women's Movement in Northwest Arkansas, 1970–1980*, 156–57.

26. One such commune near Greers Ferry, Arkansas, which had been operating since 1964, had to relocate to Little Rock in 1974 after locals vandalized their communal property. The commune, collectively known as the Dan Blocker Singers, referred to themselves as a "straight-laced" commune that had become known in the state for "its old-fashioned disapproval of drugs, alcohol, and free love and approval of hard work." The group never gained the trust of the tiny Greers Ferry community, which largely considered it cultish and foreign. See "The Group, Inc., Files Libel Suit Against Editor," *Arkansas Gazette*, 10 August 1973, final edition. Ginger Shiras, "Police Charge 9 with Nightriding at Greers Ferry," *Arkansas Gazette*, 26 August 1973, final edition.

27. Faderman, *Odd Girls and Twilight Lovers*, 239–40.

28. Faderman, *Odd Girls and Twilight Lovers*, 239–40.

29. ALFA Periodicals, box 26. "Ozark Women on Land," May, 1976, Sally Bingham Center for Women's Studies, Duke University Libraries, Division of Rare Books, Manuscripts, and Special Collections, Durham, NC. The Atlanta Lesbian Feminist Alliance (ALFA) operated from 1972 to 1994. During this time, ALFA employed both an historian as well as an archivist. In an extraordinary bit of foresight the group sought communication and newsletter exchanges with hundreds of grassroots feminist and gay organizations from around the world.

30. "Ozark Women on Land."

31. Faderman, *Odd Girls and Twilight Lovers*, 241.

32. "Ozark Women on Land." The Oregon's Women's Land Trust, founded in 1976, operated on 147 acres near the town of Canyonville in southern Oregon. The trust still operates today.

33. Ibid.

34. "Ozark Women on Land," August, 1976.

35. Ibid.

36. Ibid.

37. Ibid.

38. ALFA Periodicals, box 26, "'Dykes from Arkansas Ozarks' Want to Start 'Lesbian Nation,'" Sally Bingham Center for Women's Studies.

39. "'Dykes from Arkansas Ozarks' Want to Start 'Lesbian Nation.'"

40. "Ozark Women on Land," May, 1976.

41. Hog Farm had three communes operating in the western United States. They were located in Sunland, California; Llano, New Mexico; and Berkeley, California. Hog Farm was founded in 1965 and is ongoing. Timothy Miller, *The 60s Communes: Hippies and Beyond* (Syracuse, NJ: Syracuse University Press, 1999), 266.

42. Diana Rivers, personal interview, 20 October 2005.

43. Rivers, interview.

44. This is a very loose definition of a commune, as communes and like-living situations were very informal and loosely based. Sociologist Benjamin Zablocki provides this highly technical and useful definition: "Let us define commune as any group of five or more adult individuals (plus children, if any), the majority of whose dyads are not cemented by blood or marriage, who have decided to live together, without compulsion, focused upon the achievement of community, for which a collective household is deemed essential." See Zablocki, *Alienation and Charisma*, 6–7.

45. Rivers, interview. Nancy Vaughn, personal interview, 16 June 2005.

46. This idea was at the heart of feminism, which lesbian separatism built upon. In *The Feminine Mystique*, Betty Freidan stated that "equality and human dignity are not possible for women if they are not able to earn. Only economic independence can free a woman to marry for love, not status or financial support, or to leave a loveless, intolerable, humiliating marriage, or eat, dress, rest, and move if she plans not to marry." Building on this, a woman is also allowed to separate herself altogether from a larger society. Betty Friedan, *The Feminine Mystique* (New York: Dell Books, 1963), 370–71.

47. According to feminist theorist Shane Phelan, "separation can range from the provision of occasional women-only events to an almost completely separated life." Shane Phelan, *Identity Politics: Lesbian Feminism and the Limits of Community* (Philadelphia: Temple University Press, 1989), 52. The work also remains one of the best to trace the unstable relationship between the lesbian-feminist and the larger women's movement.

48. Listed here are the novels in order of publication: *Journey to Zelinder* (Los Angeles: Alyson Press, 1990), *Daughter of the Great Star* (Los Angles: Alyson Press, 1992), *The Hadra* (Los Angeles: Alyson Press, 1995), *Clouds of War* (Tallahassee, FL: Bella Books, 2002), and *The Red Line of Yarmald* (Tallahassee, FL: Bella Books, 2003). Rivers also published numerous short stories appearing in various lesbian-oriented magazines and journals. Both Bella Books and the Alyson Press are popular gay and

lesbian presses. The market for lesbian and radical feminist works such as the *Demeter Flower,* first published in 1970, grew exponentially as the feminist movement increased in strength and numbers. Rochelle Singer, *The Demeter Flower* (New York: St. Martin's Press, 1980). For an in depth analysis of lesbian separatism seen through popular fiction, see Sonya Andermahr, "The Politics of Separatism and Lesbian Utopian Fiction," *New Lesbian Criticism: Literary and Cultural Readings,* ed. Sally Munt (New York: Columbia University Press, 1992), 133–52. For a detailed account of the rise of the gay and lesbian press, though mainly concerning itself with the press as news and information, see Roger Strietmatter, *Unspeakable: The Rise of the Gay and Lesbian Press in America* (Boston: Faber & Faber, 1995), 154–82.

49. Donna Jo Smith writes that that "the term southern queer is redundant. Since the South is already an aberration, what is a southern queer but deviance multiplied?" If that is the case, what is to be said for the hillbilly? Donna Jo Smith, "Queering the South: Constructions for a Southern/Queer Identity," *Carryin' on in the Lesbian and Gay South,* 370.

50. *Maize: A Lesbian Country Magazine* as a magazine was "for and by lesbians." ALFA Periodicals, box 26, Sally Bingham Center for Women's Studies. Joyce Cheney, ed., *Lesbian Land* (Minneapolis: Word Weavers, 1979). Maria Christina Morelas, "Sunhawk," personal interview, 18 December 2004.

51. "On the Land," *Maize: A Lesbian Country Magazine,* Winter 9986, 12. The "On the Land" portion of the magazine appeared each season. It was an opportunity for lesbian separatist communities across America to post their stories, problems, and solutions to rural life. The date on the magazine does read "9986." This should be read as 1986, changed perhaps to reject the patriarchal calendar system, or a typo.

52. Morelas, interview.

53. "On the Land," *Maize,* Winter 9986, 13.

54. Ibid., 14.

55. Ibid., 13.

56. *Maize,* Winter 9990 (1990), 15.

57. *Maize,* Winter 9986 (1986).

58. *Maize,* Winter 9990 (1990), 15.

59. One of the more vocal critics of separatism to this point was African American feminist Audrey Lorde. Regardless of sexuality, Lorde challenged women to examine the deep relationships between racism, sexism, and homophobia. Though now a bit dated, Mari Evans's works remains the best treatment of Lorde. See Mari Evans, ed., *Black Women Writers (1950–1980): A Critical Evaluation* (New York: Anchor, 1984).

60. K. J. Zumwalt, personal interview, 30 July 2004.

61. John D'Emilio, "Capitalism and Gay Identity," *Powers of Desire: The Politics of Sexuality,* ed. Ann Snitow, Christine Stansell, and Sharon Thompson (New York: Monthly Review Press, 1983), 100, 105. For an excellent description of mass urbanization and post-industrial economics' influence on gay and lesbian identity in the United States, see D'Emilio, "Capitalism and Gay Identity," *Powers of Desire: The Politics of Sexuality* (New York: Monthly Review Press, 1983), 100–113.

62. Separatist communities can be regionally precise in their makeup. On this point, and dealing with the ALFA community in Atlanta, Georgia, see Becca Cragin, "Post-Lesbian Feminism: Documenting 'Those Cruddy Old Dykes of Yore,'" *Carryin'*

On in the Lesbian and Gay South, 285–330. On essentialism and the creation of community, see Kathy Rudy, "Radical Feminism, Lesbian Separatism, and Queer Theory," *Feminist Studies* 27.1 (Spring 2001): 191–222.

FOURTEEN

1. The best work on rural Ozark life remains the highly engaging *Hill Folks*. Brooks Blevins, *Hill Folks: A History of Arkansas Ozarkers and Their Image* (Chapel Hill: University of North Carolina Press, 2002). Susan Schaefer, *I Didn't Know That! About Eureka Springs* (Eureka Springs, AR: Ozark Mountain Press, 1997), 7–9.

2. "Good health is the greatest boon known to mankind, and in the hearts of those who found it at Eureka Springs there will forever be a tender spot for the resort. They will always cherish pleasant recollections of the place, and ever be ready to speak a kind word in its behalf." John Kearney, *Eureka Springs: The Resort of the Ozarks* (1907), 38–40. This self-published work is half local history and half tourist pamphlet.

3. Borrowing from the region's dubious past, the town attracted its share of eccentric personalities and regional celebrities. Carry A. Nation, the axe-welding personification of the American temperance movement, built a home there. For those who came to Eureka Springs for the cures and convalescence, Nation, now in old age, appealed to their spiritual needs. Fond of the peace and quiet offered by the Ozarks, she built Hatchet Hall in 1908 as a boarding house and Sunday school. Downtown saloons proudly displayed hatchet marks in their bars from Nation's occasional visits. Bonnie Lela Crump, *Carry A. Nation: Hatchet Hall, Her Last Home in Eureka Springs, Arkansas* (Eureka Springs, AR: Times-Echo, 1959), 20–21.

4. Schaefer, *I Didn't Know That! About Eureka Springs*, 32–35. Of the dozens of bathhouses that operated in Eureka Springs at the peak of the tourist trade, only two were operational in 1997, with only one, the Palace Hotel and Bathhouse, still offering medical baths and hot-water treatments. During their heyday, Eureka Springs's bathhouses offered everything from Swedish massages to hot air and electric baths, provided by "skilled and attentive" attendants.

5. Glen Jeansonne, *Gerald L. K. Smith: Minister of Hate* (New Haven, CT: Yale University Press, 1988). Also see Glen Jeansonne, "Arkansas's Minister of Hate: A Research Odyssey," *Arkansas Historical Quarterly* 59 (2000): 429–35. Jeansonne's highly accessible and thoroughly researched work on Smith remains the best available.

6. For an interesting and in-depth exposure of Smith and the prewar anti-Semitic and isolationist movements, see Max Wallace, *The American Axis: Henry Ford, Charles Lindbergh, and the Rise of the Third Reich* (New York: St. Martin's Press, 2003), 144–45, 214–315.

7. Both men had strong fascist sympathies and anti-Semitic beliefs, and both were personal friends of Smith. See Jeansonne, *Gerald L. K. Smith*, 84–86. Also see A. Scott Berg, *Lindbergh* (Berkeley, CA: Berkeley Publishing Group, 1998), 361, 385–86.

8. Jeasonne, *Gerald L. K. Smith*, 190.

9. Ibid., 190.

10. Ibid., 188–89.

11. Ibid., 191.

12. Ken Sculley, personal interview, 29 July 2004. The "milk carton" was one of

the less flattering nicknames given to the Christ of the Ozarks statue by the towns-people of Eureka Springs.

13. Robert Gilmore Jeansonne, *Ozark Baptizings, Hangings, and Other Diversions: Theatrical Folkways of Rural Missouri, 1885–1910* (Norman: University of Oklahoma Press, 1984), 13, 167. Glen Jeansonne, *Gerald L. K. Smith,* 196.

14. Glen Jeansonne, *Gerald L. K. Smith,* 201.

15. Ibid., 203.

16. The battle between Gerald L. K. Smith and the town of Eureka Springs over such issues as taxes and revenue only increased over the years. The relationship hit a particularly sour note in 1999 when members of the Smith Foundation petitioned state legislators to allow them to collect tourist tax dollars although the operation sat outside the city limits and therefore did not contribute towards the tax. Chad Hayworth, "Bill Lets Passion Play Collect Promotion Tax, Area Outside Eureka Springs, Mayor Objects," *Arkansas Democrat-Gazette,* 3 April 1999, final edition.

17. Jubilation T. Cornpone, "Ozarks Lure the Slickers . . . ," *Sentinel-Record* (Hot Springs, AR), 24 November 1968, 24. "The Great Passion Play and Allied Sacred Projects: Portraying the Agony and the Glory of the Last Week in the Life of Jesus Christ," program, (Eureka Springs, AR: Dwight Nichols, 1971).

18. "The Great Passion Play," program.

19. The verse commonly referred to as the blood curse appears in the Gospel according to Matthew, but no others. Matthew 27:25. Jeansonne, *Gerald L. K. Smith,* 197–98.

20. Harrison, interview.

21. Also built was the Sacred Arts and Bible Museum, where Smith housed his personal collection of some 6,000 Bibles in over 650 languages and dialects, including one brought over on the *Mayflower* crossing, and over a thousand pieces of art detailing the life of Jesus of Nazareth. With these came the gift shop (where one could purchase any number of souvenirs), a buffet, and snack shop as well as a lounge for bus drivers. Vernon Kay (director of sales, Gerald L. K. Smith Foundation), personal interview, 27 July 2004.

22. Roy Reed, "Hippies and Gerald L. K. Smith Make Ozark Resort Town a Model of Coexistence," *New York Times,* 27 July 1972, final edition.

23. Ibid.

24. Ginger Shiras, "Longhairs, Sacred Projects Reviving Eureka Springs," *Arkansas Gazette,* 25 June 1972, final edition.

25. Ibid., "Lack of Negroes Called Attraction."

26. During the boom years following the First World War, Eureka Springs had a rather large black population, many finding work in service jobs in the downtown bathhouses and hotels. Susan Schaefer, *Eureka Springs.*

27. Shiras, "Longhairs, Sacred Projects."

28. Ibid.

29. Ibid.

30. Ibid.

31. Reed, "Hippies and Gerald L. K. Smith Make Ozark Town a Model of Coexistence."

32. Ibid.

33. Ibid.

34. See Timothy K. Beal, *Roadside Religion: In Search of the Sacred, the Strange, and the Substance of Faith* (Boston: Beacon Press, 2005). Also, Burke O. Long, *Imagining the Holy Land: Maps, Models, and Fantasy Travels* (Bloomington: Indiana University Press, 2002).

FIFTEEN

1. "Travel/Vacation," *Ms.*, April 1976, 63.

2. Barbara Scott, telephone interview, 30 April 2006.

3. Scott, interview. Jacqueline Ann Froelich, "The Gay and Lesbian Movement in Arkansas: An Investigation Study" (master's thesis, University of Arkansas, 1995), 53–54

4. Ibid.

5. Ibid., 111.

6. Steve Roberson, personal interview, 27 July 2004.

7. Gabriel Giorgi, "Madrid En Transito" *GLQ: A Journal of Lesbian and Gay Studies* 8.1 (2202): 57–59. Giorgi writes that "gay tourism functions . . . as an articulation between discourses of political rights and transnational displacements in a landscape where national borders are currently being reformulated in both their symbolic and their practical effects."

8. Mike Rodman, "Gays Keep Low Profile, Aid Tourism," *Arkansas Democrat-Gazette* 15 August 1993, final edition.

9. Rodman, "Gays Keep Low Profile, Aid Tourism." In an article for the *Gayly Oklahoman*, the gay and lesbian newspaper serving Tulsa, Oklahoma, and the surrounding areas, reporters Donald Pile and Ray Williams marveled at the beauty of Eureka Springs and the opportunity for the gay tourist there. Commenting on the town's tourist website, www.eurekasprings.com, the authors noted that if you "click on 'alternative' it will take you to the gay section. However, if Eureka Springs is so gay friendly, why don't they just call it the 'gay and lesbian section?'" Donald Pile and Ray Williams, "Eureka Springs, Arkansas," *Gayly Oklahoman*, 1 July 2004, final edition.

10. M. V. Lee Badgett, *Money, Money, Myths, and Change: The Economic Lives of Lesbians and Gay Men* (Chicago: University of Chicago Press, 2001), 240.

11. For the best books on these towns, Boyd, *Wide Open Town: A History of Queer San Francisco;* Newton, *Cherry Grove, Fire Island: Sixty Years in America's First Gay and Lesbian Town;* and Karen Krahulik, *Provincetown: From Pilgrim Landing to Gay Resort* (New York: NYU Press, 2007).

12. On understanding these differing circumstances, B. Greene writes, "Ethnicity, culture, and sexual orientation are salient aspects of human identity about which most people have strong feelings but often find difficult to discuss openly. Attempting to understand these issues and their interactive effects is challenging." B. Greene, ed., "Ethnic and Cultural Diversity Among Lesbians and Gay Men," *Psychological Perspectives on Gay and Lesbian Issues* 3 (1997): xii.

13. Annette Pritchard, Nigel J. Morgan, Diane Sedgley, Elizabeth Kahn, and Andrew Jenkins, "Sexuality and Holiday Choices: Conversations with Gay and Lesbian Tourists," *Leisure Studies* 19 (2000): 268.

14. The most poignant work on HIV and AIDS in the rural remains Abraham

Verghese's *My Own Country,* the beginning of which deals with a very ill young man attempting to get back to his small town from New York City so that he might die at home. For AIDS and the rural, Verghese states that "no one has described the rural experience with AIDS I was seeing; a quietly burgeoning clinic, an intimate primary-care kind of clinic, a clinic with strong resemblances to a secret society with me at its head and the various novitiates and initiates dispersed among the townsfolk, disguised as bakers, shoe repairman, housewives, priests, waiters, blacksmiths, and publicans." Abraham Verghese, *My Own Country: A Doctor's Story* (New York: Vintage Books, 1995), 277. Though the work remains the most poignant concerning AIDS in the rural landscape, it has had it fair share of criticism. See Craig Wilson, "A Doctor's Story about AIDS in the 'Country,'" review of *My Own Country* by Abraham Verghese, *Washington Post,* 15 May 1994. Also see Pico Iyer, "72 Churches, and Also AIDS," review of *My Own County* by Abraham Verghese, *Time,* 6 June 1994, 70.

15. Sculley, interview.

16. Ibid.

17. Gary W. Shannon, Gerald F. Pyle, and Rashid Bashshur, *The Geography of AIDS: Origins and Course of an Epidemic* (New York: Guilford Press, 1991), 121.

18. Shannon, Pyle, and Bashshur, *The Geography of AIDS,* 121.

19. Arkansas Department of Health, *HIV/AIDS Surveillance* (31 December 2005). As to how Arkansas itself ranked disproportionately high among states with HIV/AIDS infection per capita, see page 123 of this study.

20. Meredith Raimondo, "The Next Wave: Media Maps and the 'Spread of AIDS'" (dissertation, Emory University, 1991), 252–55.

21. Ibid.

22. These auctions for goods and services is a common and successful technique for local HIV/AIDS charities.

23. Michael Haddigan, "Eureka Springs's Wedding Boom: Gay 'Marriages' Swell the Numbers," *Arkansas Times,* 18 October 1996, final edition. The weddings began the same year Clinton signed the Defense of Marriage Act.

24. Raimondo, "The Next Wave."

SIXTEEN

1. Harry Benson, "Anita Bryant: 'It's Nice to Be Vindicated,'" *People,* 7 March 1994, 270.

2. Benson, "Anita Bryant"

3. Patricia Maynews, "State's Lifestyle Appeals to Anita Bryant, Husband," *Arkansas Democrat-Gazette,* 9 April 1991, final edition.

4. "Anita Bryant Files to Get Debts in Line," *Arkansas Democrat-Gazette,* 30 April 1997, final edition.

5. Released in the Winter of 2004, Mel Gibson's *Passion* opened to a barrage of controversy and criticism as well as unabashed praise from some conservative religious groups, resembling that received by Smith and his cohorts for their production.

6. Michelle Parks, "Passion in a New Light: Mel Gibson's Blockbuster Movie Is Having an Evident Impact on Audiences and Actors at the Great Passion Play in Eureka Springs," *Arkansas Democrat-Gazette,* 6 June 2004, final edition.

7. Kay, interview. Bill King, "New Passion Play Exhibit Melds Dinosaurs with Creationism," *Lovely County Citizen* (Eureka Springs, AR), 22 July 2004, final edition.

8. Of the twenty-one "hate groups" identified in Arkansas by the Federal Bureau of Investigation and posted by the Southern Poverty Law Center, seven operate in northwest Arkansas, five within an hour's drive from Eureka Springs and one, the Christian Research Church, operating out of Eureka Springs. These groups with their radical and racist policies find rural mountain living more in tune with their own agendas of separatism and a larger distrust of society, especially of the federal government. See Southern Poverty Law Center, "Intelligence Project," http://www.splcenter.org (accessed 1 December 2004).

EPILOGUE

1. Rita Dove, *On the Bus with Rosa Parks* (New York: Norton, 1999), 40.

2. The fundraiser was organized by Clinton friend David Mixner and other prominent California gay men. Mixner traveled to Little Rock for the 1992 Clinton watch party. Later in his memoirs, Mixner wrote, "Little Rock seemed such an unlikely setting for such a historic moment. I was shocked at the small-town atmosphere of what was, after all, the capital city of Arkansas. I thought, this is what it would have been like for me if I had returned home to southern New Jersey and run for office and spent most of my time living in Trenton. At least there I would have been two hours from New York and a short ride form Philadelphia. I understood once again why gays and lesbians left their small towns to seek the anonymity and freedom of the big cities."

3. Cleninden and Nagourney, *Out for Good*, 472–74.

4. All of these promises were met with varying degrees of success. The HIV-positive speaker would be not a gay man but Elizabeth Glaser, wife of actor Paul Michael Glaser, who contracted the virus through a blood transfusion. She would be introduced by openly gay and HIV-positive Bob Hattoy. See David Mixner, *Stranger Among Friends* (New York: Bantam, 1996), 243–47. The "don't ask, don't tell" policy was generally regarded both as a calamity and a sellout of the larger gay community.

5. Cleninden and Nagourney, *Out of Good*, 572.

6. David Maraniss, "Clinton Finds New Voice of Emotion," *Washington Post*, 20 May 1992, final edition.

7. Ibid.

8. After Clinton's first presidential victory, D'Emilio stated that "just as the Clinton victory will open opportunities for us to relinquish our attachment to outsider status, it is also likely that the Clinton administration will elevate some of our community members to more visible leadership." To that, I ask D'Emilio, but what sort of visibility and on whose terms? D'Emilio, *The World Turned*, 141.

9. Washington DC: Republican National Committee, 2004. I am most grateful to Brian Greer for pointing out this reference.

10. The numbers were 468,543 for and 267,275 against. Austin Gelder, "Arkansans OK Ban on Same-Sex Unions Constitutional Amendment Easily Passes," *Arkansas Democrat-Gazette*, 3 November 2004, final edition.

11. Michael Haddigan, "Eureka Springs' Wedding Boom," *Arkansas Times*, 18 October 1996, final edition.

12. The states were Georgia, Kentucky, Michigan, Mississippi, Montana, North Dakota, Oklahoma, Oregon, and Utah. "Arkansans OK Ban," 1.

13. Sandy Brewer, City of Conway, Conway City Council, Resolution No. R-04, Conway, Arkansas, 2004.

14. Michelle Hillen, "Resolution on Gay-Pride Goes Nowhere," *Arkansas Democrat-Gazette,* 23 June 2004, final edition.

15. Casey Munck, "Manure Prank Fails to Derail Gay-Pride March," *Arkansas Democrat-Gazette,* 28 June 2004, final edition.

SELECTED BIBLIOGRAPHY

PRIMARY SOURCES

Newspapers, Newsletters, and Group Publications

Arkansas Gay Writes

Arkansas Gazette (Little Rock)

Arkansas Democrat (Little Rock)

Arkansas Democrat-Gazette (Little Rock)

Camp Robinson News (Camp Robinson, AR)

Charlotte Observer

Covered Wagon

Gayly Oklahoman (Oklahoma City)

Lincoln Ledger (Star City, AR)

Lovely County Citizen (Eureka Springs, AR)

Maize (Serafina, NM)

Marked Tree Tribune (Marked Tree, AR)

Metro Times (Detroit, MI)

Military News

New York Times

Osceola Times (Osceola, MS)

Profile (Hendrix College, Conway, AR)

Rohwer Outpost

Times-Echo (Eureka Springs, AR)

Traveller

Triangle Rising

Manuscript Collections

Harvey Goodwin Collection. Archives and Special Collections. University of Arkansas at Little Rock Library.

David Pryor Papers. Special Collections. University of Arkansas Libraries, Fayetteville.

H. I. Wilson Collection. Special Collections. University of Arkansas Libraries, Fayetteville.

Jim Johnson Papers. Arkansas History Commission, Little Rock.

Fayetteville Women's Library Collection. Special Collections. University of Arkansas Libraries, Fayetteville.

Margaret Ross Collection. Special Collections. University of Arkansas Libraries, Fayetteville.

Camp Rohwer Collection. Arkansas History Commission, Little Rock.

Atlanta Lesbian Feminist Alliance Archives and Periodicals Collection. Special Collections Library. Duke University, Durham, NC.

Arkansas State Supreme Court Cases

Conners v. State

Smith v. State. 150 Ark. 265 (1921).

Strum v. State. 168 Ark. 1012 (1925).

Picado v. Jegley

United States Supreme Court Cases

Bowers v. Hardwick. 478 U.S. 186 (1986).

Lawrence et al. v. Texas. 539 U.S. 558 (2003).

Oral History Interviews

DeColores, Miguela Borges. Personal interview. Boxley, AR. 18 December 2005.

Downey, Charlotte. Personal interview. Eureka Springs, AR. 26 July 2004.

Everett, Mike. Personal interview. Marked Tree, AR. 5 October 2002.

Fairly, Elder. Personal interview. Osceola, AR. 29 July 2003.

Harrison, Katherine. Personal interview. Eureka Springs, AR. 24 July 2004.

Holder, Ted. Personal interview. Little Rock, AR. 23 September 2001.

Howard, Robert. Personal interview. Little Rock, AR. 15 June 2003.

Johnson, Jim. Telephone interview. 2 November 2005.

Jones, Norman. Personal interview. Little Rock, AR. 31 July 2003, 12 August 2003.

Kay, Vernon. Personal interview. Eureka Springs, AR. 27 July 2004.

Lee, David. Personal interview. Maumelle, AR. 11 August 2003.

Loyd, Robert. Personal interview. Conway, AR. 8 June 2004.

Meriwether, Robert. Telephone interview. 10 July 2003.

Moroles, Maria Chistina. Personal interview. Boxley, AR. 18 December 2005.

Pharr, Suzanne. Personal interview. Knoxville, TN. 9 August 2004.

Pryor, David. Telephone interview. 11 March 2001.

Ort, Randal. Personal interview. Little Rock, AR. 8 June 2003.

Roberson, Steve. Personal interview. Eureka Springs, AR. 27 July 2004.

Rivers, Diana. Personal interview. OLHA Community, AR. 20 October 2005.

Schenck, John. Personal interview. Conway, AR. 8 June 2004.

Scott, Barbara. Telephone interview. 30 April 2006.

Sculley, Ken. Personal interview. Eureka Springs, AR. 29 July 2004.

Snyder, Vic. Telephone interview. 11 March 2001.

Vaughn, Nancy. Personal interview. OLHA Community, AR. 16 June 2005.

Zumwalt, K. J. Personal interview. Eureka Springs, AR. 30 July 2004.

BOOKS AND ARTICLES

Adam, Barry. *The Rise of the Gay and Lesbian Movement*. Boston: Twayne, 1990.

Allen, Jeffner., ed. *Lesbian Philosophies and Cultures*. Albany: State University of New York Press, 1990.

Allen, Paula Gunn. *The Sacred Hoop*. Boston: Beacon Press, 1986.

———. "Lesbians in American Indian Cultures." *Hidden From History: Reclaiming the Gay and Lesbian Past*, edited by Martin Bauml Duberman, Martha Vicinus, and George Chauncey Jr., 106–17. New York: Columbia University Press, 1989.

Allen, Robert C. *Horrible Prettiness: Burlesque and American Culture*. Chapel Hill: University of North Carolina Press, 1991.

Applebome, Peter. *Dixie Rising: How the South is Shaping American Values, Politics, and Culture*. New York: Random House, 1996.

Badgett, M. V. Lee. *Money, Money, Myths, and Change: The Economic Lives of Lesbians and Gay Men*. Chicago: University of Chicago Press, 2001.

Bailey, Beth. *From Front Porch to Back Seat: Courtship in Twentieth Century America*. Boston: Johns Hopkins University Press, 1989.

———. *Sex in the Heartland*. Cambridge, MA: Harvard University Press, 1999.

Bannon, Ann. *Odd Girl Out*. Tallahassee: Volute, 1983.

Bartley, Numan V. *The New South, 1945–1980*. Baton Rouge: Louisiana State University Press, 1995.

Barnes, Kenneth C. *Who Killed John Clayton? Political Violence and the Emergence of the New South, 1861–1893*. Durham, NC: Duke University Press, 1998.

Barnett, Walter. *Sexual Freedom and the Constitution: An Inquiry into the Constitutionality of Repressive Sex Laws*. Albuquerque: University of New Mexico Press, 1990.

Bartlett, Neil. *Who Was That Man? A Present of Oscar Wilde*, London: Serpent's Tail, 1988.

Bayes, Jane H. *Minority Politics and Ideologies in the United States*. Navoto, CA: Chandler and Sharp, 1982.

Beal, Timothy K. *Roadside Religion: In Search of the Sacred, the Strange, and the Substance of Faith*. Boston: Beacon Press, 2005.

Beemyn, Brett, ed. *Creating a Place for Ourselves: Lesbian, Gay, and Bisexual Community Histories.* New York: Routledge, 1997.

Berube, Allan. *Coming Out under Fire: A History of Gay Men and Women during World War Two.* New York: Free Press, 1990.

Birch, Elizabeth, Gary J. Gates, and Jason Ost. *Gay and Lesbian Atlas.* New York: Urban Institute Press, 2004.

Black, Earl and Merle. *Politics and Society in the South.* Cambridge, MA: Harvard University Press, 1987.

Blair, Diane D. and Jay Barth. *Arkansas Politics and Government.* Lincoln: University of Nebraska Press, 2005.

Blevins, Brooks. *Hill Folks: A History of Arkansas Ozarkers and Their Image.* Chapel Hill: University of North Carolina Press, 2002.

Boggs, Carl. *Social Movements and Political Power.* Philadelphia: Temple University Press, 1987.

Bolsterli, Margaret Jones. *Born in the Delta: Reflections on the Making of a Southern White Sensibility.* Fayetteville: University of Arkansas Press, 2000.

Bordo, Susan. *Unbearable Weight: Feminism, Western Culture, and the Body.* Berkeley: University of California Press, 1993.

Boswell, John. *Christianity, Social Tolerance, and Homosexuality: Gay People in Europe from the Beginning of the Christian Era to the Fourteenth Century.* Chicago: University of Chicago, 1980.

———. *Same-Sex Unions in Premodern Europe.* New York: Villard, 1994.

Boyd, Nan Alamilla. *Wide Open Town: A History of Queer San Francisco.* Berkeley: University of California Press, 2003.

Brandt, Allan M. *No Magic Bullet: A Social History of Venereal Disease in the United States since 1880.* Oxford: Oxford University Press, 1987.

Bravmann, Scott. *Queer Fictions of the Past: History, Culture, and Difference.* Cambridge: Cambridge University Press, 1997.

Bullough, Vern, and Bonnie Bullough. "Lesbianism in the 1920s and 1930s: A Newfound Study." *Signs: Journal of Women in Culture and Society* 2, no. 4 (1977): 895–904.

Buring, Daneel. *Lesbian and Gay Memphis: Building Communities Behind the Magnolia Curtain.* New York: Garland, 1997.

———. "Softball and Alcohol: The Limits of Lesbian Community in Memphis from the 1940s through the 1960s." *Carryin' on in the Lesbian and Gay South,* edited by John Howard, 203–23. New York: New York University Press, 1997.

Burson, Anne C. "Model and Text in Folk Drama." *Journal of American Folklore* 93 (1980), 305–31.

Butler, Judith. *Bodies that Matter: On the Discursive Limits of "Sex."* New York: Routledge, 1993.

———. *Gender Trouble.* New York: Routledge, 1999.

Chappell, David L. *Inside Agitators: White Southerners and the Civil Rights Movement.* Baltimore: Johns Hopkins University Press, 1994.

Chaney, Joyce. *Lesbian Land.* Word Weavers: Minneapolis, 1985.

Charles, Casey. *The Sharon Kowalski Case: Lesbian and Gay Rights on Trial.* Lawrence: University of Kansas Press, 2003.

Chaucey, George. *Gay New York: Gender, Urban Culture, and the Making of the Gay Male World, 1890–1940.* New York: BasicBooks, 1994.

Clinton, Bill. *My Life.* New York: Knopf, 2004.

Cobb, James Charles. *The Most Southern Place on Earth: The Mississippi Delta and the Roots of Regional Identity.* New York: Oxford University Press, 1992.

———. *The Selling of the South: The Southern Crusade for Southern Development.* Baton Rouge: Louisiana State University Press, 1982.

Cook, Blanche Wiesen. "Female Support Newtworks and Political Activism." *Chrusalis* 3 (Autumn): 43–61.

Cook, Matt. *London and the Culture of Homosexuality, 1885–1914.* Cambridge: Cambridge University Press, 2003.

Corber, Robert J. *Homosexuality in Cold War America: Resistance and the Crisis of Masculinity.* Durham, NC: Duke University Press, 1997.

Corber, Robert J., and Stephen Valocchi, eds. *Queer Studies: An Interdisciplinary Reader.* New York: Blackwell, 2002.

Cocteau, Jean. *"Barbette": mit dem Essay "Le numero Barbette."* Berlin: Borderline, 1988.

Creedon, Pamula J. eds. *Women, Media and Sport: Challenging Gender Values.* New York: SAGE, 1994.

Cruikshank, Margaret. *Lesbian Studies: Present and Future.* New York: Feminist Press, 1982.

D'Emilio, John. "Capitalism and the Gay Identity." *Powers of Desire: The Politics of Sexuality,* edited by Ann Snitow, Christine Stansell, and Sharon Thompson. New York: Monthly Review Press, 1983.

———. *Sexual Politics, Sexual Communities: The Making of a Homosexual Minority in the United States, 1940–1970.* Chicago: University of Chicago Press, 1983.

———. *Making Trouble: Essays on Gay History, Politics, and the University.* New York: Routledge, 1992.

D'Emilio, John, and Estelle Freedman. *Intimate Matters: A History of Sexuality in America.* New York: Harper and Row, 1988.

Daniel, Pete. *Lost Revolutions: The South and the 1950s.* Chapel Hill: University of North Carolina Press, 2000.

———. *Standing at the Crossroads: Southern Life since 1900.* New York: Hill and Wang, 1986.

Daniels, Roger. *Prisoners Without Trial: Japanese Americans During World War II.* New York: Hill and Wang, 1993.

DeBlack, Thomas. *With Fire and Sword: Arkansas, 1861–1874.* Fayetteville: University of Arkansas Press, 2003.

Desert, Jean-Ulrick. "Queer Space." *Queers in Space: Communities, Public Places, Sites of Resistance,* edited G. B. Ingram, A Bouthillette, and Y. Ritter. Seattle: Bay Press, 1997.

Dews, Carlos L., and Carolyn Leste Law. *Out in the South.* Philadelphia: Temple University Press, 2001.

Donovan, Timothy P., Willard B. Gatewood, and Jeannie M. Whayne, eds. *The Governors of Arkansas: Essays in Political Biography.* Fayetteville: University of Arkansas Press, 1995.

Duberman, Martin. *Stonewall.* New York: Dutton, 1993.

Duberman, Martin, Martha Vicinus, and George Chauncey, eds. *Hidden from History: Reclaiming the Gay and Lesbian Past.* New York: Penguin, 1990.

DuCille, Ann. "'Othered' Matters." *Journal of the History of Sexuality* 1, no. 1 (1990): 102–27.

Duggan, Lisa. *Sapphic Slashers: Sex, Violence, and American Modernity.* Durham, NC: Duke University Press, 2001.

Duncan, Ben. *The Same Language.* Tuscaloosa: University of Alabama Press, 2005.

Echols, Alice. *Daring to Be Bad: Radical Feminism in America, 1967–1975.* Minneapolis: University of Minnesota Press, 1989.

Ericksen, Julia A. *Kiss and Tell: Surveying Sex in the Twentieth Century.* Cambridge, MA: Harvard University Press, 1999.

Eskridge, William N., Jr. *Gaylaw: Challenging the Apartheid of the Closet.* Cambridge, MA: Harvard University Press, 1990.

———. "Law and the Construction of the Closet: American Regulation of Same-Sex Intimacy, 1880–1946." *Iowa Law Review* 82, no. 4 (May 1997): 1009–136.

Faderman, Lillian. *Surpassing the Love of Men.* New York: William Morrow, 1981.

———. *Odd Girls and Twilight Lovers: A History of Lesbian Life in Twentieth-Century America.* New York: Columbia University Press, 1991.

Feinberg, Leslie. *Transgender Warriors: Making History from Joan of Arc to Dennis Rodman.* Boston: Beacon Press, 1996.

Featherstone, Mike, ed. *Global Culture: Nationalism, Globalization, and Modernity.* London: Sage, 1990.

Foucault, Michel. *The History of Sexuality.* New York: Random, 1990.

Frantzen, Allen J. *Before the Closet: Same-Sex Love from "Beowulf" to "Angels in America."* Chicago: University of Chicago Press, 2001.

Friedan, Betty. *The Feminine Mystique.* New York: Dell Books, 1963.

Frum, David. *How We Got Here: The 70s, the Decade That Brought You Modern Life (For Better or Worse).* New York: Basic, 2000.

Gamson, Joshua. *Freaks Talk Back: Tabloid Talk Shows and Sexual Nonconformity.* Chicago: University of Chicago Press, 1998.

Gaonkar, Dilip Parameshwar, ed. *Alternative Modernities*. Durham, NC: Duke University Press, 2001.

Garber, Linda. *Identity Politics: Race, Class, and the Lesbian-Feminist Roots of Queer Theory*. New York: Columbia University Press, 2001.

Gardiner, James. *Who's a Pretty Boy Then: One Hundred and Fifty Years of Gay Life in Pictures*. London: Serpent's Tail, 1997.

Godbeer, Richard. "'The Cry of Sodom': Discourse, Intercourse, and Desire in Colonial New England." *William and Mary Quarterly* 3, no. 52 (1995): 259–84.

Gordy, Sondra. *Finding the Lost Year: What Happened when Little Rock Closed Its Public Schools*. Fayetteville: University of Arkansas Press, 2009.

Goss, Kay Collett. *The Arkansas State Constitution: A Reference Guide*. Westport, CT: Greenwood Press, 1993.

Greenberg, David F. *The Construction of Homosexuality*. Chicago: University of Chicago Press, 1988.

Gustav-Wrathall, John Donald. *Take the Young Stranger by the Hand: Same-Sex Relations and the YMCA*. Chicago: University of Chicago Press, 1998.

Gutierrez, Ramon A. *When Jesus Came, The Corn Mothers Went Away: Marriage, Sexuality, and Power in New Mexico, 1500–1846*. Berkeley: University of California Press, 1991.

Halberstam, Judith. *Female Masculinity*. Durham, NC: Duke University Press, 1998.

Halperin, David. *Saint Foucault: Towards a Gay Hagiography*. New York: Replica Books, 2000.

———. *How to Write the History of Homosexuality*. Chicago: University of Chicago Press, 2003.

Hamilton, Marybeth. "Sexual Politics and African American Music; or, Placing Little Richard in History." *History Workshop Journal* (1998): 161–76.

Harne, Lynne, and Elaine Miller, eds. *All the Rage: Reasserting Lesbian Feminism*. New York: Teachers College Press, 1996.

Harvey, David. *The Condition of Postmodernity: An Enquiry into the Origins of Cultural Change*. New York: Blackwell, 1990.

———. *Justice, Nature, and the Geography of Difference*. Cambridge: Blackwell, 1996.

Higgs, David, ed. *Queer Sites: Gay Urban Histories Since 1600*. London: Routledge, 1999.

Hoagland , Sarah Lucia, and Julia Penelope, eds. *For Lesbians Only: A Separatist Anthology*. London: Onlywomen Press, 1988.

Hodes, Martha. *White Women, Black Men: Illicit Sex in the Nineteenth-Century South*. New Haven, CT: Yale University Press, 1997.

hooks, bell. *Black Looks: Race and Representation*. Boston: South End Press, 1992.

Houlbrook, Matt. *Queer London: Perils and Pleasures in the Sexual Metropolis, 1918–1957*. Chicago: University of Chicago Press, 2005.

Howard, John, ed. *Carryin' on the Lesbian South:* New York: New York University Press, 1997.

Howard, John. *Men Like That: A Southern Queer History.* Chicago: University of Chicago Press, 2001.

——. "The Politics of Dancing under Japanese American Incarceration." *The History Workshop Journal* (2001): 121–53.

——. *Concentration Camps on the Home Front: Japanese Americans in the House of Jim Crow.* Chicago: University of Chicago Press, 2008.

Humphreys, Laud. *Tearoom Trade: Impersonal Sex in Public Places.* New York: Aldine de Gruyter, 1975.

Ignatiev, Noel. *How the Irish Became White.* New York: Routledge, 1996.

Jagose, Annamarie. *Queer Theory: An Introduction.* New York: New York University Press, 1996.

Jay, Karla, and Allen Young, eds. *Out of the Closets: Voices of Gay Liberation.* London: Gay Men's Press, 1992.

Jobes, Patrick C. *Moving Nearer to Heaven: The Illusions and Disillusions of Migrants to Scenic Rural Places.* Westport, CT: Praeger, 2000.

Jacobs, Jeffery. *New Pioneers: The Back-to-the-Land Movement and the Search for a Sustainable Future.* University Park: Pennsylvania State University Press, 1997.

Jeansonne, Glen. *Gerald L. K. Smith: Minister of Hate.* New Haven, CT: Yale University Press, 1988.

Jeansonne, Robert Gilmore. *Ozark Baptizings, Hangings, and Other Diversions: Theatrical Folkways of Rural Missouri, 1885–1910.* Norman: University of Oklahoma Press, 1984.

Jeffreys, Sheila. *The Spinster and Her Enemies: Feminism and Sexuality, 1880–1930.* London: Pandora, 1985.

Johnson, Ben F. *Arkansas and Modern America: 1930–1999.* Fayetteville, University of Arkansas Press, 2000.

Jones, Amelia. "Dis/playing the Phallus: Male Artist Perform Their Masculinities." *Art History* 17, no. 4 (1994): 575–78.

Katz, Jonathan. *Gay American History: Lesbians and Gay Men in the USA.* New York: Cromwell, 1976.

——. *Gay/Lesbian Almanac: A New Documentary.* New York: Harper and Row, 1983.

——. *Love Stories: Sex between Men before Homosexuality.* Chicago: University of Chicago Press, 2001.

Kaplan, Amy, and Donald E. Pease, eds. *Cultures of United States Imperialism.* Durham, NC: Duke University Press, 1993.

Kennedy, Elizabeth Lapovsky, and Madeline D. Davis. *Boots of Leather, Slippers of Gold: The History of a Lesbian Community.* New York: Routledge, 1993.

Kephart, William M. *Extraordinary Groups: An Examination of Unconventional Life-Styles.* New York: St. Martin's Press, 1987.

Keith, Michael, and Steve Pile, eds. *Place and the Politics of Identity.* London and New York: Routledge, 1993.

Kinsey, Alfred C., Wardell B. Pomeroy, and Clyde E. Martin. *Sexual Behavior in the Human Male*. Philadelphia: W. B. Saunders, 1948.

Kinsey, Alferd C., Wardell B. Pomeroy, Clyde E. Martin, and Paul H. Gebhard. *Sexual Behavior in the Human Female*. Philadelphia: W. B. Saunders, 1953.

Kirk, John. *Redefining the Color Line: Black Activism in Little Rock, Arkansas, 1940-1970*. Gainesville: University of Florida Press, 2002.

Kidwai, Saleem, ed. *Same-Sex Love in India: Reading from Literature and History*. New York: Palgrave, 2002.

Koedt, Anne, Ellen Levine, and Anita Rapone, eds. *Radical Feminism*. New York: Quadrangle, 1973.

Krahulik, Karen. *Provincetown: From Pilgrim Landing to Gay Resort*. New York: New York University Press, 2005.

Kunzel, Regina. *Criminal Intimacy: Prison and the Uneven History of Modern American Sexuality*. Chicago: University of Chicago Press, 2008.

de Lauretis, Teresa. "Eccentric Subjects: Feminist Theory and Historical Consciousness." *Feminist Studies* 16, no. 1 (1990).

Latour, Bruno, and Catherine Porter. *We Have Never Been Modern*. Cambridge, MA: Harvard University Press, 1993.

Lefebvre, Henri. *The Production of Space*. Trans. Donald Nicholson-Smith. Oxford: Basil Blackwell, 1991.

LeMaster, Carolyn Gray. *A Corner of the Tapestry: A History of the Jewish Experience in Arkansas, 1820s-1990s*. Fayetteville: University of Arkansas Press, 1994.

Lewin, Ellen, ed. *Inventing Lesbian Cultures in America*. Boston: Beacon, 1996.

Leyland, Winston, ed. *Gay Roots: Twenty Years of "Gay Sunshine": An Anthology of Gay History, Sex, Politics, and Culture*. San Francisco: The Gay Sunshine Press, 1991.

Long, Burke O. *Imagining the Holy Land: Maps, Models, and Fantasy Travels*. Bloomington: Indiana University Press, 2002.

Lorde, Audre. *Sister/Outsider: Essays and Speeches*. Trumansburg, NY: The Crossing Press, 1991.

McLelland, Mark J. *Male Homosexuality in Modern Japan: Cultural Myths and Social Realities*. New York: Taylor and Francis, 2000.

McNeil, W. K. *Ozark Country*. Jackson: University Press of Mississippi, 1995.

Mahar, William. *Behind the Burnt Cork Mask: Early Blackface Minstrelsy and Antebellum American Popular Culture*. Chicago: University of Illinois Press, 1994.

Manalansan, Martin F. *Global Divas: Filipino Gay Men in the Diaspora*. Durham, NC: Duke University Press, 2003.

Marcus, Eric. *Making History: The Struggle for Gay and Lesbian Equal Rights, 1945–1990: An Oral History*. New York: HarperCollins, 1992.

Marshall, John. "Pansies, Perverts, and Macho Men: Changing Conceptions of Male Homosexuality." *The Making of the Modern Homosexual*, edited by Ken Plummer. London: Hutchinson, 1981.

Maynard, Steven. "'Respect Your Elders: Know Your Past': History and the Queer Theorists." *Radical History Review* 75 (1999): 56–78.

Meyer, Leisa D. *Creating GI Jane: Sexuality and Power in the Women's Army Corps during World War II*. New York: Columbia University Press, 1996.

Middlebrook, Diane Wood. *Suits Me: The Double Life of Billy Tipton*. New York: Houghton Mifflin, 1998.

Miller, D. A. *A Place for Us: Essay on the Broadway Musical*. Cambridge, MA: Harvard University Press, 2000.

Miller, Neil. *Out in the World: Gay and Lesbian Life from Buenos Aires to Bangkok*. New York: Penguin, 1992.

Miller, Timothy. *The 60s Communes: Hippies and Beyond*. Syracuse, NJ: Syracuse University Press, 1999.

Moodie, Dunbar T. "Migrancy and Male Sexuality on the South African Gold Mines." *Hidden From History: Reclaiming the Gay and Lesbian Past*, 411–23. New York: Meridian, 1989.

Moore, Michael. *Drag! Male and Female Impersonators on Stage, Screen, and Television*. Jefferson, NC: MacFarland, 1994.

Mumford, Kevin. *Interzones: Black/White Sex Districts in Chicago and New York in the Early Twentieth Century*. New York: Columbia University Press, 1997.

Munt, Sally, ed. *New Lesbian Criticism: Literary and Cultural Readings*. New York: Columbia University Press, 1992.

Murton, Tom, and Joe Hyams. *Accomplices to the Crime*. New York: Grove Press, 1969.

Newfield, Christopher. "The Politics of Male Suffering: Masochism and Hegemony in the American Renaissance." *differences: A Journal of Feminist Culture Studies* 1, no. 3 (1989): 57–87.

Newton, Esther. *Cherry Grove, Fire Island: Sixty Years in America's First Gay and Lesbian Town*. Boston: Beacon Press, 1993.

———. *Margaret Meade Made Me Gay*. Durham, NC: Duke University Press, 2000.

———. *Mother Camp: Female Impersonators in America*. Chicago: University of Chicago Press, 1972.

Nicholson, Linda. *Gender and History*. New York: Columbia University Press, 1986.

Nissenbaum, Stephen. *A Battle for Christmas: A Cultural History of America's Most Cherished Holiday*. New York: Vintage, 1997.

Norton, Rictor. *Mother Clap's Molly House: The Gay Subculture in England, 1700-1830*. London: Gay Men's Press, 1992.

O'Brien, Michael. *Rethinking the South: Essays in Intellectual History*. Baltimore: Johns Hopkins University Press, 1988.

Orleck, Annelise. *Common Sense and a Little Fire: Women and Working-Class Politics in the United States, 1900–1965*. Chapel Hill: University of North Carolina Press, 1995.

Parker, Suzi. *Sex in the South: Unbuckling the Bible Belt*. New York: Justin, Charles and Co., 2003.

Patton, Cindy. *Globalizing AIDS*. Minneapolis: University of Minnesota Press, 2002.

Peiss, Kathy, and Christina Simmons, with Robert Padgug, eds. *Passion and Power: Sexuality in History*. Philadelphia: Temple University Press, 1989.

Pharr, Suzanne. *Homophobia: A Weapon of Sexism*. Little Rock: Chardon, 1988.

Phelan, Shane. *Identity Politics: Lesbian Feminism and the Limits of Community*. Philadelphia: Temple University Press, 1989.

Phillips, Thomas Hal. *The Bitterweed Path*. Chapel Hill: University of North Carolina Press, 1949. Introduction, John Howard, 1996.

Ponse, Barbara. *Identities in the Lesbian World: The Social Construction of the Self*. Westport, CT: Greenwood, 1978.

Price, Deb, and Joyce Murdoch. *Courting Justice: Gay Men and Lesbians and the Supreme Court*. New York: BasicBooks, 2001.

Quinn, D. Michael. *Same-Sex Dynamics among Nineteenth Century Americans: A Mormon Example*. Urbana: University of Illinois Press, 1996.

Rafferty, Milton D. *The Ozarks: Land an Life*. Norman: University of Oklahoma Press, 1980.

Reed, John Shelton. *My Tears Spoiled My Aim: And Other Reflections on Southern Culture*. New York: Harcourt, 1994.

Reed, Roy. *Faubus: The Life and Times of an American Prodigal*. Fayetteville: University of Arkansas, 1997.

Rhode, Deborah L. *Justice and Gender*. Cambridge, MA: Harvard University Press, 1989.

Riggs, Marlon T. "Ruminations of a Snap Queen: What Time is it?!" *Outlook: National Lesbian and Gay Quarterly* 12 (Spring 1991): 16.

Rivers, Diana. *Daughters of the Great Star*. Boston: Lace Publications, 1992.

Robb, Graham. *Strangers: Homosexual Love in the Nineteenth Century*. New York: Norton, 2003.

Roberts, Ron E. *The New Communes: Coming Together in America*. Englewood Cliffs, NJ: Prentice Hall, 1971.

Robinson, Charles. *Dangerous Liaison: Sex and Love in the Segregated South*. Fayetteville: University of Arkansas Press, 2004.

Rubin, Gayle S. "Thinking Sex: Notes for a Radical Theory of the Politics of Sexuality." *The Lesbian and Gay Studies Reader*, edited by Henry Abelove, Michele Aina Barale, and David M. Halperin. New York: Routledge, 1993.

Rupp, Leila J. *A Desired Past: A Short History of Same-Sex Love in America*. Chicago: University of Chicago Press, 2002.

Rupp, Leila J., and Verta Taylor. *Drag Queens at the 801 Cabaret*. Chicago: University of Chicago Press, 2003.

Russell, Ida, ed. *Jeb and Dash: A Diary of Gay Life, 1918–1945*. Boston: Faber and Faber, 1993.

Russo, Vito. *The Celluloid Closet: Homosexuality in the Movies.* New York: Harper and Row, 1987.

Rydstrom, Jens. *Sinners and Citizens: Bestiality and Homosexuality in Sweden, 1880–1950.* Chicago: University of Chicago Press, 2003.

Sang, Tze-Ian D. *The Emerging Lesbian: Female Same Sex Desire in Modern China.* Chicago: University of Chicago Press, 2003.

Schmitt, Arno, and Jehoedo Sofer, eds. *Sexuality and Eroticism Among Males in Moslem Societies.* New York: Haworth, 1992.

Schulman, Bruce J. *The Seventies: The Great Shift in American Culture, Society, and Politics.* New York: Free Press, 2001.

Schrur, James A. "Closet Crusaders: The John Committee and Homophobia, 1956–1965." *Carryin' On in the Lesbian and Gay South* edited by John Howard. New York: New York University Press, 1997.

Seabrook, Jeremy. *Love in a Different Climate: Men who Love Men in India.* London: Verso, 1999.

Sears, James T. *Rebels, Rubyfruit, and Rhinestones.* New Brunswick, NJ: Rutgers University Press, 2001.

Sedgwick, Eve Kosofsky. *The Epistemology of the Closet.* Berkeley: University of California Press, 1990.

Sedgwick, Eve Kosofsky, ed. *Tendencies.* Durham, NC: Duke University Press, 1993.

Sedgwick, Eve Kosofsky. "Queer Performativity: Henry James's *The Art of the Novel.*" *GLQ: Journal of Lesbian and Gay Studies* 1 (1993): 11.

Segrest, Mab. *My Mama's Dead Squirrel: Lesbian Essays on Southern Culture.* Ithaca, NY: Firebrand, 1985.

Shannon, Gary W., Gerald F. Pyle, Rashid Bashshur. *The Geography of AIDS: Origins and Course of an Epidemic.* New York: Guilford Press, 1991.

Shilts, Randy. *And the Band Played On.* New York: Penguin, 1988.

———. *The Mayor of Castro Street: The Life and Times of Harvey Milk.* New York: Saint Martin's Press, 1982.

Sintow, Ann, Christine Stansell, and Sharon Thompson, eds. *Powers of Desire: Politics of Sexuality.* New York: Monthly Review Press, 1983.

Smith, Calvin C. *War and Wartime Changes: The Transformation of Arkansas, 1940–1945.* Fayetteville: University of Arkansas Press, 2001.

Smith, Donna Jo. "Queering the South: Constructions for a Southern/Queer Identity." *Carryin' on in the Lesbian and Gay South,* edited by John Howard. New York: New York University, 1997.

Smith, William L. *Families and Communes: An Examination of Nontraditional Lifestyles.* London: Sage Publications, 1999.

Somerville, Sioban. *Queering the Color Line: Race and the Invention of Homosexuality in American Culture.* Durham, NC: Duke University Press, 2000.

Spargo, Tamsin. *Foucault and Queer Theory.* New York: Icon, 2000.

Spitzberg, Irving J. *Racial Politics in Little Rock, 1954–1964*. New York: Garland, 1987.

Stockley, Grif. *Blood in Their Eyes: The Elaine Race Massacres of 1919*. Fayetteville: University of Arkansas Press, 1999.

Stein, Marc. *City of Brotherly and Sisterly Loves: The Making of Lesbian and Gay Communities in Greater Philadelphia, 1945–1972*. Chicago: University of Chicago Press, 2000.

Streitmatter, Rodger. *Unspeakable: The Rise of the Gay and Lesbian Press in America*. Boston: Faber and Faber, 1995.

Terkel, Studs. *Hard Times: An Oral History of the Great Depression*. New York: New Press, 1986.

Terry, Jennifer. *An American Obsession: Science, Medicine, and Homosexuality in Modern Society*. Chicago: University of Chicago Press, 1999.

Thompson, W. Brock. "A Crime Unfit to Be Named': Arkansas and Sodomy," *Arkansas Historical Quarterly* 61 (2002): 255–71.

Timmons, Stuart. *The Trouble with Harry Hay: Founder of the Modern Gay Movement*. Boston: Alyson Publications, 1990.

Tinkcom, Matthew. *Working Like a Homosexual: Camp, Capital, Cinema*. Durham, NC: Duke University Press, 2002.

Tripp, C. A., and Jean Baker. *The Intimate World of Abraham Lincoln*. New York: Free Press, 2005.

Turner, Mark. *Backward Glances: Cruising Queer Streets in London and New York*. London: Reaktion Books, 2003.

Turner, Victor. *The Anthropology of Performance*. New York: PAJ Publications, 1987.

Turner, William B. *Genealogy of Queer Theory*. Chicago: Temple University Press, 2000.

Vanita, Ruth, ed., *Queering India: Same Sex Desire and Eroticism in Indian Culture and Society*. New York: Rutledge, 2001.

Verghese, Abraham. *My Own Country: A Doctor's Story*. New York: Vintage Books, 1995.

Wallace, Max. *The American Axis: Henry Ford, Charles Linbergh, and the Rise of the Third Reich*. New York: St. Martin's Press, 2003.

Ward, John L. *Winthrop Rockefeller, Philanthropist*. Fayetteville: University of Arkansas Press, 1990.

Warner, Michael, ed. *Fear of a Queer Planet*. Minneapolis: University of Minnesota Press, 1993.

———. *The Trouble With Normal: Sex, Politics, and the Ethics of Queer Life*. Cambridge, MA: Harvard University Press, 2000.

Watney, Simon. "AIDS and the Politics of Queer Diaspora." *Negotiating Lesbian and Gay Subjects*, edited by M. Dorenkamp and R. Henke. New York: New York University Press, 1995.

Weeks, Jeffery. *Coming Out: Homosexual Politics in Britain from the Nineteenth Century to the Present*. London: Quartet, 1979.

Wiess, Andrea, and Greta Schiller. *Before Stonewall: The Making of a Gay and Lesbian Community.* Tallahassee: Naiad Press, 1988.

Whayne, Jeannie M. *The Arkansas Delta: Land of Paradox.* Fayetteville: University of Arkansas Press, 1993.

———. *A New Plantation South: Land, Labor, and Federal Favor in Twentieth-Century Arkansas.* Charlottesville: University of Virginia Press, 1996.

Whayne, Jeannie M., et al. *Arkansas: A Narrative History.* Fayetteville: University of Arkansas Press, 2002.

White, Edmund. *States of Desire: Travels in Gay America.* New York: E. P. Dutton, 1980.

White, Kevin. *The First Sexual Revolution: The Emergence of Male Heterosexuality in Modern America.* New York: New York University Press, 1993.

Wilcox, Clyde, Kenneth Wald, and Craig A. Rimmerman, eds. *The Politics of Gay Rights.* Chicago: University of Chicago Press, 2000.

Williams, Walter L. *The Spirit and the Flesh: Sexual Diversity in American Indian Culture.* Boston: Beacon Press, 1986.

Woods, Gregory. *A History of Gay Literature: The Male Tradition.* New Haven, CT: Yale University Press, 1998.

Woods, Randall Bennett. *Fulbright: A Biography.* Cambridge: Cambridge University Press, 1995.

Woodside, Jane Xenia Harris. "The Womanless Wedding: An American Folk Drama." Master's thesis, University of North Carolina, Chapel Hill, 1997.

Woodward, C. Vann. *Origins of the New South, 1877–1913.* Baton Rouge: Louisiana State University Press, 1951.

Wright, Les, ed. *The Bear Book: Readings in the History and Evolution of a Gay Male Subculture.* New York: Harrington Park Press, 1997.

Young, Iris Marion. *Justice and the Politics of Difference.* Princeton: Princeton University Press, 1990.

Zablocki, Benjamin. *Alienation and Charisma: A Study of Contemporary American Communes.* London: Free Press, 1980.

Zimmerman, Bonnie, and Toni A. H. McNaron. *The New Lesbian Studies: Into the Twenty-first Century.* New York, City University of New York, 1996.

INDEX

African Americans: Arkansas free black population, 204n9; civil rights movement and, 206n1; courting of by Winthrop Rockefeller, 90; depiction of by blackface, 26, 196n39; Jim Crow and, 82; low population of in Eureka Springs, 163, 170, 220n26; post–Civil War, Reconstruction population growth of, 86–87; rape fears, violence against, 26, 87, 92; in relation to this study, 189; Second World War and mobilization of, 39; segregation within gay bars, 57–58; separatism, 214n12, 218n59; sodomy law targeting of, 82, 86–87, 104, 93; treatment of black gay males by, 200n17

AIDS czar, 183, 223n4

AIDS/HIV: Arkansas's rate of infection, 123, 166, 212n2; Eureka Springs and, 172–75; first reported case in Arkansas, 123; forging of gay identity, 124, 176; impact on the rural, the South, 172–75, 201n5, 221–22n14; information on and testing for provided by gay bars, 67; Pulaski County, rate in, 212n2; pushing the urban to rural migration, 172; rural fundraising for, 174–75; sodomy law and the manipulation of public fears of, 114–15, 123n3; sodomy law arrest and court-ordered testing for, 114–15, 124; Vic Snyder and sodomy law argument, 111, 123

Alabama, 56, 154; sodomy law in, 203–4n19; southern queer network and, 168

alcohol, 52, 60, 98, 99

alternative modernity, 9, 40, 71, 136, 156

American Civil Liberties Union (ACLU), 95, 115–16, 116, 203n19,

American Indians: Caddo Indians and same-sex desire, 7–8; European terminology for, 191n4, 191n5

Americans with Disabilities Act, 117, 211n35

Appalachia, 105, 173

Arco Iris, 149–52, 154, 155, 169, 219n19; ingenuity of, 150–51; plea for diversity by, 152

Arkansas, 189; geographical description of, 12; in framing this study, 9–11; industrialization and, 40, 90; perception of, self-perception of, 4; polarization of gender and race in, 25

cities and towns: Arkadelphia, 51, 101; Bee Branch, 63; Berryville, 175, 178; Cave City, 175; Clarendon, 49; Clarksville, 141; Conway, 32, 110–11, 112, 126, 127; gay pride parade and, 186–189; England, 190; Eureka Springs, 131, 134–35, 137, 143–44, 152, 154–56, 157–59, "gay capital of the Ozarks," 177; African American population and, 162–63, 220n26; Christian tourism and, 158–61; city government friendly towards gays and lesbians, 175–76, 177; Civil War veterans and, 157; downtown/uptown divide, 168, 172, 177, 180; gay and lesbian tourism and, 165, 167, 169–70, 178–80, 221n9; hippie community and, 162–165, 167, 174; popular health retreat, 157–58; Fayetteville, 67, 135, 137, 148, 175, 184; Fort Smith, 84; Graysonia, 83; Gurdon, 83; Hamburg, 102; Harrison, 6–7; Hot Springs, 51, 53, 54, 55, 57,

65, 67, 199n8; Little Rock, 12,
35, 36, 39–40, 55; gay bars in 55;
Marked Tree, 24, 118; Marvell,
5; Mena, 40; Pocahontas, 95;
Prescot , 83; Russellville, 115;
Star City, 107; Stuttgart, 97;
Texarkana, 55, 101, 113;
Wilson, 25–28; and the new
plantation system, 25
counties: Boone, 173; Carroll, 173;
Madison, 173; Monroe, 45, 46;
Newton, 147, 154; Pope, 143;
Pulaski, 212n2; Sebastian, 84
See also rural space; urban space
Arkansas Baptist Association, 112
Arkansas criminal code, 81, 97
Arkansas Criminal Code Revision
Commission, 81, 97–98, 201n7
Arkansas Democrat, 75, 117; antigay tone
of, suicide and, 124
Arkansas Democrat-Gazette, 170
Arkansas Gazette, 76, 101, 112, 116, 123,
124; "nickname the state" contest, 4
Arkansas Faith, 90, 91
Arkansas Gay and Lesbian Taskforce,
114, 210n16, 211n40
Arkansas Highway Department, 116,
117, 122, 211n36, 211n87
Arkansas Industrial Development
Commission, 81
Arkansas Marriage Amendment
Committee, 185
Arkansas River, 12, 35, 56, 65, 132
Arkansas State Teacher's College, 2
Arkansas Supreme Court, 84, 85, 88,
100, 115, 119, 120
Arkansas Territory, 8
Arkansas Times, 101
Arkansas Traveler, 138, 214n6
Atlanta Lesbian Feminist Alliance, 144–
45, 216n29
autohistory, 13, 192n15
automobiles: American fascination
with, 109, 121; cruising and, 52–54,
57; freedom provided by, 55, 57;
gay identity and, 100, 200n11; sig-
nals and, 54; used for queer net-
working, 10, 53–54, 121

bachelor, use of term, 6
back-to-land movement, 140–41, 143–
44, 216n23
Badgett, M. V. Lee, 170
Barnett, Walter, 79–80
Barnsdall, Oklahoma, 106
bars: AIDS testing and, 67; class division
and, 54; drag in, 58, 67; facilitation
of community and identity
through, 8, 40, 56, 67–68, 175;
operating near hotels, 55; racial
divides in, 57–58; rules against displayed affection in, 56–57; rural
and urban, 57. See also specific bars
Barth, Jay, 205n3
Bartlett, Neil, 125
bases, army. See military bases
Bassey, Shirley, 59
Beauvoir, Simone de, 29
Bentley, Wilbur C. "Dub," 99
berdache, 191n4, 191n5
Berkes, Milton, 96, 206n3
Berube, Alan, 32
bestiality, 80, 102, 111, 208n30; inclusion
of in sodomy law, 104–5
Bethesda, Maryland, 51, 53
bigamy, 46, 48, 198n7
Black, James "Sammy," 98–100
Black Cat, Tulsa, Oklahoma, 132–33, 134
blackface minstrelsy, 26–27, 196n39
black politicians, 86–87
Blair, Diane, 205n3
Blystone, Bryan, 113
Bogard, David, 118–19
Bowers v. Hardwick, 75–82, 119–20
Bowers, Michael, 75
Branson, Missouri, 160, 178
Brass Rail, Little Rock, Arkansas, 55–56
Bravmann, Scott, 200–201n23
Breakfast at Tiffany's, 68
Brewer, Sandy, 187, 188
Brown v. Board of Education, 39
Bryant, Anita, 81; Arkansas perform-
ance, poor showing at, 108; back-
ing of the Gerald L. K. Smith
Foundation, 177; bankruptcy and,
178; controversy with Lincoln
Ledger (Star City, AR) and, 107–8;

creation of the "Save Our Children" campaign, 107, 177; Eureka Springs failure and, 178; honored by Arkansas legislature, 106; negative view of, 108; opposition to Miami/Dade County discrimination ordinance, 107; orange juice spokeswoman, 106; praised by Arkansas legislature, 106; relocation to Eureka Springs, poor showings at, 177–78; ridiculousness of, 178

Burger, Warren, 76, 202n5

Burns Park, 124

Bush, Reagan, 64

Butler, Judith, 196n38, 198n16

Caddo Indian Tribe, 7

California Democratic Primary (1992), 183

camp, 68–69, 201n10

Campbell, Jay, 113, 114, 115

Campbell, John William, 205n14

Camp Pike, 32

Camp Robinson, 32, 35

Camp Rowher Recreation Association, 19

Carlin, Jimmy, 44

Carr, Opal, 205n14

cars. See automobile

Carter, Lynda, 63, 66

Carter, Norman, 112

Cash, Pete, 83–84

Centers for Disease Control, 173

Center Street Bar, Eureka Springs, 175–76

Central High School, Little Rock, 39–40, 89, 90, 93

Charles, Casey, 13, 192n15

Charlotte, North Carolina, 60–61

Chauncey, George, 11

cheerleaders, 194n16; Powder-Puff football and, 17–18

Cherry Grove, Fire Island, New York, 171

Chicago, Illinois, 5, 56, 184

Christian Coalition of Arkansas, 111

Christian Nationalist Party, Christian Nationalist Crusade, 159

Christian Research Church, 223n8

Christian tourism, 160–62, 165, 170, 180

Christ of the Ozarks, statue, 159–60, 165, 179

churches: Conway gay-pride parade and, 187–88; Eureka Springs and, 161; fostering queer behavior and, 45; race and class divisions, 39; and southern life, 9, 48; venue for drag, 24–25, 34, 58, 68; womanless weddings and, 10

Church of Christ, 46, 48

civil rights movement, 10, 39, 82, 88, 104, 154; sexuality and, 200n17, 206n12, 208n28

Civil War, 86, 87, 104, 157

class, 213n2; class distinction in gay community, 54–55, 170, 171; lesbians and, 132–33, 144, 146, 164, 213n2; rural drag and, 70

Clinton, Bill: 1992 Democratic primary and election of, 183–84, 223n8; appointment of AIDS czar, 183–84; as attorney general, 102–3; Defense of Marriage Act and, 118, 223n8

cold war era, 41, 52; climate of paranoia, 41, 45; growing fear of sexual deviancy, 41, 197n44

colleges and universities: drag and, 32, 43, 64–65; homophobia at, 79–80, 137–40.

Collier, Albert "Tom," 106

Collinwood, Tennessee, 47,

coming out, 140, 173–74

Commonwealth College, Mena, Arkansas, 40, 197n42

communes/communities, 8, 10, 135, 140, 141–42, 143–49, 151–56, 165, 170, 172, 217n44, 218n62; difference between, 148; difficulties with, 144–46; locations of, 215n19, 216n24, 217n14; money issues and, 145; rural skills necessary for, 145–46

Constitution, Arkansas State, 81, 103–4, 105, 118, 119

Constitution, United States, 75–76

Continental, Little Rock, Arkansas, 56, 200n13

Cooper Union, School of Art, New York, 147

Cox, Jerry, 185

Cross, John, 162–63a

cross-dressing, 5, 32, 49, 63, 119. *See also* drag

cruising, 122; definition of, 209n4; internet and, 67; signals for, 53–54; use of automobiles and, 52

Cullman, Alabama, 54

Cummins Prison Farm, 43–44, 46, 47, 197n4

Dade County, Dade County Metro Commission, Florida, 107

Dallas, Texas, 60, 150, 173, 180

Daniel, Pete, 28, 197n44

DeColores, Maria Christina Moroles (Sunhawk), 149–52, 169

DeColores, Miguela-Borges, 149–52, 169

Defense of Marriage Act, 185, 222n23

D'Emilio, John, 11, 206n11, 223n8

Democratic National Convention, 1992, 184

Democratic National Committee, 184

Dennis, Ross, 107–8

Dinosaur World, 179

discourse, 7, 70, 78–79, 82, 92–93, 104, 127; law and, 86–88, 203n18, 206n1

Discovery, Little Rock, Arkansas, 51, 61, 64, 65, 67, 68

disease, 212n3

Diversity Weekend, Eureka Springs, 175

The Donna Reed Show, 43

Doobie Plantation, 143

Doty, Mark, 63

Dove, Rita, 183

Dowd, Wayne, 112–13

Downey, Charlotte, 118, 131–35, 169

drag, 6, 9, 10, 11, 18, 19–71, 197n1; accompanying blackface, 26–27; declining popularity of rural drag, 43; didactic nature of, 30–31; displaying racial and gender transgressions, 26, 69, 196n38;

entertainment value of, 27; popularity in the rural, 58; popularity of in southern gay bars, 60, 61, 67, 68, 70–71, 156, 175; used as college hazing, 195n27

drag kings, 198n15

drag queens: cost of performing, 202n11; professionalism of, queer entrepreneurialism and, 59, 60, 64–65, 195n36, 200n18; rules against plastic surgery, 69

Drummer's Club, 56

Dry, Charlie, 178

Dukes of Hazzard, 63

Dupont Circle, Washington DC, 51

Earnhart, Milt, 103

English common law, 78, 82, 86, 97

essentialism, 155

evangelicalism, 165

Everett, Mike, 118, 211n40

Factory, 65, 67, 71

Fatted Calf, New Orleans, Louisiana, 167

Faubus, Orval, 39–40, 90, 92; southern progressive roots and, 39–40

Fayetteville Women's Center, 137–40, 141 213n2, 213n3, 214n11; location of, 137; mission of, 137, 213n1, 213n2; turmoil and, 138–39, 214n11

Federal Bureau of Investigation (FBI), 159, 223n8

Feminine Mystique, 217n46

feminism, 46, 64, 135, 137, 138, 141, 196n36, 214n12, 217n46

First World War, 158

Flagg, Fannie, 193–94n15

folk drama: definition of, 193n7; womanless weddings and, 20, 29

football, 17–18

Ford, Henry, 159

Ford, Tennessee Ernie, 159

Fore Runners Hotel, Grand Duchess Ballroom, 177

USS *Forrestal,* 52, 199n5

Fort Caffee, Arkansas, 32

Foucault, Michel, 88, 195n29, 203n18
Freedman, Estelle, 11
Freidan, Betty, 217n46
Fried Green Tomatoes and the Whistle Stop Café, 193n15

Gar Hole, 56
Garner, Tyron, 119
gay and lesbian history: difficulties in researching, 192n14; importance of, 212–13n9; limits to, 189
gay bars. *See* bars. *See specific gay bars*
Gay Community News, 112
gender, 8, 17, 18, 20–21, 23, 25–26, 28–30, 38, 44, 48, 64, 69, 70, 155; gender transgressions and performance, 20–30
Gender Trouble, 196n38, 198n16
Gentry, Hugh, 98
Georgia, 71, 75, 77, 78, 90; sodomy laws and, 75–78, 202n1
Gibson, Mel, 170, 220n5
GI drag, 32–35, 38
Girl Talk, 71
Givens, Art, 101
The Golden Girls, 126
Goodwin, Harvey, "Harvey Lee," 35–36, 61; popularity and professionalism of, 35–36
Grady Manning Hotel, 55
Grant, G. L., 84
Great Depression, 6, 163
Great Passion Play, 160–162, 179–180; anti-Semitism and, 162, 179
Greenwich Village, New York City, 154

Hale, David, 115, 124
Hall, Jacquelyn Dowd, 26
Hall, John, Jr., 99
Hardwick, Michael, 75
Harris County, Texas, 120
Harrison, Katy, 213n4
Harvey, H. E., 141, 215n15
Hay, Harry, 214n12
Henderson, Willie, 98–100
Hendrix College, Conway, Arkansas, 32, 43, 63, 195n27

Henry, Aaron, 216n12
Henslee, Lee, 46–48
Hepburn, Audrey, 68
hermaphrodite, 191n4
highways: interstates, 109–10, 121; queer networks and, 57, 125, 173
hippies, 154, 158, 162–64, 167, 174
history, southern, 11
history, gay and lesbian. *See* gay and lesbian history
Hitler, Adolf, 108
HIV/AIDS. *See* AIDS
Hodges, Jan, 114
Hog Mountain Georgia, 142
Hollins, A. H., 46
hotels: Eureka Springs and, 157–58, 162, 164, 167–69; queer networks and, 8, 55–56, 167–68, 173
Hot Springs National Park, 53
Houston, Harry 35
Houston, Texas, 168, 171, 173, 180
Howard, John: departure from *Men Like That,* 11; writing gay and lesbian history, 192n14
Howard, Robert, 5–6, 109–10, 113, 123–24, 126
Huckleberry Farm, 143
Hudson, James E., 90–93
Human Rights Campaign, 183
Humphreys, Laud, 109, 121–25, 209n1

Imber, Annabelle Clinton, 119
Independence Baptist Association, 100
identity formation/politics, 124, 146, 179–81, 184, 221n12
Interstate 40 (I-40), 109, 121, 126, 127. *See also* highways
interstate rest areas: arrest and police involvement at, 109–17; popularity for cruising, 121–23. *See also* Morgan rest area
interstates. *See* highways
Ivers, David, 118

Jackson, Mississippi, 70, 168
Jackson, Sam, 83–84
Jacobson, Jay, 116

jail, as a public space, 98–100, 207n13. *See also* prisons
Jameson, W. C., 191n1
Japanese Americans, 19, 38–39, 43, 193n1
Jeansonne, Glen, 219n5
Jerome, Camp, 38, 43, 193n1, 196n39
Jim Crow, 82, 208n28
Johnson, "Justice Jim": 1966 governor's race and, 89–93; playing on racial and sexual fears, 90–93; White Citizen's Council and, 90
Jones, Earl, 101
Jones, Norman, 51–55, 57–62, 184
Joplin, Missouri, 175
Joutel, Henri, 7

Kennedy, Anthony, 120, 211n45
Kent State University, 143
Key West, Florida, 171, 172
Kierkegaard, Soren, 3
Kinsey, Alfred, 49
Kirby, William, 99, 207n13
Kristie, Norma. *See* Norman Jones
Ku Klux Klan, 60, 87

Ladies Home Journal, 108
Lambda Legal Defense and Education Fund, 81, 118, 120, 184, 203n12
Lambertson v. People, 85
La Salle, René-Robert Cavelier, Sieur de: encounters with gay Indians, 7–8, 191n5; rumors of homosexuality, 191n4
Lawrence, John Geddes, 119
Lawrence v. Texas, 119–20
Laws, Ike Allen, 115
Leave it to Beaver, 49
LeBlanc, Vernon, 167, 175
Lee, David: as Fonda Cox as Fonda Le Femme, 63–66, 68–71; on the popularity of drag in the south, 7
lesbian fiction. *See* fiction
Lesbian Rap Group, 138. *See also* Razordykes
lesbian separatism. *See* separatism
lesbian utopian fiction. *See* fiction

Life (magazine), 91, 205n6
Lincoln Ledger (Star City, Arkansas), 107–8
Lindbergh, Charles, 159
Little Rock City Jail. *See* jail
longhairs. See hippies
Long, Huey, 158
loitering, 209–10n6
Los Angeles, California, 183
Lowery, Mark, 111–12
Lyons, Gene, 205n4

Maize Magazine, 149, 151
Manire, Bryan, 118
Maraniss, David, 184
Marion Hotel, 56
marriage: portrayed in womanless weddings, 19, 25, 30; as a sacred institution, 48, 75, 100; same-sex marriage and, 185–86, 222n23
masculinity, 18, 20, 24, 25, 28, 30–32, 34, 38, 45, 49; civil rights movement and, 206n12; performance and, 20, 24, 25, 69, 194–95n26, 198n15
Massachusetts Supreme Judicial Court, 185
Max Factor makeup, 59
McCain, Randy, 118
McGowan, C. B., 20
Memphis, Tennessee, 71, 109, 184
Meriwether, Robert, 32
Miami, Florida, 106, 107
Miami Vice, 126
Miles, John, 111
military bases, 32–35. *See* Camp Robinson; Camp Pike; Fort Chaffee
miscegenation, 87, 92, 104, 208n28
Miss Gay America Pageant, 60–62, 64, 184
Mississippi River, 184
Mixner, David, 223n2
Mobile, Alabama, 168
Model Penal Code, 98
Mondale, Walter, 183
Moral Majority, 104

Morgan rest area, 109–17, 121–27; condition of, 211n36; description of, 209n3; traffic at, 211n37

mountains, 10, 155, 157, 223n8

Ms. magazine, 141, 167

Mulberry Cemetery, England, Arkansas, 190

Murphy, N. B. Nap, 102

Nashville, Tennessee, 59, 71

Native Americans. *See* American Indians

navy, 51, 52, 53

New Girl/Old Girl Wedding, 2

New Holy Land, 179

New Orleans Hotel, Eureka Springs, 167, 168, 172–73, 178

New Orleans, Louisiana, 5, 56, 109, 142, 143, 167, 173, 216n21

newspapers, 215n16. *See also Arkansas Democrat; Arkansas Democrat-Gazette; Arkansas Gazette*

Newton, Esther, 11, 141–42, 201n10

New York Times, 164

Norcross, Jim, 200n13

Norman Carter, 112

North Arkansas Railroad, 6

Oklahoma State University, Stillwater, 132

old maid/spinster, 6

oral history, 12, 135, 189, 199n1, 199n1

Oregon, 96, 147, 185

Oregon Women's Land Trust, 145

Ort, Randall, 117

Ouachita Baptist University, Arkadelphia, Arkansas, 51

Ouachita Mountains, 12

Our Place, Hot Springs, Arkansas, 67

Our Place, Tulsa, Oklahoma, 132, 134

Our World magazine, 176

Ozark AIDS Resources and Services, 174

Ozark Land Holders Association (OLHA), 147–49

Ozarks Mountains, 12, 131, 141, 171, 172; AIDS cases in, 173, 180, 134, 135

Ozark Women on Land, 144–47; financial troubles and, 145; infighting in, 144–45

Palace Theater, Los Angeles, California, 183

Partain, David, 84

passing, 5. *See also* cross-dressing

The Passion of the Christ, 179, 220n5

Peek, Jerry, 59, 60

Pennsylvania, 95

People magazine, 177

Perez-Carrera, Clary, 152–55, 169

Pharr, Suzanne, 142, 180

Phelan, Shane, 217n47

Picado, Elaine, 118

Picado v. Jegley, 118–119, 131

The Pit, 56, 200n13

police: raids and sting operations, 123; use of decoys (entrapment) and, 123

Powder-Puff football, 17–18

prisons. *See* Cummins; Tucker; jail

private space, 81, 99, 105, 148

Provincetown, Massachusetts, 171

Pryor, David, 95; forgetfulness of, 208n32

Pryor, Mark, 119

public space, 58, 81, 98, 100, 103, 121–23, 158, 207n13

Put Your Hand in the Hand of the Man from Galilee (Hymn), 158

Quakers, 95

Quarter Bar, New Orleans Hotel, Eureka Springs, 168, 175

queer, 8, 191n6; use of term, 8–9, 273n14

queer theory, 196n38

race: as an analytical rubric, 11, 12, 171, 189; Arkansas and, 40; class and, 12, 27, 70; gay bars and, 57, 58; segregation and, 25; sodomy law and, 86–87; the south and, 28, 38, 39; within gender and sexuality, 25, 26, 40, 90–93. *See specific racial groups*

Radical Faeries, 214n12
Raimondo, Meredith, 176
Ranchino, Jim, 101
rape: fear of, 26; in prison, 44
Raspberry, William, 76
Razorbacks, University of Arkansas
    mascot, 3, 138, 139
Razordykes, 139–40
Real, Jerry, 70
Reconstruction, 86–88, 89
Red Cross, 24
Reed, Donna, 43
Rehoboth Beach, Delaware, 171
Republicans for Better Government, 91
Republican Party, Arkansas, 87, 89, 90
Republican National Committee, 185–
    86; GOP antigay mailer, 186
rest areas. *See* interstate rest areas
Rivers, Diana, 147–49; complete of les-
    bian fantasy fiction, 218n48
Roark, Thomas, 107
Roberson, Steve, 168–69, 171–72, 174
Robinson Center Auditorium, 35, 108
Rockefeller, John D., 89
Rockefeller, Winthrop, 89–93; 1966 gov-
    ernor's race and, 89–93; Arkansas
    Industrial Development Commis-
    sion and, 90; rumors of alco-
    holism/homosexuality, 89, 90, 92
Rockefeller Public Enemy No. 1, 91
Roe v. Wade, 76
Ron's Place, 71
Roosevelt, Franklin, 36, 193n1
Rohwer, Camp, 19–20, 34, 38, 43, 193n1
Rohwer Outpost, 19, 20
Royal Lion's Club, 56, 60
Rubin, Gayle, 208n29
rural space, 141, 170, 171, 199–200n10;
    as analytical rubric, 11; as queer
    space, 57; migration to, 134, 160;
    mocking of 104–5; representations
    of, 105
Rustin, Bayard, 206n12

San Francisco, California, 36, 40, 56, 61,
    70, 134, 170, 172, 174, 210n16
Sassafras, 147–50
Save Our Children, 107, 177

schools: as venue for drag, 10, 17–18, 25,
    39; segregation and, 39–40. *See also*
    Central High School
Scott, Barbara, 167–68
Scully, Ken, 172, 174, 178
The Secret Life of Walter Winchell, 91
Second World War: African Americans
    and, 39; effect on drag, 38, 195n35;
    mobilization and, 7, 39, 40–41,
    195n29
Sedgwick, Eve Kosofsky, 210n10
separatism, 141–42, 148, 155–56,
    214n12, 217n46, 217n49, 218n59;
    definition of, 217n47; difficulties
    with, 144
sexology, 49, 199n17, 199n18
Sexuality in the Human Male, 49
Shapp, Milton, 96
Sheppard of the Hills, 160
Smith, Dixie, 84
Smith, Gerald L. K.: Eureka Springs
    and, 158–65, 168, 177–80, 220n16;
    anti-Semitism and, 159, 161, 219n7;
    Christian tourism and, 163, 165,
    177, 220n21; dislike of hippie sub-
    culture, 162–64; friction with
    Eureka Springs, 220n16
Smith, Kate, 159
Smith v. State (1921), 80, 85
Snyder, Vic, 110–12, 114, 118, 123,
    210n16
Society of Friends. *See* Quakers
sodomy laws: ambiguity of term, 77,
    103–4; Arkansas sodomy law, 77–
    80; Arkansas Territory and, 86; bes-
    tiality and, 102, 104–5; derived
    from English common law, 78;
    fluid definition of, 87–88; legal con-
    sequences, social stigma of, 79,
    203n17, 203–204n19; miscegena-
    tion and, 104; targeting of African
    Americans by, 86–87, 104
softball, 132, 213n3
Southern Exposure, 70
Southern Poverty Law Center, 223n8
space: as analytical rubric, 81, 105; cre-
    ation of gay space, 122
spinster/old maid, 6

Stancil, Bill, 101–3
Stephenson, Wellington, 6
Stillwater, Oklahoma, 132
Stokey, Vernon, 118
Stonewall Riots, 187, 189, 200–201n23
Stoneybrook, 147
Streisand, Barbra, 58
Strum, John, 83
Strum v. State (1925), 83, 84, 87
suicide, 124
supremacy. *See* white supremacy

tearoom, 121–23, 125
Thompson, A. G., 19
Those Rockefeller Brothers, 92
Times-Echo (Eureka Springs), 162–63
Tinker Air Force Base, Oklahoma City,
    Oklahoma, 131
tourism, gay and lesbian, 167, 165,
    169–70, 179–80
Townsand, George, 118
transgenderism, 62
Triangle Rising, 210n16
Tucker Prison Farm, 43–47, 197n2; age
    of prisoners, 197n4; brutality and,
    43–44; drag and cross-dressing,
    facilitation of, 44–45; rape, 44
Tucker, Jim Guy, 102
Tulsa, Oklahoma, 131
Tyer, Arlo, 101
Tyra Banks Show, 71
Tyson, R. C., 83

University of Arkansas, Fayetteville,
    Arkansas, 137–40, 195n27, 203n17
University of Central Arkansas,
    Conway, Arkansas, 2
urban space: AIDS and, 172, 174; city as
    jungle, 93; gay and lesbian history
    and, 192n9; gay identity and, 135,
    154; migration from, 168, 180; seen
    as the "privileged metropolis," 9
Urban League, National, 91
U.S. Supreme Court, 75–80, 120, 184

Van Rippey, David, Dorothy, 45–50, 71,
    93
Vietnam War, 51, 163

Wakeland, Franchesca, 60
Warwick, Dionne, 58
Washington Post, the, 184
Washington DC, 36, 51, 54, 172, 185
Waters, John, 200n10
Waynesboro, Tennessee, 47
Weeks, Jeffrey, 104
White Citizens Council, 90
White River Valley, 148
white supremacy, 93
White, Byron R., 76
White, Robin, 118
whites: class and racial divisions and, 54,
    57–58; Eureka Springs and, 162;
    normalcy and, 41, 48, 87; racial
    transgression and, 6, 26–30;
    schools, 25; sodomy laws and, 86,
    104, 119; supremacy. *See also* white
    supremacy; womanless weddings
white supremacy, 28–29, 38–39, 93
Wilde, Oscar, vi, 125
Williams, Manny, 167, 175
Wilson, Nick, 103
womanless weddings, womanless
    beauty pageants, 19–23, 26–29, 61;
    carnivalesque, burlesque, nature
    of, 20–21, 193n6, 194n24; costumes
    for, 19; didactic nature of, 26–29; as
    folk drama, 20, 193n7; fundraising
    popularity of, 23; parody of
    Protestant wedding, 19; script and
    dialogue for, 22–23, 31
Wonder Woman, 63, 66, 68
Wood, J., 85

Yancey, Larry, 95, 106

Zumwalt, K. J., 155

BROCK THOMPSON received his PhD in American studies at King's College London. A native Arkansan, he now lives in Washington DC and works at the Library of Congress.